EVENING TII

CW00725209

Big Game Dat
Final League 1
Final Junior Ta
Bank of Scotla
Bell's Scottish
Leading Execu
Season 2003-:

Compiled by PHILIP JOYCE and FRASER GIBSON
Published by Newsquest (Herald and Times) Ltd.,
200 Renfield Street, Glasgow, G2 3QB.

ISBN: 0-903-21607-8

BIG GAME DATES

WORLD CUP QUALIFIERS

SCOTLAND v Slovenia	Wednesday, September 8, 2004
SCOTLAND v Norway	Saturday, October 9, 2004
Moldova v SCOTLAND	Wednesday, October 13, 2004
Italy v SCOTLAND	Saturday, March 26, 2005
SCOTLAND v Moldova	Saturday, June 4, 2005
Belarus v SCOTLAND	Wednesday, June 8, 2005
SCOTLAND v Italy	Saturday, September 3, 2005
Norway v SCOTLAND	Wednesday, September 7, 2005
SCOTLAND v Belarus	Saturday, October 8, 2005
Slovenia v SCOTLAND	Wednesday, October 12, 2005

INTERNATIONAL CHALLENGE MATCHES

SCOTLAND v Hungary	Wednesday, August 18, 2004
SCOTLAND away match	Thursday, September 2, 2004
SCOTLAND v Sweden	Wednesday, November 17, 2004

FUTURE CUP 2005

Germany v SCOTLAND	Tuesday, December 7, 2004
SCOTLAND v Poland	Tuesday, February 22, 2005
Austria v SCOTLAND	Tuesday, April 19, 2005
SCOTLAND v TURKEY	Tuesday, may 31, 2005

UEFA UNDER-21 CHAMPIONSHIP

SCOTLAND v Slovenia	Tuesday, September 7, 2004
SCOTLAND v Norway	Friday, October 8, 2004
Moldova v SCOTLAND	Tuesday, October 12, 2004
Italy v SCOTLAND	Friday, March 25, 2005
SCOTLAND v Moldova	Friday, June 3, 2005
Belarus v SCOTLAND	Tuesday, June 7, 2005
SCOTLAND v Italy	Friday, September 2, 2005
Norway v SCOTLAND	Tuesday, September 6, 2005
SCOTLAND v Belarus	Friday, October 7, 2005
Slovenia v SCOTLAND	Tuesday, October 11, 2005

WOMEN'S EUROPEAN CHAMPIONSHIP QUALIFIERS

SCOTLAND v Czech Republic	Sunday, September 5, 2004

CIS LEAGUE CUP

FIRST ROUND	Tuesday, August 10, 2004
SECOND ROUND	Tuesday, August 24, 2004
THIRD ROUND	Wednesday, September 22, 2004
QUARTER-FINALS	Wednesday, November 10, 2004
SEMI-FINALS	Tuesday, February 1, 2005
FINAL	Sunday, March 20, 2005

BELL'S CUP

FIRST ROUND	Saturday, July 31, 2004
SECOND ROUND	Tuesday, August 31, 2004
THIRD ROUND	Tuesday, September 14, 2004
SEMI-FINALS	Tuesday, September 28, 2004
FINAL	Sunday, October 31, 2004

TENNENT'S SCOTTISH CUP

FIRST ROUND	Saturday, November 20, 2004
SECOND ROUND	Saturday, December 11, 2004
THIRD ROUND	Saturday, January 8, 2005
FOURTH ROUND	Saturday, February 5, 2005
QUARTER-FINALS	Saturday, February 26, 2005

SEMI-FINALS ....Saturday/Sunday, April 9/10, 2005
FINAL..Saturday, May 28, 2005
EUROPEAN CHAMPIONS LEAGUE (Tuesdays/Wednesdays)
FIRST QUALIFYING ROUND.................................July 14 and 21, 2004
SECOND QUALIFYING ROUND ....July 28 and August 4, 2004
THIRD QUALIFYING ROUND ....August 10/11 and August 24/25, 2004
GROUP STAGE.........September 14/15, September 28/29, October 19/20,
November 2/3, November 23/24, December 7/8.
FIRST KNOCKOUT ROUND ....February 22/23 and March 8/9, 2005
QUARTER-FINALS ....April 5/6 and April 12/13, 2005
SEMI-FINALS ....April 26/27 and May 3/4, 2005
FINAL...Wednesday, May 25, 2005 (at the Atatürk Olympic Stadium, Istanbul)
UEFA CUP (Wednesdays/Thursdays)
FIRST QUALIFYING ROUND......................................July 15 and 29, 2004
SECOND QUALIFYING ROUND..........................August 12 and 26, 2004
FIRST ROUND ....September 16 and 30, 2004
GROUP STAGE ....October 21, November 11, Novermber 25,
December 1/2, December 15/16
FIRST KNOCKOUT ROUND............February 16/17 and February 24, 2005
SECOND KNOCKOUT ROUND...............March 10 and March 16/17, 2005
QUARTER-FINALS ....April 7 and 14, 2005
SEMI-FINALS ....April 28 and May 5, 2005
FINAL...Wednesday, May 18, 2005 (at the José Alvalade Stadium, Lisbon)

FINAL LEAGUE TABLES 2003-2004

BANK OF SCOTLAND PREMIER LEAGUE

	P	W	D	L	F	A	Pt
Celtic	38	31	5	2	105	25	98
Rangers	38	25	6	7	76	33	81
Hearts	38	19	11	8	56	40	68
Dunfermline	38	14	11	13	45	52	53
Dundee Utd	38	13	10	15	47	60	49
Motherwell	38	12	10	16	42	49	46
Dundee	38	12	10	16	48	57	46
Hibernian	38	11	11	16	41	60	44
Livingston	38	13	5	20	48	57	43
Kilmarnock	38	12	6	20	51	74	42
Aberdeen	38	9	7	22	39	63	34
Partick Th	38	6	8	24	39	67	26

BELL'S DIVISION ONE

	P	W	D	L	F	A	Pt
Inverness CT	36	21	7	8	67	33	70
Clyde	36	20	9	7	64	40	69
St Johnstone	36	15	12	9	59	45	57
Falkirk	36	15	10	11	43	37	55
QofSouth	36	15	9	12	46	48	54
Ross Co	36	12	13	11	49	41	49
St Mirren	36	9	14	13	39	46	41
Raith Rov	36	8	10	18	37	57	34
Ayr Utd	36	6	13	17	37	58	31
Brechin City	36	6	9	21	37	73	27

BELL'S DIVISION TWO

	P	W	D	L	F	A	Pt
Airdrie Utd	36	20	10	6	64	36	70
Hamilton	36	18	8	10	70	47	62
Dumbarton	36	18	6	12	56	41	60
Morton	36	16	11	9	66	58	59
Berwick	36	14	6	16	61	67	48
Forfar Ath	36	12	11	13	49	57	47
Alloa	36	12	8	16	55	55	44
Arbroath	36	11	10	15	41	57	43
East Fife	36	11	8	17	38	45	41
Sten'muir	36	7	4	25	28	65	25

BELL'S DIVISION THREE

	P	W	D	L	F	A	Pt
Stranraer	36	24	7	5	87	30	79
Stirling Alb	36	23	8	5	78	27	77
Gretna	36	20	8	8	59	39	68
Peterhead	36	18	7	11	67	37	61
C'denbeath	36	15	10	11	46	39	55
Montrose	36	12	12	12	52	63	48
Queen's Pk	36	10	11	15	41	53	41
Albion Rov	36	12	4	20	66	75	40
Elgin City	36	6	7	23	48	93	25
E Stirling	36	2	2	32	30	118	8

WESTERN REGION SJFA LEAGUES
LEAGUE 2003-2004

CALEDONIAN SUPER PREMIER DIVISION

	P	W	D	L	F	A	Pts
Kilwinning	22	16	4	2	55	26	52
Arthurlie	22	15	4	3	53	24	49
Pollok	22	14	3	5	42	29	45
Cumnock	22	11	7	4	53	34	40
Glenafton	22	10	4	8	38	26	34
Maryhill	22	9	4	9	36	33	31
*Troon	22	8	6	8	33	38	27
Auchinleck	22	4	8	10	26	34	20
Johnstone	22	4	6	12	27	50	18
Larkhall	22	3	8	11	29	47	17
Neilston	22	4	4	14	32	49	16
Kilbirnie	22	2	6	14	22	56	12

*Points deducted.

ABERCORN CENTRAL DISTRICT LEAGUE FIRST DIVISION

	P	W	D	L	F	A	Pts
Cambuslang	22	14	3	5	62	31	45
Rob Roy	22	14	2	6	48	31	44
Greenock	22	12	4	6	50	37	40
Vale of Leven	22	11	3	8	63	43	36
East Kilbride	22	10	4	8	50	41	34
Dunipace	22	10	3	9	41	40	33
Vale of Clyde	22	10	3	9	42	47	33
St Anthony's	22	9	5	8	52	50	32
Glencairn	22	8	5	9	34	30	29
Port Glasgow	22	5	7	10	35	47	22
Lanark Utd	22	5	4	13	29	44	19
Perthshire	22	1	3	18	22	87	6

ABERCORN CENTRAL DISTRICT LEAGUE SECOND DIVISION

	P	W	D	L	F	A	Pts
Clydebank	24	20	2	2	66	16	62
Carluke Rov	24	18	4	2	77	28	58
Yoker	24	17	4	3	61	23	55
Lesmahagow	24	14	4	6	53	30	46
Blantyre V	24	13	2	9	52	44	41
Forth W	24	9	6	9	43	42	33
Ashfield	24	9	6	9	40	46	33
St Roch's	24	10	2	12	44	45	32
Royal Albert	24	7	6	11	44	56	27
Thorniewood	24	8	1	15	39	55	25
Wishaw	24	6	4	14	38	40	22
Stonehouse	24	3	2	19	30	81	11
Coltness Utd	24	0	1	23	16	96	1

ROCKWARE SUPER LEAGUE FIRST DIVISION

	P	W	D	L	F	A	Pts
Bellshill	22	14	4	4	45	22	46
Renfrew	22	12	7	3	51	23	43
Shotts	22	12	7	3	42	20	43
Kilsyth Rov	22	10	4	8	36	30	34
Beith	22	9	6	7	43	35	33
Petershill	22	9	3	10	39	40	30
Irvine M	22	8	5	9	23	24	29
Hurlford U	22	8	3	11	38	53	27
Lugar Bos	22	5	7	10	30	40	22
Cumb'nld	22	6	3	13	26	44	21
Benburb	22	5	5	12	28	52	20
Shettleston	22	3	8	11	31	49	17

KILWINNING boss Mark Shanks led his side to the Super Premier title

ROCKWARE AYRSHIRE DISTRICT LEAGUE

	P	W	D	L	F	A	Pts
Maybole	24	18	4	2	68	27	58
Saltcoats V	24	17	3	4	82	29	54
Irvine Vics	24	14	4	6	77	44	46
Annbank U	24	14	3	7	50	38	45
Kello Rov	24	13	4	7	56	38	43
Largs Th	24	13	2	9	60	44	41
Darvel	24	10	5	9	50	52	35
Craigmark	24	7	4	13	38	59	25
Ardrossan	24	5	8	11	37	51	23
Whitletts	24	7	2	15	52	77	23
Muirkirk	24	4	5	15	38	64	17
Ardeer Th	24	4	5	15	34	63	17
Dalry Th	24	4	3	17	31	87	15

BANK OF SCOTLAND
SCOTTISH PREMIER LEAGUE 2004-2005
FIXTURES SUBJECT TO CHANGE FOR LIVE TV COVERAGE
AND CORRECT AT TIME OF GOING TO PRESS

Saturday, August 7, 2004
Aberdeen v Rangers
Celtic v Motherwell
Dundee v Hearts
Dunfermline v Dundee Utd
Hibernian v Kilmarnock
Livingston v Inverness CT

Saturday, August 14
Dundee Utd v Dundee
Hearts v Aberdeen
Kilmarnock v Celtic
Motherwell v Hibernian
Rangers v Livingston

Sunday, August 15
Inverness CT v Dunfermline

Saturday, August 21
Dundee v Motherwell
Dunfermline v Aberdeen
Hearts v Kilmarnock
Inverness CT v Celtic
Livingston v Dundee Utd
Rangers v Hibernian

Saturday, August 28
Aberdeen v Livingston
Celtic v Rangers
Dundee Utd v Inverness CT
Hibernian v Dundee
Motherwell v Hearts

Sunday, August 29
Kilmarnock v Dunfermline

Saturday, September 11
Celtic v Dundee
Dundee Utd v Aberdeen
Dunfermline v Motherwell
Hearts v Rangers
Inverness CT v Hibernian
Livingston v Kilmarnock

Saturday, September 18
Dundee v Livingston
Hibernian v Celtic
Kilmarnock v Aberdeen
Motherwell v Dundee Utd
Rangers v Inverness CT

Sunday, September 19
Dunfermline v Hearts

Saturday, September 25
Aberdeen v Hibernian
Celtic v Dunfermline
Dundee v Rangers
Hearts v Inverness CT
Kilmarnock v Dundee Utd
Livingston v Motherwell

Saturday, October 2
Aberdeen v Dundee
Dundee Utd v Celtic
Dunfermline v Hibernian
Inverness CT v Motherwell
Rangers v Kilmarnock

Sunday, October 3
Hearts v Livingston

Saturday, October 16
Celtic v Hearts
Dundee v Kilmarnock
Hibernian v Dundee Utd
Inverness CT v Aberdeen
Livingston v Dunfermline
Motherwell v Rangers

Saturday, October 23
Aberdeen v Motherwell
Dundee v Dunfermline
Hearts v Hibernian
Kilmarnock v Inverness CT
Livingston v Celtic
Rangers v Dundee Utd

Tuesday, October 26
Dundee Utd v Hearts

Wednesday, October 27
Celtic v Aberdeen
Dunfermline v Rangers
Hibernian v Livingston
Inverness CT v Dundee
Motherwell v Kilmarnock

Saturday, October 30
Dundee Utd v Dunfermline
Hearts v Dundee
Inverness CT v Livingston
Kilmarnock v Hibernian
Motherwell v Celtic
Rangers v Aberdeen

Saturday, November 6
Aberdeen v Hearts
Celtic v Kilmarnock
Dundee v Dundee Utd
Dunfermline v Inverness CT
Hibernian v Motherwell
Livingston v Rangers

Saturday, November 13
Aberdeen v Dunfermline
Celtic v Inverness CT
Dundee Utd v Livingston
Hibernian v Rangers
Kilmarnock v Hearts
Motherwell v Dundee

Saturday, November 20
Dundee v Hibernian
Dunfermline v Kilmarnock
Hearts v Motherwell
Inverness CT v Dundee Utd
Livingston v Aberdeen
Rangers v Celtic

Saturday, November 27
Aberdeen v Dundee Utd
Dundee v Celtic
Hibernian v Inverness CT
Kilmarnock v Livingston
Motherwell v Dunfermline
Rangers v Hearts

Saturday, December 4
Aberdeen v Kilmarnock
Celtic v Hibernian
Dundee Utd v Motherwell
Hearts v Dunfermline
Inverness CT v Rangers
Livingston v Dundee

Saturday, December 11
Dundee Utd v Kilmarnock
Dunfermline v Celtic
Hibernian v Aberdeen
Inverness CT v Hearts
Motherwell v Livingston
Rangers v Dundee

Saturday, December 18
Celtic v Dundee Utd
Dundee v Aberdeen
Hibernian v Dunfermline
Kilmarnock v Rangers
Livingston v Hearts
Motherwell v Inverness CT

Monday, December 27
Aberdeen v Inverness CT
Dundee Utd v Hibernian
Dunfermline v Livingston
Hearts v Celtic
Kilmarnock v Dundee
Rangers v Motherwell

Saturday, January 1, 2005
Celtic v Livingston
Dundee Utd v Rangers
Dunfermline v Dundee
Hibernian v Hearts
Inverness CT v Kilmarnock
Motherwell v Aberdeen

Saturday, January 15
Aberdeen v Celtic
Dundee v Inverness CT
Hearts v Dundee Utd
Kilmarnock v Motherwell
Livingston v Hibernian
Rangers v Dunfermline

Saturday, January 22
Aberdeen v Rangers
Celtic v Motherwell
Dundee v Hearts
Dunfermline v Dundee Utd
Hibernian v Kilmarnock
Livingston v Inverness CT

Saturday, January 29
Dundee Utd v Dundee
Hearts v Aberdeen
Inverness CT v Dunfermline
Kilmarnock v Celtic
Motherwell v Hibernian
Rangers v Livingston

Saturday, February 12
Dundee v Motherwell
Dunfermline v Aberdeen
Hearts v Kilmarnock
Inverness CT v Celtic
Livingston v Dundee Utd
Rangers v Hibernian

Saturday, February 19
Aberdeen v Livingston
Celtic v Rangers
Dundee Utd v Inverness CT
Hibernian v Dundee
Kilmarnock v Dunfermline
Motherwell v Hearts

Tuesday, March 1
Dundee Utd v Aberdeen

Wednesday, March 2
Celtic v Dundee
Dunfermline v Motherwell
Hearts v Rangers
Inverness CT v Hibernian
Livingston v Kilmarnock

Saturday, March 5
Dundee v Livingston
Dunfermline v Hearts

Hibernian v Celtic
Kilmarnock v Aberdeen
Motherwell v Dundee Utd
Rangers v Inverness CT

Saturday, March 12
Aberdeen v Hibernian
Celtic v Dunfermline
Dundee v Rangers
Hearts v Inverness CT
Kilmarnock v Dundee Utd
Livingston v Motherwell

Saturday, March 19
Aberdeen v Dundee
Dundee Utd v Celtic
Dunfermline v Hibernian
Hearts v Livingston
Inverness CT v Motherwell
Rangers v Kilmarnock

Saturday, April 2
Celtic v Hearts
Dundee v Kilmarnock
Hibernian v Dundee Utd
Inverness CT v Aberdeen
Livingston v Dunfermline
Motherwell v Rangers

Saturday, April 9
Aberdeen v Motherwell
Dundee v Dunfermline
Hearts v Hibernian
Kilmarnock v Inverness CT
Livingston v Celtic
Rangers v Dundee Utd

Saturday, April 16
Celtic v Aberdeen
Dundee Utd v Hearts
Dunfermline v Rangers
Hibernian v Livingston
Inverness CT v Dundee
Motherwell v Kilmarnock

LEAGUE WILL NOW SPLIT IN TWO FOR FINAL FIVE GAMES.
DATES TO BE ARRANGED.

BELL'S LEAGUE DIVISION ONE 2004-2005

Saturday, August 7, 2004
Airdrie Utd v St Johnstone
Clyde v Partick
Hamilton v Raith
Qof S v Ross County
St Mirren v Falkirk

Saturday, August 14
Falkirk v Hamilton
Partick v Airdrie Utd
Raith v Clyde
Ross County v St Mirren
St Johnstone v QofS

Saturday, August 21
Airdrie Utd v Raith
Clyde v Ross County
Hamilton v Partick
QofS v Falkirk
St Mirren v St Johnstone

Saturday, August 28
Falkirk v Airdrie Utd
QofS v Clyde
Ross County v Partick
St Johnstone v Raith
St Mirren v Hamilton

Saturday, September 4
Airdrie Utd v QofS
Clyde v St Mirren
Hamilton v St Johnstone
Partick v Falkirk
Raith v Ross County

Saturday, September 11
Clyde v Airdrie Utd
Falkirk v Raith
QofS v Hamilton
Ross County v St Johnstone
St Mirren v Partick

Saturday, September 18
Airdrie Utd v Ross County
Hamilton v Clyde
Partick v QofS
Raith v St Mirren
St Johnstone v Falkirk

Saturday, September 25
Falkirk v Clyde
Hamilton v Ross County
Raith v QofS
St Johnstone v Partick
St Mirren v Airdrie Utd

Saturday, October 2
Airdrie Utd v Hamilton
Clyde v St Johnstone
Partick v Raith
QofS v St Mirren
Ross County v Falkirk

Saturday, October 16
Airdrie Utd v Partick
Clyde v Raith
Hamilton v Falkirk
QofS v St Johnstone
St Mirren v Ross County

Saturday, October 23
Falkirk v St Mirren
Partick v Clyde
Raith v Hamilton
Ross County v QofS
St Johnstone v Airdrie Utd

Saturday, October 30
Airdrie Utd v Falkirk
Clyde v QofS
Hamilton v St Mirren
Partick v Ross County
Raith v St Johnstone

Saturday, November 6
Falkirk v Partick
QofS v Airdrie Utd
Ross County v Raith
St Johnstone v Hamilton
St Mirren v Clyde

Saturday, November 13
Airdrie Utd v Clyde
Hamilton v QofS
Partick v St Mirren
Raith v Falkirk
St Johnstone v Ross County

Saturday, November 20
Clyde v Hamilton
Falkirk v St Johnstone
QofS v Partick
Ross County v Airdrie Utd
St Mirren v Raith

Saturday, November 27
Falkirk v Ross County
Hamilton v Airdrie Utd
Raith v Partick
St Johnstone v Clyde
St Mirren v QofS

Saturday, December 4
Airdrie Utd v St Mirren
Clyde v Falkirk
Partick v St Johnstone
QofS v Raith
Ross County v Hamilton

Saturday, December 11
Airdrie Utd v St Johnstone
Clyde v Partick
Hamilton v Raith
QofS v Ross County
St Mirren v Falkirk

Saturday, December 18
Falkirk v QofS
Partick v Hamilton
Raith v Airdrie Utd
Ross County v Clyde
St Johnstone v St Mirren

Sunday, December 26
Falkirk v Airdrie Utd
QofS v Clyde
Ross County v Partick
St Johnstone v Raith
St Mirren v Hamilton

Wednesday, December 29
Airdrie Utd v QofS
Clyde v St Mirren
Hamilton v St Johnstone
Partick v Falkirk
Raith v Ross County

Saturday, January 1, 2005
Clyde v Airdrie Utd
Falkirk v Raith
QofS v Hamilton
Ross County v St Johnstone
St Mirren v Partick

Saturday, January 15
Airdrie Utd v Ross County
Hamilton v Clyde
Partick v QofS
Raith v St Mirren
St Johnstone v Falkirk

Saturday, January 22
Falkirk v Clyde
Hamilton v Ross County
Raith v QofS
St Johnstone v Partick
St Mirren v Airdrie Utd

Saturday, January 29
Airdrie Utd v Hamilton
Clyde v St Johnstone
Partick v Raith
QofS v St Mirren
Ross County v Falkirk

Saturday, February 12
Falkirk v Hamilton
Partick v Airdrie Utd
Raith v Clyde
Ross County v St Mirren
St Johnstone v QofS

Saturday, February 19
Airdrie Utd v Raith
Clyde v Ross County
Hamilton v Partick
QofS v Falkirk
St Mirren v St Johnstone

Saturday, March 5
Falkirk v Partick
QofS v Airdrie Utd
Ross County v Raith
St Johnstone v Hamilton
St Mirren v Clyde

Saturday, March 12
Airdrie Utd v Falkirk
Clyde v QofS
Hamilton v St Mirren
Partick v Ross County
Raith v St Johnstone

Saturday, March 19
Airdrie Utd v Clyde
Hamilton v QofS
Partick v St Mirren
Raith v Falkirk
St Johnstone v Ross County

Saturday, April 2
Clyde v Hamilton
Falkirk v St Johnstone
QofS v Partick
Ross County v Airdrie Utd
St Mirren v Raith

Saturday, April 9
Falkirk v Ross County
Hamilton v Airdrie Utd
Raith v Partick
St Johnstone v Clyde
St Mirren v QofS

Saturday, April 16
Airdrie Utd v St Mirren
Clyde v Falkirk
Partick v St Johnstone
QofS v Raith
Ross County v Hamilton

Saturday, April 23
Falkirk v St Mirren
Partick v Clyde
Raith v Hamilton
Ross County v QofS
St Johnstone v Airdrie Utd

Saturday, April 30
Airdrie Utd v Partick
Clyde v Raith
Hamilton v Falkirk
QofS v St Johnstone
St Mirren v Ross County

Saturday, May 7
Falkirk v QofS
Partick v Hamilton
Raith v Airdrie Utd
Ross County v Clyde
St Johnstone v St Mirren

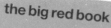

BELL'S LEAGUE
DIVISION TWO 2004-2005

Saturday, August 7, 2004
Berwick v Morton
Dumbarton v Ayr
Forfar v Brechin
Stirling v Arbroath
Stranraer v Alloa

Saturday, August 14
Alloa v Forfar
Arbroath v Dumbarton
Ayr v Berwick
Brechin v Stirling
Morton v Stranraer

Saturday, August 21
Berwick v Brechin
Dumbarton v Morton
Forfar v Arbroath
Stirling v Alloa
Stranraer v Ayr

Saturday, August 28
Arbroath v Stranraer
Ayr v Morton
Brechin v Alloa
Dumbarton v Forfar
Stirling v Berwick

Saturday, September 4
Alloa v Ayr
Berwick v Dumbarton
Forfar v Stirling
Morton v Arbroath
Stranraer v Brechin

Saturday, September 11
Ayr v Forfar
Berwick v Alloa
Brechin v Arbroath
Dumbarton v Stranraer
Stirling v Morton

Saturday, September 18
Alloa v Dumbarton
Arbroath v Ayr
Forfar v Berwick
Morton v Brechin
Stranraer v Stirling

Saturday, September 25
Alloa v Morton
Ayr v Brechin
Berwick v Arbroath
Dumbarton v Stirling
Forfar v Stranraer

Saturday, October 2
Arbroath v Alloa
Brechin v Dumbarton
Morton v Forfar
Stirling v Ayr
Stranraer v Berwick

Saturday, October 16
Berwick v Ayr
Dumbarton v Arbroath
Forfar v Alloa
Stirling v Brechin
Stranraer v Morton

Saturday, October 23
Alloa v Stranraer
Arbroath v Stirling
Ayr v Dumbarton
Brechin v Forfar
Morton v Berwick

Saturday, October 30
Alloa v Brechin
Berwick v Stirling
Forfar v Dumbarton
Morton v Ayr
Stranraer v Arbroath

Saturday, November 6
Arbroath v Morton
Ayr v Alloa
Brechin v Stranraer
Dumbarton v Berwick
Stirling v Forfar

Saturday, November 13
Alloa v Berwick
Arbroath v Brechin
Forfar v Ayr
Morton v Stirling
Stranraer v Dumbarton

Saturday, November 27
Ayr v Arbroath
Berwick v Forfar
Brechin v Morton
Dumbarton v Alloa
Stirling v Stranraer

Saturday, December 4
Arbroath v Berwick
Brechin v Ayr
Morton v Alloa
Stirling v Dumbarton
Stranraer v Forfar

Saturday, December 18
Alloa v Arbroath
Ayr v Stirling
Berwick v Stranraer
Dumbarton v Brechin
Forfar v Morton

Monday, December 27
Berwick v Morton
Dumbarton v Ayr
Forfar v Brechin
Stirling v Arbroath
Stranraer v Alloa

Saturday, January 1, 2005
Alloa v Stirling
Arbroath v Forfar
Ayr v Stranraer
Brechin v Berwick
Morton v Dumbarton

Monday, January 3
Arbroath v Stranraer
Ayr v Morton
Brechin v Alloa
Dumbarton v Forfar
Stirling v Berwick

Saturday, January 15
Alloa v Ayr
Berwick v Dumbarton
Forfar v Stirling
Morton v Arbroath
Stranraer v Brechin

Saturday, January 22
Ayr v Forfar
Berwick v Alloa
Brechin v Arbroath
Dumbarton v Stranraer
Stirling v Morton

Saturday, January 29
Alloa v Dumbarton
Arbroath v Ayr
Forfar v Berwick
Morton v Brechin
Stranraer v Stirling

Saturday, February 5
Alloa v Morton
Ayr v Brechin
Berwick v Arbroath
Dumbarton v Stirling
Forfar v Stranraer

Saturday, February 12
Arbroath v Alloa
Brechin v Dumbarton
Morton v Forfar
Stirling v Ayr
Stranraer v Berwick

Saturday, February 19
Berwick v Brechin
Dumbarton v Morton
Forfar v Arbroath
Stirling v Alloa
Stranraer v Ayr

Saturday, February 26
Alloa v Forfar
Arbroath v Dumbarton
Ayr v Berwick
Brechin v Stirling
Morton v Stranraer

Saturday, March 5
Arbroath v Morton
Ayr v Alloa
Brechin v Stranraer
Dumbarton v Berwick
Stirling v Forfar

Saturday, March 12
Alloa v Brechin
Berwick v Stirling
Forfar v Dumbarton
Morton v Ayr
Stranraer v Arbroath

Saturday, March 19
Alloa v Berwick
Arbroath v Brechin
Forfar v Ayr
Morton v Stirling
Stranraer v Dumbarton

Saturday, April 2
Ayr v Arbroath
Berwick v Forfar
Brechin v Morton
Dumbarton v Alloa
Stirling v Stranraer

Saturday, April 9
Alloa v Arbroath
Ayr v Stirling
Berwick v Stranraer
Dumbarton v Brechin
Forfar v Morton

Saturday, April 16
Arbroath v Berwick
Brechin v Ayr
Morton v Alloa
Stirling v Dumbarton
Stranraer v Forfar

Saturday, April 23
Alloa v Stirling
Arbroath v Forfar
Ayr v Stranraer
Brechin v Berwick
Morton v Dumbarton

Saturday, April 30
Berwick v Ayr
Dumbarton v Arbroath
Forfar v Alloa
Stirling v Brechin
Stranraer v Morton

Saturday, May 7
Alloa v Stranraer
Arbroath v Stirling
Ayr v Dumbarton
Brechin v Forfar
Morton v Berwick

BELL'S LEAGUE
DIVISION THREE 2004-2005

Saturday, August 7, 2004
East Fife v Montrose
Gretna v Albion
Peterhead v East Stirling
Queen's Park v Cowdenbeath
Stenhousemuir v Elgin

Saturday, August 14
Albion v East Fife
Cowdenbeath v Stenhousemuir
East Stirling v Gretna
Elgin v Queen's Park
Montrose v Peterhead

Saturday, August 21
East Fife v Cowdenbeath
Gretna v Montrose
Peterhead v Elgin
Queen's Park v Albion
Stenhousemuir v East Stirling

Saturday, August 28
Albion v Peterhead
Cowdenbeath v East Stirling
East Fife v Stenhousemuir
Elgin v Montrose
Queen's Park v Gretna

Saturday, September 4
East Stirling v Elgin
Gretna v Cowdenbeath
Montrose v Albion
Peterhead v East Fife
Stenhousemuir v Queen's Park

Saturday, September 11
Albion v Stenhousemuir
Cowdenbeath v Elgin
East Fife v East Stirling
Peterhead v Gretna
Queen's Park v Montrose

Saturday, September 18
East Stirling v Queen's Park
Elgin v Albion
Gretna v East Fife
Montrose v Cowdenbeath
Stenhousemuir v Peterhead

Saturday, September 25
Albion v East Stirling
East Fife v Queen's Park
Gretna v Elgin
Montrose v Stenhousemuir
Peterhead v Cowdenbeath

Saturday, October 2
Cowdenbeath v Albion
East Stirling v Montrose
Elgin v East Fife
Queen's Park v Peterhead
Stenhousemuir v Gretna

Saturday, October 16
East Fife v Albion
Gretna v East Stirling
Peterhead v Montrose
Queen's Park v Elgin
Stenhousemuir v Cowdenbeath

Saturday, October 23
Albion v Gretna
Cowdenbeath v Queen's Park
East Stirling v Peterhead
Elgin v Stenhousemuir
Montrose v East Fife

Saturday, October 30
East Stirling v Cowdenbeath
Gretna v Queen's Park
Montrose v Elgin
Peterhead v Albion
Stenhousemuir v East Fife

Saturday, November 6
Albion v Montrose
Cowdenbeath v Gretna
East Fife v Peterhead
Elgin v East Stirling
Queen's Park v Stenhousemuir

Saturday, November 13
East Stirling v East Fife
Elgin v Cowdenbeath
Gretna v Peterhead
Montrose v Queen's Park
Stenhousemuir v Albion

Saturday, November 27
Albion v Elgin
Cowdenbeath v Montrose
East Fife v Gretna
Peterhead v Stenhousemuir
Queen's Park v East Stirling

Saturday, December 4
Cowdenbeath v Peterhead
East Stirling v Albion
Elgin v Gretna
Queen's Park v East Fife
Stenhousemuir v Montrose

Saturday, December 18
Albion v Cowdenbeath
East Fife v Elgin
Gretna v Stenhousemuir
Montrose v East Stirling
Peterhead v Queen's Park

Monday, December 27
East Fife v Montrose
Gretna v Albion
Peterhead v East Stirling
Queen's Park v Cowdenbeath
Stenhousemuir v Elgin

Saturday, January 1, 2005
Albion v Queen's Park

Cowdenbeath v East Fife
East Stirling v Stenhousemuir
Elgin v Peterhead
Montrose v Gretna

Monday, January 3
Albion v Peterhead
Cowdenbeath v East Stirling
East Fife v Stenhousemuir
Elgin v Montrose
Queen's Park v Gretna

Saturday, January 15
East Stirling v Elgin
Gretna v Cowdenbeath
Montrose v Albion
Peterhead v East Fife
Stenhousemuir v Queen's Park

Saturday, January 22
Albion v Stenhousemuir
Cowdenbeath v Elgin
East Fife v East Stirling
Peterhead v Gretna
Queen's Park v Montrose

Saturday, January 29
East Stirling v Queen's Park
Elgin v Albion
Gretna v East Fife
Montrose v Cowdenbeath
Stenhousemuir v Peterhead

Saturday, February 5
Albion v East Stirling
East Fife v Queen's Park
Gretna v Elgin
Montrose v Stenhousemuir
Peterhead v Cowdenbeath

Saturday, February 12
Cowdenbeath v Albion
East Stirling v Montrose
Elgin v East Fife

Queen's Park v Peterhead
Stenhousemuir v Gretna

Saturday, February 19
East Fife v Cowdenbeath
Gretna v Montrose
Peterhead v Elgin
Queen's Park v Albion
Stenhousemuir v East Stirling

Saturday, February 26
Albion v East Fife
Cowdenbeath v Stenhousemuir
East Stirling v Gretna
Elgin v Queen's Park
Montrose v Peterhead

Saturday, March 5
Albion v Montrose
Cowdenbeath v Gretna
East Fife v Peterhead
Elgin v East Stirling
Queen's Park v Stenhousemuir

Saturday, March 12
East Stirling v Cowdenbeath
Gretna v Queen's Park
Montrose v Elgin
Peterhead v Albion
Stenhousemuir v East Fife

Saturday, March 19
East Stirling v East Fife
Elgin v Cowdenbeath
Gretna v Peterhead
Montrose v Queen's Park
Stenhousemuir v Albion

Saturday, April 2
Albion v Elgin

Cowdenbeath v Montrose
East Fife v Gretna
Peterhead v Stenhousemuir
Queen's Park v East Stirling

Saturday, April 9
Albion v Cowdenbeath
East Fife v Elgin
Gretna v Stenhousemuir
Montrose v East Stirling
Peterhead v Queen's Park

Saturday, April 16
Cowdenbeath v Peterhead
East Stirling v Albion
Elgin v Gretna
Queen's Park v East Fife
Stenhousemuir v Montrose

Saturday, April 23
Albion v Queen's Park
Cowdenbeath v East Fife
East Stirling v Stenhousemuir
Elgin v Peterhead
Montrose v Gretna

Saturday, April 30
East Fife v Albion
Gretna v East Stirling
Peterhead v Montrose
Queen's Park v Elgin
Stenhousemuir v Cowdenbeath

Saturday, May 7
Albion v Gretna
Cowdenbeath v Queen's Park
East Stirling v Peterhead
Elgin v Stenhousemuir
Montrose v East Fife

LEADING EXECUTIVES/SECRETARIES

SCOTTISH FA – D. Taylor, Chief Executive, Hampden Park, Glasgow, G42 9AY. Tel: 0141 616 6000. Website: scottishfa.co.uk

SCOTTISH PREMIER LEAGUE – Lex Gold, Chairman, Hampden Park, Glasgow, G42 9DE. 0141 620 4140. Website: scotprem.com

SCOTTISH FOOTBALL LEAGUE – P. Donald, Secretary, Hampden Park, Glasgow, G42 9EB. Tel: 0141 620 4160. Website: scottishfootballleague.com

ENGLISH FA – M. Palios, Chief Executive, 25 Soho Square, London, W1D 4FA. Tel: 0207 262 4542. Website: thefa.com

ENGLISH PREMIER LEAGUE – R. Scudamore, Chief Executive, 11 Connaught Place, London, W2 2ET. Tel: 0207 298 1600. Website: 4thegame.com

ENGLISH FOOTBALL LEAGUE – B. Mawhinney, Chairman, Edward VII Quay, Navigation Way, Preston, PR2 2YF. Tel: 01772 325800. Website: football-league.co.uk

FA OF WALES – D. Collins, Chief Executive, 3 Westgate Street, Cardiff, CF10 1DP. Tel: 02920 372325. Website: faw.org.uk

NORTHERN IRELAND FA – D. I. Bowen, General Secretary, 20 Windsor Avenue, Belfast, BT9 6EE. Tel: 02890 669458. Website: irishfa.com

IRISH LEAGUE – H. Wallace, Secretary, 96 University Street, Belfast, BT7 1HE. Tel: 02890 242888. Website: irish-league.co.uk

FA OF IRELAND – K. Fahy, General Secretary, 80 Merrion Square, Dublin 2, Eire. Tel: 00 353 1 6766864. Website: fai.ie

FOOTBALL LEAGUE OF IRELAND – B. Dillon, Chairman, 80 Merrion Square, Dublin 2, Eire. Tel: 00 353 1 6765120. Website: fai.ie

FIFA – S. Blatter, President, FIFA House, PO Box 85, 8030, Zurich, Switzerland. 00 411 384 9595. Website: fifa.com

UEFA – L Olsson, Chief Executive, Route de Geneve 46, CH-1260 Nyon 2, Switzerland. Tel: 00 41 22 994 4444. Website: uefa.com

SCOTTISH PROFESSIONAL FOOTBALLERS' ASSOCIATION – A. Higgins, Secretary, Fountain House, 1/3 Woodside Crescent, Glasgow, G3 7UJ. 0141 332 8641.

SCOTTISH JUNIOR FA – T. Johnston, Secretary, Hampden Park, Glasgow, G42 9DD. Tel: 0141 620 4560. Website: scottish-juniors.co.uk

WEST OF SCOTLAND REGION – S Robertson. Secretary. 01698 266 725. Website: scottish-juniors.co.uk

SCOTTISH WOMENS' FA – Ms M McGonigle, Executive Administrator. Hampden Park, Glasgow G42. Tel: 0141 620 4580.

K7X

FOOTRALL COMPLEX & BAR

- ⚽ **Five and Seven a-side Pitches**
- ⚽ Casual and Block Bookings available
- ⚽ **Kids Nestle Allstars Football Parties**
- ⚽ Free Function Room Hire
- ⚽ **Junior Football Coaching with the Scottish Football Association**
- ⚽ Adult and Junior Leagues
- ⚽ Café/Bar

**K7X Ltd, Rouken Glen Park,
Rouken Glen Road, Glasgow, G46 6UG
T: 0141 621 4459   F 0141 620 3613
info@ k7x.co.uk   www.k7x.co.uk**

2003-2004 REVIEW OF THE SEASON

JULY

3: Celtic striker Craig Beattie signs new three-year contract.

8: Rangers manager Alex McLeish hands trials to David May and Emerson Thome.

11: Celtic defender Stanislav Varga signs a new two-year deal.

14: Blackburn complete £1.4million signing of Rangers defender Lorenzo Amoruso on a three-year deal.

15: Rangers offer a trial to former Aston Villa defender Alan Wright.

16: Scotland striker Stevie Thompson hits both goals as Rangers kick off their tour of Germany with a 2-0 win over Greuther Furth.

17: Early goals from Stilian Petrov and Henrik Larsson earn Celtic a 2-1 victory in a friendly at Fulham.

18: Dundee defender Zura Khizanishvili signs a three-year deal with Rangers.

19: Rangers run out comfortable 5-1 victors against German Fourth Division side Auerbach in the Wernesgruner Cup. Ronald de Boer fires Rangers to a 1-0 victory over FC Erzgebirge in their second 45-minute game of the day.

23: Manchester United blitz Celtic 4-0 in their friendly at Seahawks Stadium in Seattle in front of a 66,722 crowd.

24: Sunderland's Emerson Thome released from his trial with Rangers, along with fellow trialist David May.

26: Rangers lose 3-2 in a friendly with Everton. Chris Sutton bags the only goal as Celtic wrap up pre-season tour with a 1-0 win over Boca Juniors in Cleveland.

28: Celtic striker Chris Sutton handed a one-match ban – bringing his total to five after his double red card against Kilmarnock – for bringing the game into disrepute after he accused Dunfermline of 'lying down' to Rangers to hand them the 2002-03 SPL title following Celtic's win over Killie.

30: Celtic win their Champions League second qualifying round first leg tie against FBK Kaunas 4-0 in Lithuania with goals from Henrik Larsson, Chris Sutton, Shaun Maloney and Liam Miller.

AUGUST

2: Celtic play out a 1-1 draw with Arsenal at Parkhead.

4: Rangers sign former Parma and Bologna Italian defender Paolo Vanoli.

5: Neil McCann leaves Rangers for Southampton for £1.5m as Gers sign former Manchester United and Blackburn defender Henning Berg on a one-year deal. Arsenal outclass Rangers to record a 3-0 Ibrox victory.

6: Celtic book their place in the final qualifying stages of the Champions League when

2003-2004 REVIEW OF THE SEASON

they dump Kaunas out of the competition. A Darius Gvildys own goal in the 21st minute gives Celtic a 1-0 win on the night and a 5-0 aggregate victory.

9: Dunfermline deny Celtic three points in a goalless draw on the opening day of the campaign. Champions Rangers thump 10-man Kilmarnock 4-0 to get their season off to a flying start.

13: Celtic take a massive step towards the group stage of the Champions League by romping to an impressive 4-0 win over MTK Hungaria. Henrik Larsson, Didier Agathe, Stilian Petrov and Chris Sutton are on target for Martin O'Neill's side. Rangers are outclassed on their own patch by FC Copenhagen in a 1-1 draw at Ibrox. Peter Lovenkrands scores to keep intact Rangers' unbeaten home record in European competition that stretches back to 1999.

14: Sunderland manager Mick McCarthy completes the signing of Celtic midfielder Colin Healy on a two-year deal.

16: Celtic notch up their first league win of the new season in style by a 5-0 margin over Dundee United.

22: Rangers manager Alex McLeish confirms Barry Ferguson wants to leave the club as soon as possible.

27: Chris Sutton secures a 1-0 win (5-0 aggregate) at home to MTK Hungaria to guarantee a Champions League place.

A late strike by Shota Arveladze fires Rangers into the Champions League for the first time in three seasons as they beat FC Copenhagen 2-1 – a 3-2 aggregate success.

28: Uefa hand a historic Fair Play award to Celtic fans. Celtic's fans are recognised as a result of the Uefa Cup final, when 70,000 supporters descended on Seville for the match against Porto.

29: Blackburn complete their £7.5million move for Rangers midfielder Barry Ferguson. Rangers sign Brazilian midfielder Emerson. Kevin Muscat joins Millwall on a three-year contract from Rangers.

30: Rangers snap up striker Egil Ostenstad from Blackburn Rovers on a one-year deal. Hat-trick hero Henrik Larsson sends Martin O'Neill's side to the top of the Premier League for the first time this season with a 5-1 win over Livingston.

SEPTEMBER

1: Motherwell sell prize asset James McFadden to Everton for £1.5million. Celtic swoop for Sunderland defender Michael Gray on a four-month loan deal.

6: Goals from Neil McCann, Paul Dickov and James McFadden hand Scotland a

2003-2004 REVIEW OF THE SEASON

3-1 win over the Faroe Islands at the National Stadium in Euro 2004 qualifying.

8: Free agents Dani and Ivan de la Pena train with Celtic as Martin O'Neill attempts to boost his squad for the Champions League.

10: Scotland crash 2-1 to Germany in Euro 2004 qualifying at the Westfalen Stadium in Dortmund.

16: Peter Lovenkrands' deflected shot 11 minutes from time earns Rangers a 2-1 comeback victory over Stuttgart in the Champions League at Ibrox.

17: Bayern Munich come from behind to beat Celtic 2-1 in the Olympic Stadium.

25: Rangers manager Alex McLeish finally signs his new deal, tying him to the Ibrox club until 2007.

30: Liam Miller and Chris Sutton kick-start Celtic's Champions League campaign with a 2-0 win over Lyon.

OCTOBER

1: Rangers go top of Champions League Group E thanks to a 1-1 draw with Panathinaikos in Athens.

4: A deflected strike from John Hartson 20 seconds into the second half gives Celtic a 1-0 victory in the opening Old Firm derby of the season.

11: A Darren Fletcher strike on 69 minutes against Lithuania

wins Scotland a Euro 2004 qualifying play-off spot against Holland.

19: Rangers held 1-1 at Motherwell

21: Celtic squander a golden opportunity to earn their first Champions League away win as 10-man Anderlecht snatch a 1-0 victory.

22: Rangers lose to a Phil Neville goal at home to Manchester United.

25: Rangers drop points for the second successive week after they follow up Sunday's defeat at Motherwell with a goalless stalemate at Livingston.

28: A Christian Nerlinger hat-trick ensures that Rangers get back to winning ways when they dump Forfar out of the CIS Insurance Cup with a 6-0 win.

NOVEMBER

4: Ruud van Nistelrooy ends his barren scoring spell with a brace in Manchester United's 3-0 win which condemns Rangers to back-to-back defeats in the Battle of Britain.

5: Liam Miller inspires Celtic at Parkhead as they revive their Champions League campaign with a crushing 3-1 defeat of Anderlecht.

15: Scotland shock Holland at Hampden as a James McFadden goal hands Berti Vogts' men a 1-0 Euro 2004

2003-2004 REVIEW OF THE SEASON

play-off lead after the first leg.

16: Scotland Under-21s lose out in 2-0 in Croatia in the first leg of their European Championship play-off.

18: A goal from Garry O'Connor for a 1-0 victory is not enough as Scotland Under-21s crash 2-1 on aggregate to Croatia in their European Championship play-off second leg.

19: Holland are rampant as they snuff out Scottish Euro 2004 play-off hopes with a 6-0 (6-1 on aggregate) triumph at Amsterdam ArenA in the second leg.

24: Dundee are placed into administration.

25: Bayern Munich claim a goalless draw with Celtic at Parkhead.

26: Rangers' slim hopes of reaching the Champions league knockout stages are extinguished once and for all by a 1-0 defeat in Stuttgart. John Coughlin steps down as St Mirren manager.

30: Gerry Collins sacked as manager of Partick Thistle.

DECEMBER

1: Peter Hetherston resigns as Albion Rovers manager.

3: Chris Burke scores a stunning solo goal on his debut as Rangers beat St Johnstone 3-0 to reach the semi-finals of the CIS Insurance Cup.

4: Craig Beattie and Jamie Smith steal the show from managerless Partick as Celtic stroll into the quarter-final of the CIS Insurance Cup with a 2-0 win at Firhill.

9: Rangers are dumped out of Europe after Panathinaikos produce a scintillating second-half display to earn a 3-1 win at Ibrox.

10: A late penalty condemns Celtic to a 3-2 defeat in Lyon and also sends them out of the Champions League.

12: Fifa award the 2003 Fair Play Award to Celtic supporters for their conduct at the Uefa Cup Final in May.

13: Celtic crawl eight points clear of Rangers at the top of the SPL table with a 3-2 win over Dundee. Celtic set a new club milestone of 15 straight victories in the process.

14: Rangers manager Alex McLeish confirms Auxerre defender Jean-Alain Boumsong has signed a pre-contract agreement with the Ibrox side. Rangers' season takes another turn for the worse when Paolo Vanoli's bizarre own goal confirms their first league defeat to Dunfermline in 30 years. Their 2-0 loss has a massive impact on the SPL championship as Celtic, who beat Dundee on Saturday, have now seen their eight-point advantage remain intact.

18: Nineteen-year-old Kevin Thomson scores the goal

2003-2004 REVIEW OF THE SEASON

which sends Celtic tumbling to their first domestic defeat of the season as Hibs pull off a stunning 2-1 win. Thomson's strike is enough to book his side a place in the CIS Insurance Cup semi-finals against Rangers. Gus MacPherson replaces John Coughlin as boss of St Mirren.

23: Gerry Britton and Derek Whyte are confirmed as the joint replacement bosses for Gerry Collins at Partick Thistle.

24: Rangers winger Chris Burke agrees terms on a three-year contract extension.

27: Chris Sutton and John Hartson both score twice as Celtic hit 10-man Hibernian for six at Parkhead to move 11 points clear of Rangers at the top of the SPL.

31: Celtic manager Martin O'Neill awarded OBE. Fulham complete the loan signing of Celtic midfielder Bobby Petta until the end of the current season. Dundee and Rangers agree a fee for midfielder Gavin Rae and he signs for Gers.

JANUARY

3: Celtic move 11 points clear of Rangers at the top of the SPL with a comfortable 3-0 victory at Parkhead.

9: Manchester United finalise a pre-contract agreement for Celtic midfielder Liam Miller. Celtic complete the signing of

Stephen Pearson from Motherwell for £350,000.

10: Second-half goals from John Hartson and Paul Lambert ensure an out-of-sorts Celtic make the fourth round of the Tennent's Scottish Cup against Ross County. Holders Rangers book a place in the next round of the as well with a 2-0 win at Hibernian.

14: Bob Malcolm signs a one-year contract extension at Rangers.

15: Steve Guppy rejoins Leicester on a short-term contract until the end of the season.

19: Celtic striker Craig Beattie puts pen to paper on a new three-year deal at the Parkhead club.

22: Scottish Premier League clubs who go into administration after this season will suffer a 10-point deduction and be banned from signing new players.

26: Holland international Frank de Boer signs for Rangers until the end of the season.

28: Celtic manager Martin O'Neill confirms that he has allowed out-of-favour goalkeeper Magnus Hedman to join Italian side Ancona on loan until the end of the season.

30: Southampton complete the signing of left-back Stephen Crainey from Celtic for an undisclosed fee.

2003-2004 REVIEW OF THE SEASON

31: Celtic stretch their lead over Rangers at the top of the Bank of Scotland Premier League to 14 points with a 5-1 victory over Kilmarnock.

FEBRUARY

4: Livingston are placed in administration.

5: Hibernian book their place in the CIS Insurance Cup final with a penalty shoot-out victory over holders Rangers. Frank de Boer trundles a spot-kick against a post as the Gers lose the shoot-out 4-3 following a 1-1 draw.

7: Stilian Petrov shatters Hearts for the second time in three weeks with a double as Celtic cruise into the quarter-final of the Tennent's Scottish Cup with a 3-0 win.

8: Rangers keep their season alive with a 2-0 win at Kilmarnock thanks to second-half goals from Ronald de Boer and Shota Arveladze.

10: Rangers fine Fernando Ricksen £10,000 for elbowing Hibs player Derek Riordan during a cup semi-final

14: Celtic come from behind against Dundee United with two late goals to extend their lead over Rangers to 13 points. Shaun Maloney and Chris Sutton's rescue act extends the Hoops' winning league run to 23 games, equalling a 40-year-old British record in the process.

22: Martin O'Neill's record-breaking Celtic stars destroy Morton's 40-year league winning feat with a 4-1 victory at Firhill over Partick Thistle. Chris Sutton and Stanislav Varga both celebrate with doubles as Celtic stretch their winning run to an incredible 24 games. That beats the Greenock side's milestone in 1963/64.

24: Celtic striker Shaun Maloney faces up to nine months on the sidelines after an arthroscopy showed a ruptured anterior cruciate ligament. The Scotland Under-21 forward was injured five minutes into an Under-21 game against Partick Thistle.

26: The Scottish Premier League confirm that broadcasters Setanta have won the bidding war to televise live games on a lucrative four-year deal. Celtic continue their Uefa Cup pursuit with a comfortable 3-0 win over Teplice at Parkhead.

29: Mark Kerr and Andy McLaren earn Dundee United their first victory over Rangers in almost three years in a 2-0 triumph at Tannadice. The result sees last year's Treble winners fall even further behind Celtic in a championship race that has already seen bookies pay up on the Hoops, who moved 16 points clear by hammering Livingston.

2003-2004 REVIEW OF THE SEASON

MARCH

2: The Scottish Football Association fine referee Stuart Dougal after he was caught on camera swearing at Rangers midfielder Christian Nerlinger last month during the Light Blues' 1-0 win at Partick Thistle.

3: Celtic reach the fourth round of the Uefa Cup, despite a 1-0 second-leg defeat by Teplice, winning 3-1 on aggregate.

7: Rangers' season came to a painful conclusion with a 1-0 defeat at the hands of bitter rivals Celtic in the Scottish Cup quarter-final clash at Parkhead. Henrik Larsson is again the ruthless hitman who effectively killed off any trophy hopes that Alex McLeish might have had, with the championship also surely out of reach.

10: Alex McLeish begins the clear-out of players the fans have been demanding - with Nuno Capucho, Emerson and Christian Nerlinger the first to be told they have no futures at Ibrox. Henning Berg and Michael Mols will also leave at the end of the season when their contracts expire.

11: Three players are red-carded as 10-man Celtic punish a wasteful and indisciplined Barcelona side 1-0 at Parkhead. After Barca squander three glorious first-half chances, Robert Douglas and Thiago Motta are dismissed following a clash in the tunnel. And Javier Saviola also sees red just after the break, before Celtic snatch the Uefa Cup fourth-round, first-leg win through Alan Thompson's strike.

16: Rangers defender Fernando Ricksen is handed a ban by the Scottish FA. The SFA use video evidence against a player for only the third time in their history after charging the Dutch international with violent conduct. Television cameras caught Ricksen elbowing Hibernian's Derek Riordan in the CIS Cup semi-final at Hampden Park on February 1.

17: Rangers manager Alex McLeish continues his clear-out of surplus players by allowing Egil Ostenstad to return to Norway.

21: Henrik Larsson enhances his legendary status at Parkhead with a classy double as his side destroy Hibs 4-0 at Easter Road. Didier Agathe also bags a brace as the champions-elect regain their 19-point lead over Rangers at the top of the SPL. Larsson becomes the club's all-time third top scorer after going beyond Stevie Chalmers' record of 231 goals.

24: Rangers defender Fernando Ricksen rejects the offer of an extended contract at Ibrox,

2003-2004 REVIEW OF THE SEASON

according to his agent, Henk van Ginkel. Rangers defender Alan Hutton signs a new three-year deal after scoring his first goal for the club on Tuesday night.

25: Celtic pull off one of the greatest results in their history, holding on for a 1-0 aggregate win over Barcelona.

26: Celtic goalkeeper David Marshall signs a new four-year deal with the Parkhead club.

27: Celtic midfielder Alan Thompson in England squad for friendly v Sweden in Gothenburg.

28: Celtic rack up their fourth Old Firm victory of the season and their fifth in a row as a 2-1 win inflicts more misery on last season's Treble winners Rangers.

30: SPL board meeting approves Division One leaders Clyde's plans to groundshare at Kilmarnock after denying the Bully Wee and Inverness more time to meet the SPL stadium criteria.

APRIL

1: Celtic defender John Kennedy facing a year out after his Scotland debut ended in agony. The 20-year-old was the victim of a crunching tackle by Wolves striker Vio Ganea just 14 minutes into the defeat against Romania at Hampden Park. Kennedy was stretchered off

and the club feared ligament damage – and those fears were confirmed.

3: Celtic score twice in an incredible final three minutes to deny Hearts a famous victory and save their incredible unbeaten record in a dramatic 2-2 draw at Parkhead. A last-gasp Didier Agathe strike put them a point closer the Premier League trophy and keeps intact a fantastic home run which stretches back to August 2001 and 76 games.

7: Chris Sutton and Alan Thompson sign new two-year contract extensions with Celtic. Striker Sutton and midfielder Thompson, who made his England debut against Sweden last week, pledge their immediate futures to the Hoops until 2007.

8: Celtic's Uefa Cup quarter-final first leg against Villarreal finishes 1-1 at Parkhead. The Spanish side take the lead in the eighth minute through Jose Moreno Josico and test the Hoops in the first half with some dangerous counter-attacking moves. But Celtic buck up in the second half, denying Villarreal possession and deservedly equalise in the 63rd minute with a Henrik Larsson header.

11: Treble-chasing Celtic seize on some calamitous Livingston defending at Hampden Park to book their place in the Tennent's Scottish

2003-2004 REVIEW OF THE SEASON

Cup Final with a 3-1 success.

14: Celtic's Uefa Cup flame finally flicker out after their defence and attack fail to shine in a 2-0 defeat at Villarreal. Sonny Anderson and Roger Garcia capitalise on some sloppy play in the Hoops backline by Bobo Balde and Joos Valgaeren in each half to guide Villarreal into the last four in a 3-1 aggregate triumph.

Colin McMenamin comes off the bench to fire another nail into Rangers' coffin of a season as Livingston earned a 1-1 draw. Last year's Treble winners knew that Celtic would be put on championship-clinching alert at Kilmarnock on Sunday if they slipped up at Almondvale, as they had done earlier in the season. Michael Mols gives Rangers a half-time lead but youngster McMenamin's equaliser with 10 minutes remaining a reward for a second half that the home side dominated.

17: Livingston defender Marvin Andrews signs a pre-contract agreement with Rangers.

18: Martin O'Neill's Celtic heal the pain of Spain by wrapping up their third Premier League title in four years with a controversial victory at Kilmarnock. Celtic were hurting after their Uefa Cup quarter-final exit to Villarreal but Stilian Petrov's 32nd-minute goal moves them an unassailable 16 points clear of Rangers at the top of the league.

20: Former Celtic goalkeeper Ronnie Simpson dies at the age of 73 after suffering a heart attack. The ex-Queen's Park player kept goal for the Hoops in their historic 1967 European Cup Final win over Inter Milan in Lisbon. Jackie McNamara signs a one-year extension to his current Celtic deal, tying him to the club until the summer of 2005.

21: Celtic's hopes of going through an entire SPL campaign unbeaten are crushed by an entirely unexpected 2-1 home defeat at the hands of Aberdeen. Motherwell come out of administration.

24: Substitute Jason Scotland comes off the bench to fire two second-half goals and earn Dundee United a point from a thrilling 3-3 draw with Rangers.

Celtic's Chris Sutton named SPFA Player of the Year with team-mate Stephen Pearson young Player of the Year. Other awards go to Clyde forward Ian Harty, Forfar's Paul Tosh, and Stranraer midfielder Michael Moore, who land the top prizes for the Bell's First, Second and Third Divisions respectively.

30: Henrik Larsson comes out

2003-2004 REVIEW OF THE SEASON

of international retirement to play for Sweden.

MAY

3: Rangers confirm they have parted company with Christian Nerlinger after the German agrees a pay-off settlement.

3: Celtic manager Martin O'Neill wins the Scottish Football Writers' Manager of the Year Award. The Hoops' Jackie McNamara is SFWA Player of the Year .

0: Monaco striker Dado Prso signs a pre-contract deal to join Rangers.

5: Inverness clinch Division One title with home win against St Johnstone on the final day of the season. Caley boss John Robertson calls for the board to move forward with plans to groundshare with Aberdeen.

9: Wolves midfielder Alex Rae puts pen to paper on a pre-contract agreement to join Rangers.

22: A brace from Henrik Larsson in his final game for Celtic and a Stilian Petrov strike gives Celtic a 3-1 Scottish Cup triumph over Dunfermline and clinches The Double.

4: Tony Mowbray is named as Hibs boss to replace Bobby Williamson.

7: Inverness reach agreement with the Dons over ground-share at Pittodrie. Partick Thistle chairman Tom Hughes promises he will not give up the club's place in the SPL without a fight.

28: Dunfermline manager Jimmy Calderwood leaves to take over as Aberdeen manager from the sacked Steve Paterson.

JUNE

1: Inverness fail to get enough votes to join Scottish Premier League and Partick stay in, but Caley chairman Ken Mackie vows to appeal against the ruling.

2: Caley verbally inform the Scottish Football Association of their intention to appeal against the decision.

3: Two SPL clubs request another meeting to discuss promotion and relegation issue, to the surprise of Partick.

5: Allan Preston is named as new Livingston boss.

17: Davie Hay takes over as manager of Dunfermline.

18: Partick launch legal proceedings in an attempt to stop a second vote taking place.

22: Partick fail in their bid to seek an interim interdict just minutes before the meeting at Hampden Park is due to begin. SPL votes 10-2 in favour to allow Inverness to join league.

HIGH AND MIGHTY: Aberdeen's Markus Heikkinen and Nuno Capucho, of Rangers, jump for the ball

ABERDEEN

NICKNAME:	The Dons
COLOURS:	Red and white
GROUND:	Pittodrie
TELEPHONE:	01224 650400
FAX:	01224 644173
WEBSITE:	afc.co.uk
CAPACITY:	22,199
RECORD ATT:	45,061 (v Hearts, 1954)
RECORD VICTORY:	13-0 (v Peterhead, 1923)
RECORD DEFEAT:	0-8 (v Celtic, 1965)
MANAGER:	Jimmy Calderwood
CHIEF EXECUTIVE:	Keith Wyness
CHAIRMAN:	Stewart Milne
MOST LEAGUE	
GOALS (1 SEASON):	38, Benny Yorston, 1929-30
GOALS (OVERALL):	199, Joe Harper

HONOURS

LEAGUE CHAMPIONSHIP (4): Division 1 – 1954-55. Premier Division – 1979-80, 1983-84, 1984-85. SCOTTISH CUP (7): 1947, 1970, 1982, 1983, 1984, 1986, 1990. LEAGUE CUP (5): 1955-56, 1976-77, 1985-86, 1989-90, 1995-96. EUROPEAN CUP-WINNERS' CUP: 1983. EUROPEAN SUPER CUP: 1983-84.

LEAGUE RESULTS 2003-2004

Hearts 2 Aberdeen 0	Dundee Utd 3 Aberdeen 2
Aberdeen 2 Rangers 3	Aberdeen 1 Celtic 3
Aberdeen 1 Dunfermline 2	Hearts 1 berdeen 0
Hibernian 1 Aberdeen 1	Aberdeen 1 Rangers 1
Aberdeen 2 Partick 1	Aberdeen 2 Dunfermline 0
Dundee 2 Aberdeen 0	Motherwell 1 Aberdeen 0
Aberdeen 0 Livingston 3	Hibernian 0 Aberdeen 1
Kilmarnock 1 Aberdeen 3	Aberdeen 0 Partick 0
Aberdeen 0 Dundee Utd 1	Dundee 1 Aberdeen 1
Celtic 4 Aberdeen 0	Aberdeen 1 Livingston 2
Aberdeen 0 Motherwell 3	Kilmarnock 3 Aberdeen 1
Aberdeen 0 Hearts 1	Aberdeen 3 Dundee Utd 0
Rangers 3 Aberdeen 0	Aberdeen 0 Motherwell 2
Dunfermline 2 Aberdeen 2	Celtic 1 Aberdeen 2
Aberdeen 3 Hibernian 1	Livingston 2 Aberdeen 0
Partick 0 Aberdeen 3	Partick 2 Aberdeen 0
Aberdeen 2 Dundee 2	Aberdeen 0 Hibernian 1
Livingston 1 Aberdeen 1	Kilmarnock 4 Aberdeen 0
Aberdeen 3 Kilmarnock 1	Aberdeen 1 Dundee 2

AIRDRIE UNITED

NICKNAME:	The Diamonds
COLOURS:	White and red
GROUND:	Excelsior Stadium
TELEPHONE No:	07710 230775
FAX No:	0141 221 1497
WEBSITE:	airdrieunitedfc.com
CAPACITY:	10,170
RECORD ATT:	5709 (v Morton, 2004)
RECORD VICTORY:	6-0 (v Berwick, 2004)
RECORD DEFEAT:	1-6 (v Morton, 2003)
FOUNDED:	2002
MANAGER:	Sandy Stewart
CHAIRMAN:	Jim Ballantyne
MOST LEAGUE GOALS (1 SEASON):	18, Jerome Vareille, 2002-03

HONOURS

LEAGUE CHAMPIONSHIP: Second Division – 2003-04.

LEAGUE RESULTS 2003-2004

Morton 3 Airdrie Utd 1
Airdrie Utd 1 Alloa 0
Hamilton 2 Airdrie Utd 1
Airdrie Utd 2 Dumbarton 0
East Fife 3 Airdrie Utd 1
Airdrie Utd 2 Arbroath 1
Berwick 0 Airdrie Utd 1
Forfar 1 Airdrie Utd 1
Alloa 1 Airdrie Utd 4
Airdrie Utd 2 Stenhousemuir 0
Airdrie Utd 1 Morton 6
Airdrie Utd 1 East Fife 1
Dumbarton 2 Airdrie Utd 0
Arbroath 1 Airdrie Utd 1
Airdrie Utd 1 Berwick 1
Airdrie Utd 3 Forfar 3
Stenhousemuir 0 Airdrie Utd 1
Airdrie Utd 0 Arbroath 1

East Fife 0 Airdrie Utd 1
Airdrie Utd 1 Dumbarton 1
Airdrie Utd 4 Stenhousemuir 0
Airdrie Utd 3 Hamilton 0
Airdrie Utd 2 Alloa 1
Morton 1 Airdrie Utd 1
Hamilton 0 Airdrie Utd 1
Berwick 1 Airdrie Utd 1
Forfar 1 Airdrie Utd 3
Dumbarton 1 Airdrie Utd 2
Airdrie Utd 2 East Fife 1
Airdrie Utd 6 Berwick 0
Arbroath 0 Airdrie Utd 4
Stenhousemuir 0 Airdrie Utd 3
Airdrie Utd 2 Forfar 2
Airdrie Utd 1 Hamilton 1
Alloa 0 Airdrie Utd 1
Airdrie Utd 2 Morton 0

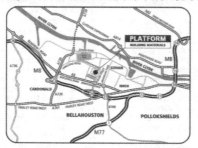

ALBION ROVERS

NICKNAME:	The Rovers
COLOURS:	Yellow and red
GROUND:	Cliftonhill Stadium
TELEPHONE No:	01236 606334
FAX No:	01236 606334
CAPACITY:	2496
RECORD ATT:	27,381
	(v Rangers, 1936)
RECORD VICTORY:	12-0 (v Airdriehill, 1887)
RECORD DEFEAT:	1-11 (v Partick Thistle, 1993)
MANAGER:	Kevin McAllister
CHAIRMAN:	Andrew Dick
MOST LEAGUE	
GOALS (1 SEASON):	41, Jim Renwick, 1932-33

HONOURS

LEAGUE CHAMPIONSHIP: Division II – 1933-34. Second Division – 1988-89.

LEAGUE RESULTS 2003-2004

Albion 1 Stranraer 1
Cowdenbeath 1 Albion 4
Albion 3 Queen's Park 1
Gretna 3 Albion 1
Albion 1 Elgin City 2
Albion 0 Montrose 1
Stirling 2 Albion 1
Albion 2 Peterhead 0
Albion 5 East Stirling 0
Elgin City 1 Albion 5
Albion 1 Cowdenbeath 2
Stranraer 5 Albion 0
Montrose 1 Albion 0
Albion 1 Gretna 3
Albion 0 Stirling 3
Peterhead 2 Albion 1
East Stirling 3 Albion 4
Queen's Park 1 Albion 1

Stirling 3 Albion 0
Albion 3 Montrose 0
Gretna 3 Albion 0
Albion 1 Stranraer 4
Elgin City 1 Albion 2
Cowdenbeath 1 Albion 1
Albion 5 East Stirling 1
Albion 3 Queen's Park 1
Albion 3 Peterhead 3
Montrose 3 Albion 1
Albion 1 Gretna 2
Peterhead 5 Albion 0
Albion 3 Stirling 5
Albion 1 Elgin City 2
East Stirling 1 Albion 8
Queen's Park 0 Albion 1
Albion 2 Cowdenbeath 4
Stranraer 4 Albion 0

ALLOA

NICKNAME:	The Wasps
COLOURS:	Gold and black
GROUND:	Recreation Park
TELEPHONE No:	01259 722695
FAX No:	01259 210886
WEBSITE:	alloaathletic.co.uk
CAPACITY:	3142
RECORD ATT:	13,000
	(v Dunfermline, 1939)
RECORD VICTORY:	9-2 (v Forfar, 1933)
RECORD DEFEAT:	0-10 (v Dundee, 1937)
MANAGER:	Tom Hendrie
CHAIRMAN:	David R Murray
MOST LEAGUE	
GOALS (1 SEASON):	49, William Crilley, 1921-22

HONOURS
LEAGUE CHAMPIONS: Division II – 1921-22. Third Division – 1997-98. BELL'S CHALLENGE CUP: 1999-00.

LEAGUE RESULTS 2003-2004

Alloa 1 Dumbarton 2	East Fife 0 Alloa 1
Airdrie Utd 1 Alloa 0	Alloa 4 Forfar 0
Alloa 2 Stenhousemuir 2	Alloa 4 Arbroath 0
Berwick 3 Alloa 2	Berwick 3 Alloa 1
Alloa 2 Arbroath 2	Alloa 3 Morton 3
East Fife 0 Alloa 1	Airdrie Utd 2 Alloa 1
Alloa 1 Forfar 1	Alloa 1 Stenhousemuir 0
Hamilton 3 Alloa 4	Hamilton 0 Alloa 1
Alloa 1 Airdrie Utd 4	Arbroath 2 Alloa 1
Alloa 0 Morton 1	Alloa 4 Berwick 2
Dumbarton 1 Alloa 0	Morton 2 Alloa 2
Arbroath 3 Alloa 1	Alloa 1 East Fife 1
Alloa 2 Berwick 3	Forfar 2 Alloa 0
Alloa 2 East Fife 0	Morton 2 Alloa 1
Forfar 1 Alloa 1	Alloa 1 Hamilton 1
Alloa 1 Hamilton 3	Stenhousemuir 0 Alloa 1
Stenhousemuir 1 Alloa 3	Alloa 0 Airdrie Utd 1
Alloa 3 Dumbarton 0	Dumbarton 3 Alloa 1

ARBROATH

NICKNAME:	The Red Lichties
COLOURS:	Maroon and white
GROUND:	Gayfield Park
TELEPHONE No:	01241 872157
FAX No:	01241 431125
WEBSITE:	arbroathfc.co.uk
CAPACITY:	4125
RECORD ATT:	13,510 (v Rangers, 1952)
RECORD VICTORY:	36-0 (v Bon Accord, 1885)
RECORD DEFEAT:	1-9 (v Celtic, 1993)
MANAGER:	Steve Kirk
CHAIRMAN:	John D Christison
MOST LEAGUE GOALS (1 SEASON):	45, Dave Easson, 1958-59

LEAGUE RESULTS 2003-2004

Arbroath 1 Berwick 0
Dumbarton 1 Arbroath 1
Arbroath 0 Forfar 0
Arbroath 2 Hamilton 2
Alloa 2 Arbroath 2
Airdrie Utd 2 Arbroath 1
Arbroath 0 Morton 4
Stenhousemuir 1 Arbroath 0
Arbroath 0 East Fife 1
Arbroath 2 Dumbarton 1
Berwick 3 Arbroath 0
Arbroath 3 Alloa 1
Hamilton 2 Arbroath 0
Arbroath 1 Airdrie Utd 1
Morton 6 Arbroath 4
Arbroath 2 Stenhousemuir 1
East Fife 0 Arbroath 1
Arbroath 1 Berwick 2

Airdrie Utd 0 Arbroath 1
Arbroath 2 Morton 2
Alloa 4 Arbroath 0
Arbroath 0 Hamilton 2
Arbroath 0 East Fife 0
Dumbarton 1 Arbroath 0
Arbroath 0 Forfar 1
Forfar 2 Arbroath 2
Arbroath 2 Alloa 1
Hamilton 2 Arbroath 2
Stenhousemuir 0 Arbroath 3
Morton 1 Arbroath 0
Arbroath 0 Airdrie Utd 4
East Fife 1 Arbroath 2
Arbroath 1 Stenhousemuir 1
Forfar 1 Arbroath 2
Arbroath 0 Dumbarton 3
Berwick 1 Arbroath 3

AYR UNITED

NICKNAME: The Honest Men
COLOURS: White and black
GROUND: Somerset Park
TELEPHONE No: 0871 222 1910
FAX No: 01292 281314
CAPACITY: 10,184
RECORD ATT: 25,225
(v Rangers, 1969)

RECORD VICTORY: 11-1 (v Dumbarton, 1952)
RECORD DEFEAT: 0-9 (v Rangers, 1929; v Hearts, 1931; v Third Lanark, 1954)

MANAGER: Campbell Money
CHAIRMAN: David Capperauld
MOST LEAGUE
GOALS (1 SEASON): 66, Jimmy Smith, 1927-28
GOALS (OVERALL): 213, Peter Price, 1955-61

HONOURS

LEAGUE CHAMPIONS: Division II (6) – 1911-12, 1912-13, 1927-28, 1936-37, 1958-59, 1965-66. Second Division (2) – 1987-88, 1996-97.

LEAGUE RESULTS 2003-2004

Clyde 3 Ayr 0	Ayr 1 Raith 0
Ayr 1 Falkirk 1	Ayr 1 Queen of Sth 1
Raith 1 Ayr 1	Inverness CT 2 Ayr 1
Ayr 1 Queen of Sth 4	Ross County 1 Ayr 1
Inverness CT 1 Ayr 0	Ayr 1 Brechin 3
Ross County 2 Ayr 2	St Johnstone 3 Ayr 0
Ayr 3 Brechin 2	Ayr 2 St Mirren 0
St Johnstone 1 Ayr 1	Ayr 2 Falkirk 3
Ayr 0 St Mirren 2	Raith 2 Ayr 1
Falkirk 0 Ayr 1	Ayr 1 Inverness CT 1
Ayr 2 Clyde 2	Queen of Sth 0 Ayr 0
Ayr 0 Inverness CT 3	Brechin 0 Ayr 3
Queen of Sth 1 Ayr 0	Ayr 1 Ross County 2
Brechin 3 Ayr 1	St Mirren 4 Ayr 1
Ayr 1 Ross County 3	Ayr 1 St Johnstone 1
St Mirren 3 Ayr 2	Ayr 1 Clyde 1
Ayr 1 St Johnstone 1	Falkirk 0 Ayr 0
Clyde 2 Ayr 1	Ayr 1 Raith 1

BERWICK RANGERS

NICKNAME:	The Borderers
COLOURS:	Black and gold
GROUND:	Shielfield Park
TELEPHONE No:	01289 307424
FAX No:	01289 309424
CAPACITY:	4131
RECORD ATT:	13,365 (v Rangers, 1967)
RECORD VICTORY:	8-1 (v Forfar Athletic, 1965; Vale of Leithen, 1966)
RECORD DEFEAT:	1-9 (v Hamilton, 1980)
MANAGER:	Paul Smith
CHAIRMAN:	Robert Wilson
MOST LEAGUE GOALS (1 SEASON):	38, Ken Bowron, 1963-64

HONOURS
LEAGUE CHAMPIONSHIP: Second Division – 1978-79

LEAGUE RESULTS 2003-2004

Arbroath 1 Berwick 0
Berwick 3 Hamilton 1
East Fife 3 Berwick 1
Berwick 3 Alloa 2
Dumbarton 1 Berwick 1
Stenh'semuir 0 Berwick 3
Berwick 0 Airdrie Utd 1
Morton 1 Berwick 3
Berwick 0 Forfar 4
Hamilton 2 Berwick 2
Berwick 3 Arbroath 0
Berwick 1 Dumbarton 4
Alloa 2 Berwick 3
Berwick 2 Stenh'semuir 1
Airdrie Utd 1 Berwick 1
Berwick 2 Morton 3
Forfar 1 Berwick 5
Berwick 0 East Fife 2

Arbroath 1 Berwick 2
Stenh'semuir 3 Berwick 1
Dumbarton 4 Berwick 1
Berwick 3 Alloa 1
Berwick 3 Forfar 1
Berwick 2 Hamilton 4
East Fife 2 Berwick 2
Berwick 1 Airdrie Utd 1
Morton 2 Berwick 1
Alloa 4 Berwick 2
Berwick 1 Dumbarton 2
Airdrie Utd 6 Berwick 0
Berwick 3 Stenh'semuir 0
Forfar 0 Berwick 2
Berwick 2 Morton 0
Berwick 1 East Fife 1
Hamilton 2 Berwick 0
Berwick 1 Arbroath 3

BRECHIN CITY

NICKNAME:	The City
COLOURS:	Red and white
GROUND:	Glebe Park
TELEPHONE No:	01356 622856
FAX No:	01356 625667
WEBSITE:	brechincity.co.uk
CAPACITY:	3960
RECORD ATT:	8122
	(v Aberdeen, 1973)
RECORD VICTORY:	12-1 (v Thornhill, 1926)
RECORD DEFEAT:	0-10 (v Airdrie, Albion Rovers,
	Cowdenbeath, all 1937-38)
MANAGER:	Dick Campbell
CHAIRMAN:	David Birse
MOST LEAGUE	
GOALS (1 SEASON):	26, W McIntosh, 1959-60

HONOURS

LEAGUE CHAMPIONSHIP: Second Division (2) – 1982-83, 1989-90. Third Division – 2001-02. C Division – 1953-54.

LEAGUE RESULTS 2003-2004

Ross County 4 Brechin 0	Brechin 1 Clyde 3
Brechin 0 Raith 3	St Johnstone 2 Brechin 2
Clyde 2 Brechin 1	Brechin 2 St Mirren 0
St Johnstone 3 Brechin 1	Brechin 2 Inverness CT 4
Brechin 1 St Mirren 1	Ayr 1 Brechin 2
Brechin 0 nverness CT 2	Brechin 2 Queen of Sth 1
Ayr 3 Brechin 2	Falkirk 5 Brechin 0
Brechin 0 Queen of Sth 1	Brechin 1 Raith
Falkirk 3 Brechin 0	Clyde 0 Brechin 0
Raith 2 Brechin 1	St Mirren 3 Brechin 3
Brechin 4 Ross County 2	Brechin 0 St Johnstone 2
St Mirren 0 Brechin 0	Brechin 0 Ayr 3
Brechin 0 St Johnstone 1	Inverness CT 1 Brechin 0
Brechin 3 Ayr 1	Brechin 0 Falkirk 1
Inverness CT 5 Brechin 0	Queen of Sth 2 Brechin 2
Brechin 2 Falkirk 2	Brechin 1 Ross County 0
Queen of Sth 1 Brechin 0	Raith 1 Brechin 1
Ross County 2 Brechin 1	Brechin 2 Clyde 5

CELTIC

NICKNAME:	The Bhoys
COLOURS:	Green and white
GROUND:	Celtic Park
TELEPHONE No:	0141 556 2611
FAX No:	0141 551 8106
WEBSITE:	celticfc.co.uk
CAPACITY:	60,506
RECORD ATT:	92,000
	(v Rangers, 1938)
RECORD VICTORY:	11-0 (v Dundee, 1895)
RECORD DEFEAT:	0-8 (v Motherwell, 1937)
MANAGER:	Martin O'Neill
CHIEF EXECUTIVE:	Peter Lawwell
MOST LEAGUE	
GOALS (1 SEASON):	50, Jimmy McGrory, 1935-36
GOALS (OVERALL):	472, Jimmy McGrory, 1922-37

HONOURS

LEAGUE CHAMPIONS (39): 1892-93, 1893-94, 1895-96, 1897-98, 1904-05, 1905-06, 1906-07, 1907-08, 1908-09, 1909-10, 1913-14, 1914-15, 1915-16, 1916-17, 1918-19, 1921-22, 1925-26, 1935-36, 1937-38, 1953-54, 1965-66, 1966-67, 1967-68, 1968-69, 1969-70, 1970-71, 1971-72, 1972-73, 1973-74, 1976-77, 1978-79, 1980-81, 1981-82, 1985-86, 1987-88, 1997-98, 2000-01, 2001-02, 2003-2004.

SCOTTISH CUP WINNERS (32): 1892, 1899, 1900, 1904, 1907, 1908, 1911, 1912, 1914, 1923, 1925, 1927, 1931, 1933, 1937, 1951, 1954, 1965, 1967, 1969, 1971, 1972, 1974, 1975, 1977, 1980, 1985, 1988, 1989, 1985, 2001, 2004.

LEAGUE CUP WINNERS (12): 1956-57, 1957-58, 1965-66, 1966-67, 1967-68, 1968-69, 1969-70, 1974-75, 1982-83, 1997-98, 1999-00, 2000-01.

EUROPEAN CUP WINNERS: 1966-67.

DAVID MARSHALL   **CHRIS SUTTON**

LEAGUE RESULTS 2003-2004

Dunfermline 0 Celtic 0
Celtic 5 Dundee Utd 0
Partick 1 Celtic 2
Celtic 5 Livingston 1
Dundee 0 Celtic 1
Celtic 3 Motherwell 0
Hibernian 1 Celtic 2
Rangers 0 Celtic 1
Celtic 5 Hearts 0
Celtic 4 Aberdeen 0
Kilmarnock 0 Celtic 5
Celtic 5 Dunfermline 0
Dundee Utd 1 Celtic 5
Celtic 3 Partick 1
Livingston 0 Celtic 2
Celtic 3 Dundee 2
Motherwell 0 Celtic 2
Celtic 6 Hibernian 0
Celtic 3 Rangers 0

Hearts 0 Celtic 1
Aberdeen 1 Celtic 3
Celtic 5 Kilmarnock 1
Dunfermline 1 Celtic 4
Celtic 2 Dundee Utd 1
Partick 1 Celtic 4
Celtic 5 Livingston 1
Celtic 1 Motherwell 1
Dundee 1 Celtic 2
Hibernian 0 Celtic 4
Rangers 1 Celtic 2
Celtic 2 Hearts 2
Kilmarnock 0 Celtic 1
Celtic 1 Aberdeen 2
Hearts 1 Celtic 1
Celtic 1 Dunfermline 2
Celtic 1 Rangers 0
Motherwell 1 Celtic 1
Celtic 2 Dundee Utd 1

CLYDE

NICKNAME: The Bully Wee
COLOURS: White and red
GROUND: Broadwood Stadium

TELEPHONE No: 01236 451511
FAX No: 01236 733490
WEBSITE: clydefc.co.uk
CAPACITY: 8029
RECORD ATT: 52,000 (v Rangers, 1908, at Shawfield)
RECORD VICTORY: 11-1 (v Cowdenbeath, 1951)
RECORD DEFEAT: 0-11 (v Dumbarton 1879, Rangers, 1880)
FOUNDED: 1878
MANAGER: Vacant
MOST LEAGUE GOALS (1 SEASON): 32, Bill Boyd, 1932-33

HONOURS

LEAGUE CHAMPIONS: Division II (5) – 1904-05, 1951-52, 1956-57, 1961-62, 1972-73. Second Division (4) – 1977-78, 1981-82, 1992-93, 1999-00. SCOTTISH CUP (3): 1939, 1955, 1958.

LEAGUE RESULTS 2003-2004

Clyde 3 Ayr 0	Brechin 1 Clyde 3
Inverness CT 0 Clyde 0	St Mirren 2 Clyde 3
Clyde 2 Brechin 1	Clyde 4 Falkirk 2
St Mirren 2 Clyde 1	Clyde 1 Ross County 0
Clyde 2 St Johnstone 0	Raith 0 Clyde 2
Clyde 1 Falkirk 2	Clyde 2 St Johnstone 3
Queen of Sth 4 Clyde 1	Queen of Sth 1 Clyde 2
Clyde 2 Ross County 2	Clyde 0 Brechin 0
Raith 0 Clyde 1	Inverness CT 3 Clyde 1
Ayr 2 Clyde 2	St Johnstone 1 Clyde 3
Clyde 1 Inverness CT 0	Clyde 2 St Mirren 2
St Johnstone 3 Clyde 0	Clyde 2 Queen of Sth 0
Clyde 2 St Mirren 0	Falkirk 1 Clyde 1
Clyde 3 Queen of Sth 1	Clyde 4 Raith 1
Falkirk 0 Clyde 2	Ross County 0 Clyde 0
Clyde 0 Raith 0	Ayr 1 Clyde 1
Ross County 0 Clyde 1	Clyde 1 Inverness CT 2
Clyde 2 Ayr 1	Brechin 2 Clyde 5

COWDENBEATH

NICKNAME:	The Blue Brazil
COLOURS:	Royal blue and white
GROUND:	Central Park
TELEPHONE No:	01383 610166
FAX No:	01383 512132
WEBSITE:	cowden beathfc.com
CAPACITY:	4370
RECORD ATT:	25,586 (v Rangers, 1949)
RECORD VICTORY:	12-0 (v Johnstone, 1928)
RECORD DEFEAT:	1-11 (v Clyde, 1951)
FOUNDED:	1881
MANAGER:	Keith Wright
CHAIRMAN:	Gordon McDougall
MOST LEAGUE GOALS (1 SEASON):	54, Rab Walls 1938-39

HONOURS

LEAGUE CHAMPIONSHIP: Division II (3) – 1913-14, 1914-15, 1938-39.

LEAGUE RESULTS 2003-2004

Stirling 0 Cowdenbeath 0
Cowdenbeath 1 Albion 4
Montrose 1 Cowdenbeath 3
East Stirling 1 Cowdenbeath 1
Cowdenbeath 0 Queen's Pk 1
Cowdenbeath 0 Gretna 1
Elgin City 0 Cowdenbeath 4
Cowdenbeath 0 Stranraer 1
Peterhead 0 Cowdenbeath 1
Albion 1 Cowdenbeath 2
Cowdenbeath 2 Stirling 0
Queen's Pk 0 Cowdenbeath 2
Cowdenbeath 2 East Stirling 1
Gretna 1 Cowdenbeath 0
Cowdenbeath 0 Elgin City 2
Stranraer 2 Cowdenbeath 0
Cowdenbeath 2 Peterhead 0
Cowdenbeath 3 Montrose 3

Stirling 1 Cowdenbeath 1
Cowdenbeath 1 Gretna 2
Cowdenbeath 5 Queen's Pk 1
East Stirling 0 Cowdenbeath 1
Peterhead 0 Cowdenbeath 0
Cowdenbeath 1 Albion 1
Cowdenbeath 1 Stranraer 2
Montrose 1 Cowdenbeath 1
Elgin City 0 Cowdenbeath 0
Queen's Pk 1 Cowdenbeath 2
Cowdenbeath 2 East Stirling 0
Cowdenbeath 2 Elgin City 0
Gretna 0 Cowdenbeath 1
Cowdenbeath 0 Peterhead 3
Stranraer 1 Cowdenbeath 0
Cowdenbeath 0 Montrose 0
Albion 2 Cowdenbeath 4
Cowdenbeath 0 Stirling 5

DUMBARTON

NICKNAME: The Sons
COLOURS: White, black and gold

GROUND: Strathclyde Homes Stadium

TELEPHONE No: 01389 762569
FAX No: 01389 762629
WEBSITE: dumbartonfootballclub.com
CAPACITY: 2020
RECORD ATT: 18,000 (v Raith Rovers, 1957)
RECORD VICTORY: 13-1 (v Kirkintilloch, 1888)
RECORD DEFEAT: 1-11 (v Albion Rovers, 1926; v Ayr United, 1952)

FOUNDED: 1872
MANAGER: Brian Fairley
CHAIRMAN: Ian MacFarlane
GOALS (1 SEASON): 38, Kenny Wilson, 1971-72

HONOURS

LEAGUE CHAMPIONS: Division I (2) – 1890-91 (shared with Rangers), 1891-92. Division II (2) – 1910-11, 1971-72. Second Division – 1991-92. **SCOTTISH CUP:** 1883.

LEAGUE RESULTS 2003-2004

Alloa 1 Dumbarton 2
Dumbarton 1 Arbroath 1
Morton 2 Dumbarton 2
Airdrie Utd 2 Dumbarton 0
Dumbarton 1 Berwick 1
Forfar 3 Dumbarton 1
Dumbarton 0 Stenhousemuir 1
East Fife 1 Dumbarton 0
Dumbarton 0 Hamilton 3
Arbroath 2 Dumbarton 1
Dumbarton 1 Alloa 0
Berwick 1 Dumbarton 4
Dumbarton 2 Airdrie Utd 0
Stenhousemuir 1 Dumbarton 1
Dumbarton 3 East Fife 1
Dumbarton 1 Morton 0
Dumbarton 2 Forfar 1
Alloa 3 Dumbarton 0

Forfar 1 Dumbarton 0
Dumbarton 4 Berwick 1
Airdrie Utd 1 Dumbarton 1
Dumbarton 2 Hamilton 0
Dumbarton 1 Arbroath 1
Hamilton 2 Dumbarton 0
Morton 3 Dumbarton 2
East Fife 1 Dumbarton 3
Dumbarton 4 Stenhousemuir 0
Dumbarton 1 Airdrie Utd 2
Berwick 1 Dumbarton 2
Stenhousemuir 1 Dumbarton 2
Dumbarton 1 Forfar 1
Hamilton 2 Dumbarton 1
Dumbarton 1 East Fife 0
Dumbarton 3 Morton 0
Arbroath 0 Dumbarton 3
Dumbarton 3 Alloa 1

DUNDEE

NICKNAME: The Dark Blues
COLOURS: Dark blue, red and white
GROUND: Dens Park
TELEPHONE No: 01382 826104
FAX No: 01382 832284
WEBSITE: thedees.co.uk
CAPACITY: 11,200
RECORD ATT: 43,024 (v Rangers, 1953)
RECORD VICTORY: 10-0 (v Alloa, 1957; v Dunfermline, 1957)
RECORD DEFEAT: 0-11 (v Celtic, 1895)
MANAGER: Jim Duffy
CHIEF EXECUTIVE: Peter Marr
CHAIRMAN: Bob Brannan
MOST LEAGUE GOALS (1 SEASON): 38, Dave Halliday, 1923-24
GOALS (OVERALL): 113, Alan Gilzean

HONOURS

LEAGUE CHAMPIONS: 1961-62. First Division (3) – 1978-79, 1991-92, 1997-98. Division II – 1946-47. SCOTTISH CUP: 1910. LEAGUE CUP WINNERS (3): 1951-52, 1952-53, 1973-74.

LEAGUE RESULTS 2003-2004

Motherwell 0 Dundee 3	Partick 1 Dundee 2
Dundee 0 Dunfermline 2	Dundee 2 Dundee Utd 1
Dundee 2 Livingston	Hibernian 1 Dundee 1
Kilmarnock 1 Dundee 1	Motherwell 5 Dundee 3
Dundee 0 Celtic 1	Dundee 0 Dunfermline 1
Dundee 2 Aberdeen 0	Dundee 1 Livingston 0
Rangers 3 Dundee 1	Kilmarnock 4 Dundee 2
Hearts 2 Dundee 2	Dundee 1 Aberdeen 1
Dundee 1 Partick 0	Dundee 1 Celtic 2
Dundee Utd 1 Dundee 1	Rangers 4 Dundee 0
Dundee 1 Hibernian 1	Hearts 3 Dundee 1
Dundee 0 Motherwell 1	Dundee 2 Partick 1
Dunfermline 2 Dundee 0	Dundee Utd 2 Dundee 2
Livingston 1 Dundee 1	Dundee 2 Hibernian 2
Dundee 1 Kilmarnock 2	Partick 0 Dundee 1
Celtic 3 Dundee 2	Hibernian 1 Dundee 0
Aberdeen 2 Dundee 2	Dundee 2 Kilmarnock 0
Dundee 0 Rangers 2	Dundee 2 Livingston 0
Dundee 1 Hearts 2	Aberdeen 1 Dundee 2

DUNDEE UNITED

NICKNAME: The Terrors
COLOURS: Tangerine and black

GROUND: Tannadice Park
TELEPHONE No: 01382 833166
FAX No: 01382 889398
WEBSITE: dundeeunitedfc.co.uk
CAPACITY: 14,209
RECORD ATT: 28,000 (v Barcelona, 1966)
RECORD VICTORY: 14-0 (v Nithsdale, 1931)
RECORD DEFEAT: 1-12 (v Motherwell, 1954)
MANAGER: Ian McCall
CHAIRMAN: Eddie Thompson
MOST LEAGUE GOALS (1 SEASON): 41, John Coyle, 1955-56
GOALS (OVERALL): 158, Peter Mackay

HONOURS

LEAGUE CHAMPIONS: 1982-83. Division 2 (2) – 1924-25, 1928-29. SCOTTISH CUP: 1994. LEAGUE CUP (2): 1979-80, 1980-81.

LEAGUE RESULTS 2003-2004

Dundee Utd 1 Hibernian 2
Celtic 5 Dundee Utd 0
Hearts 3 Dundee Utd 0
Dundee Utd 1 Rangers 3
Livingston 0 Dundee Utd 0
Partick 0 Dundee Utd 20
Dundee Utd 1 Kilmarnock 1
Dundee Utd 0 Motherwell 2
Aberdeen 0 Dundee Utd 1
Dundee Utd 1 Dundee 1
Dunfermline 2 Dundee Utd 0
Hibernian 2 Dundee Utd 2
Dundee Utd 1 Celtic 5
Dundee Utd 2 Hearts 1
Rangers 2 Dundee Utd 1
Dundee Utd 2 Livingston 0
Dundee Utd 0 Partick 0
Kilmarnock 0 Dundee Utd 2
Motherwell 3 Dundee Utd 1

Dundee Utd 3 Aberdeen 2
Dundee 2 Dundee Utd 1
Dundee Utd 1 Dunfermline 0
Dundee Utd 0 Hibernian 0
Celtic 2 Dundee Utd 1
Hearts 3 Dundee Utd 1
Dundee Utd 2 Rangers 0
Partick 1 Dundee Utd 1
Dundee Utd 4 Kilmarnock 1
Livingston 2 Dundee Utd 3
Dundee Utd 1 Motherwell 0
Aberdeen 3 Dundee Utd 0
Dundee Utd 2 Dundee 2
Dunfermline 1 Dundee Utd 1
Dundee Utd 3 Rangers 3
Dundee Utd 0 Hearts 2
Motherwell 0 Dundee Utd 1
Dundee Utd 3 Dunfermline 2
Celtic 2 Dundee Utd 1

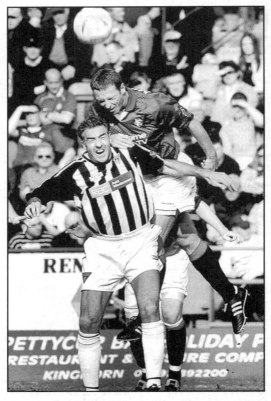

**WELL ABOVE PAR: Rangers defender Craig
Moore climbs high to clear the ball from
Dunfermline striker Craig Brewster**

DUNFERMLINE

NICKNAME:	The Pars	
COLOURS:	Black and white	
GROUND:	East End Park	
TELEPHONE No:	01383 724295	
FAX No:	01383 723468	
WEBSITE:	dafc.co.uk	
CAPACITY:	12,509	
RECORD ATT:	27,816 (v Celtic, 1968)	
RECORD VICTORY:	11-2 (v Stenhousemuir, 1930)	
RECORD DEFEAT:	0-10 (v Dundee, 1947)	
MANAGER:	Davie Hay	
CHAIRMAN:	John Yorkston	
CHIEF EXECUTIVE:	Elaine Cromwell	
MOST LEAGUE		
GOALS (1 SEASON):	53, Bobby Skinner, 1925-26	

HONOURS

LEAGUE CHAMPIONS: Division II – 1925-26. Second Division – 1985-86. First Division (2) – 1988-89, 1995-96. **SCOTTISH CUP** (2): 1961, 1968.

LEAGUE RESULTS 2003-2004

Dunfermline 0 Celtic 0	Kilmarnock 1 Dunfermline 1
Dundee 0 Dunfermline 2	Dunfermline 1 Motherwell 0
Aberdeen 1 Dunfermline 2	Dundee Utd 1 Dunfermline 0
Hearts 1 Dunfermline 0	Dunfermline 1 Celtic 4
Rangers 4 Dunfermline 0	Dundee 0 Dunfermline 2
Dunfermline 0 Hibernian 0	Aberdeen 2 Dunfermline 0
Dunfermline 2 Partick 1	Dunfermline 0 Hearts 0
Livingston 0 Dunfermline 0	Dunfermline 1 Partick 0
Dunfermline 2 Kilmarnock 3	Rangers 4 Dunfermline 1
Dunfermline 2 Dundee Utd 0	Livingston 0 Dunfermline 0
Celtic 5 Dunfermline 0	Dunfermline 2 Kilmarnock 1
Dunfermline 2 Dundee 0	Dunfermline 1 Hibernian 1
Motherwell 2 Dunfermline 2	Motherwell 1 Dunfermline 0
Dunfermline 2 Aberdeen 2	Dunfermline 1 Dundee Utd 1
Dunfermline 2 Hearts 1	Dunfermline 3 Motherwell 0
Dunfermline 2 Rangers 0	Celtic 1 Dunfermline 2
Hibernian 1 Dunfermline 0	Hearts 2 Dunfermline 1
Partick 4 Dunfermline 1	Dundee Utd 3 Dunfermline 2
Dunfermline 2 Livingston 2	Dunfermline 2 Rangers 3

EAST FIFE

NICKNAME:	The Fifers
COLOURS:	Amber and black
GROUND:	New Bayview Stadium
TELEPHONE No:	01333 426323
FAX No:	01333 426376
WEBSITE:	eastfife.org
CAPACITY:	1992
RECORD ATT:	22,515 (v Raith Rovers,1950)
RECORD VICTORY:	13-2 (v Edinburgh City, 1937)
RECORD DEFEAT:	0-9 (v Hearts, 1957)
MANAGER:	Jim Moffat
CHAIRMAN:	J Derrick Brown
MOST LEAGUE GOALS (1 SEASON):	42, Jock Wood, 1926-27

HONOURS

LEAGUE CHAMPIONSHIP: Division II – 1947-48. **SCOTTISH CUP:** 1938. **LEAGUE CUP (3):** 1947-48, 1949-50, 1953-54.

LEAGUE RESULTS 2003-2004

East Fife 3 Stenh'semuir 2	East Fife 1 Stenh'semuir 0
Forfar 0 East Fife 1	East Fife 0 Alloa 1
East Fife 3 Berwick 1	Hamilton 1 East Fife 0
Morton 2 East Fife 1	East Fife 0 Airdrie Utd 1
East Fife 3 Airdrie Utd 1	Morton 1 East Fife 1
East Fife 0 Alloa 1	Arbroath 0 East Fife 0
Hamilton 2 East Fife 2	Forfar 1 East Fife 0
East Fife 1 Dumbarton 0	East Fife 2 Berwick 2
Arbroath 0 East Fife 1	East Fife 1 Dumbarton 3
East Fife 2 Forfar 3	East Fife 1 Morton 0
Stenh'semuir 3 East Fife 0	Airdrie Utd 2 East Fife 1
Airdrie Utd 1 East Fife 1	East Fife 2 Hamilton 3
East Fife 0 Morton 0	Alloa 1 East Fife 1
Alloa 2 East Fife 0	East Fife 1 Arbroath 2
East Fife 2 Hamilton 3	Dumbarton 1 East Fife 0
Dumbarton 3 East Fife 1	Berwick 1 East Fife 1
East Fife 0 Arbroath 1	East Fife 2 Forfar 0
Berwick 0 East Fife 2	Stenh'semuir 0 East Fife 1

EAST STIRLINGSHIRE

NICKNAME:	The Shire
COLOURS:	Black and white
GROUND:	Firs Park
TELEPHONE No:	01324 623583
FAX No:	01324 637862
CAPACITY:	816
RECORD ATT:	12,000
	(v Partick Thistle, 1921)
RECORD VICTORY:	11-2 (v Vale of Bannock, 1888)
RECORD DEFEAT:	1-12 (v Dundee United, 1936)
HEAD COACH:	Dennis Newall
CHIEF EXECUTIVE:	Les Thomson
CHAIRMAN:	Alan Mackin
MOST LEAGUE GOALS (1 SEASON):	36, Malcolm Morrison, 1938-39

HONOURS
LEAGUE CHAMPIONSHIP: Division II – 1931-32. C Division – 1947-48.

LEAGUE RESULTS 2003-2004

Elgin City 3 East Stirling 1	Elgin City 3 East Stirling 0
East Stirling 1 Montrose 1	Peterhead 6 East Stirling 0
Stirling 5 East Stirling 1	Stranraer 7 East Stirling 1
East Stirling 1 Cowdenbeath 1	East Stirling 0 Cowdenbeath 1
Stranraer 4 East Stirling 0	East Stirling 2 Gretna 4
Peterhead 2 East Stirling 0	East Stirling 2 Queen's Park 4
East Stirling 1 Queen's Park 2	East Stirling 1 Montrose 4
Albion 5 East Stirling 0	Albion 5 East Stirling 1
East Stirling 0 Gretna 1	Stirling 6 East Stirling 0
Montrose 5 East Stirling 1	East Stirling 1 Stranraer 2
East Stirling 3 Elgin City 1	Cowdenbeath 2 East Stirling 0
East Stirling 1 Stranraer 4	Queen's Park 1 East Stirling 0
Cowdenbeath 2 East Stirling 1	East Stirling 0 Peterhead 3
East Stirling 1 Peterhead 3	Gretna 5 East Stirling 1
Queen's Park 3 East Stirling 0	East Stirling 1 Albion 8
East Stirling 3 Albion 4	East Stirling 0 Stirling 3
Gretna 2 East Stirling 1	Montrose 1 East Stirling 0
East Stirling 2 Stirling 4	East Stirling 2 Elgin City 1

ELGIN CITY

NICKNAME:	The City
COLOURS:	Black and white
GROUND:	Borough Briggs
TELEPHONE No:	01343 551114
FAX No:	01343 547921
CAPACITY:	4962
RECORD ATT:	12,608
	(v Arbroath,1968)
RECORD VICTORY:	18-1 (v Brora Rangers, 1960)
RECORD DEFEAT:	1-14 (v Hearts, 1939)
MANAGER:	David Robertson
CHAIRMAN:	Denis Miller
MOST LEAGUE	
GOALS (1 SEASON):	66, Willie Grant, 1960-61

LEAGUE RESULTS 2003-2004

Elgin City 3 East Stirling 1	Elgin City 3 East Stirling 0
Queen's Park 5 Elgin City 2	Stranraer 6 Elgin City 0
Elgin City 2 Peterhead 3	Elgin City 1 Gretna 1
Montrose 3 Elgin City 3	Montrose 4 Elgin City 3
Albion 1 Elgin City 2	Elgin City 1 Albion 2
Elgin City 3 Gretna 3	Queen's Park 4 Elgin City 0
Stranraer 4 Elgin City 3	Stirling 6 Elgin City 1
Elgin City 0 Cowdenbeath 4	Elgin City 1 Peterhead 0
Stirling 3 Elgin City 0	Elgin City 0 Cowdenbeath 0
Elgin City 1 Albion 3	Gretna 2 Elgin City 1
Elgin City 2 Queen's Park 2	Elgin City 2 Montrose 1
East Stirling 3 Elgin City 1	Cowdenbeath 2 Elgin City 0
Gretna 2 Elgin City 2	Elgin City 0 Stranraer 0
Elgin City 2 Montrose 3	Albion 1 Elgin City 2
Elgin City 1 Stranraer 3	Elgin City 0 Stirling 1
Cowdenbeath 3 Elgin City 2	Peterhead 3 Elgin City 1
Elgin City 0 Stirling 2	Elgin City 1 Queen's Park 3
Peterhead 5 Elgin City 1	East Stirling 2 Elgin City 1

FALKIRK

NICKNAME:	The Bairns
COLOURS:	Navy Blue and white
GROUND:	to be confirmed
TELEPHONE No:	01324 624121
FAX No:	01324 612418
WEBSITE:	falkirkfc.co.uk
CAPACITY:	7608
RECORD ATT:	23,100 (v Celtic, 1953)
RECORD VICTORY:	12-1 (v Laurieston, 1893)
RECORD DEFEAT:	1-11 (v Airdrie, 1951)
HEAD COACH:	John Hughes
DIRECTOR OF FOOTBALL:	Alex Totten
CHAIRMAN:	W. Martin Ritchie
MOST LEAGUE GOALS (1 SEASON):	43, Evelyn Morrison, 1928-29
GOALS (OVERALL):	86, Dougie Moran, 1957-61, 1964-67

Est. 1876

HONOURS

LEAGUE CHAMPIONS: Division II (3) – 1935-36, 1969-70, 1974-75. First Division (3) – 1990-91, 1993-94, 2002-03. Second Division – 1979-80. SCOTTISH CUP (2): 1913, 1957. LEAGUE CHALLENGE CUP: 1997-98. B&Q CUP: 1993-94.

LEAGUE RESULTS 2003-2004

Falkirk 2 Inverness CT 1	Raith 2 Falkirk 0
Ayr 1 Falkirk 1	Falkirk 2 Ross County 0
Falkirk 0 Queen of Sth 0	Clyde 4 Falkirk
Raith 0 Falkirk 1	St Mirren 1 Falkirk 1
Falkirk 0 Ross County 2	Falkirk 5 Brechin 0
Clyde 1 Falkirk 2	Falkirk 2 Inverness CT 1
Falkirk 0 St Johnstone 3	Ayr 2 Falkirk 3
St Mirren 0 Falkirk 0	Falkirk 0 St Johnstone 1
Falkirk 3 Brechin 0	Falkirk 0 Queen of Sth 2
Falkirk 0 Ayr 1	Ross County 1 Falkirk 1
Inverness CT 1 Falkirk 2	Falkirk 1 Raith 0
Ross County 1 Falkirk 2	St Johnstone 2 Falkirk 1
Falkirk 3 Raith 2	Falkirk 1 Clyde 1
St Johnstone 0 Falkirk 4	Brechin 0 Falkirk 1
Falkirk 0 Clyde 2	Falkirk 1 St Mirren 0
Brechin 2 Falkirk 2	Inverness CT 0 Falkirk 0
Falkirk 0 St Mirren 0	Falkirk 0 Ayr 0
Queen of Sth 2 Falkirk 0	Queen of Sth 1 Falkirk 0

JAMES McFADDEN nets the only goal of the Euro 2004 play-off first leg with Holland

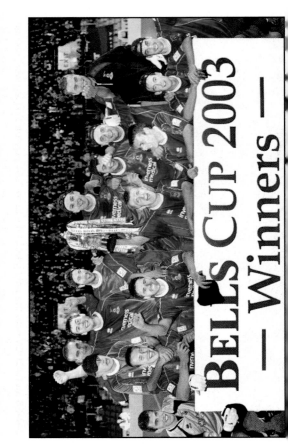

BELLS CUP 2003
— Winners —

FORFAR ATHLETIC

NICKNAME:	The Loons
COLOURS:	Sky blue and navy
GROUND:	Station Park
TELEPHONE:	01307 463576
FAX:	01307 466956
WEBSITE:	forfarathletic.co.uk
CAPACITY:	4640
RECORD ATT:	10,780
	(v Rangers, 1970)
RECORD VICTORY:	14-1 (v Lindertis, 1888)
RECORD DEFEAT:	2-12 (v King's Park, 1930)
MANAGER:	Ray Stewart
CHAIRMAN:	David McGregor
MOST LEAGUE	
GOALS (1 SEASON):	45, Dave Kilgour, 1929-30

HONOURS

LEAGUE CHAMPIONSHIP: Second Division – 1983-84. Third Division – 1994-95.

LEAGUE RESULTS 200   04

Hamilton 1 Forfar 2
Forfar 0 East Fife 1
Arbroath 0 Forfar 0
Stenhousemuir 2 Forfar 0
Forfar 2 Morton 3
Forfar 3 Dumbarton 1
Alloa 1 Forfar 1
Forfar 1 Airdrie Utd 1
Berwick 0 Forfar 4
East Fife 2 Forfar 3
Forfar 4 Hamilton 3
Morton 1 Forfar 1
Forfar 2 Stenhousemuir 0
Forfar 1 Alloa 1
Airdrie Utd 3 Forfar 3
Forfar 1 Berwick 5
Dumbarton 2 Forfar 1
Hamilton 2 Forfar 1

Forfar 2 Dumbarton 0
Alloa 4 Forfar 0
Forfar 2 Morton 1
Stenhousemuir 0 Forfar 2
Berwick 3 Forfar 1
Forfar 1 East Fife 0
Arbroath 0 Forfar 1
Forfar 2 Arbroath 2
Forfar 1 Airdrie Utd 3
Forfar 1 Stenhousemuir 1
Morton 1 Forfar 1
Dumbarton 1 Forfar 1
Forfar 2 Alloa 0
Forfar 0 Berwick 2
Airdrie Utd 2 Forfar 2
Forfar 1 Arbroath 2
East Fife 2 Forfar 0
Forfar 0 Hamilton 4

GRETNA

NICKNAME:	Black and Whites
COLOURS:	Black and white
GROUND:	Raydale Park
TELEPHONE No:	01461 337602
FAX No:	01461 338047
WEBSITE:	gretnafootballclub.co.uk
CAPACITY:	2200
RECORD ATT:	2307 (v Rochdale, 1991)
RECORD VICTORY:	20-0 (v Siloth, 1962-63)
RECORD DEFEAT:	2-9 (v Ashton Utd, Unibond League Div 1, 2000-01)
MANAGER:	Rowan Alexander
CHAIRMAN:	Ron MacGregor
MOST LEAGUE GOALS (OVERALL):	101, Denis Smith

GRETNA F.C.

HONOURS

NORTHERN LEAGUE CHAMPIONS: First Division: 1990-91 1991-92. **CARLISLE DISTRICT LEAGUE CHAMPIONS:** 28 times

LEAGUE RESULTS 2003-2004

Gretna 1 Queen's Park 1	Gretna 0 Queen's Park 1
Peterhead 2 Gretna 0	Cowdenbeath 1 Gretna 2
Gretna 1 Stranraer 1	Elgin City 1 Gretna 1
Gretna 3 Albion 1	Gretna 3 Albion 0
Elgin City 3 Gretna 3	East Stirling 2 Gretna 4
Cowdenbeath 0 Gretna 1	Gretna 1 Montrose 2
Gretna 0 Stirling 1	Gretna 1 Stirling 0
Gretna 1 Montrose 1	Peterhead 2 Gretna 1
East Stirling 0 Gretna 1	Gretna 0 Stranraer 0
Gretna 3 Peterhead 2	Gretna 2 Elgin City 1
Queen's Park 0 Gretna 1	Albion 1 Gretna 2
Gretna 2 Elgin City 2	Stirling 0 Gretna 1
Albion 1 Gretna 3	Gretna 0 Cowdenbeath 1
Gretna 1 Cowdenbeath 0	Gretna 5 East Stirling 1
Stirling 0 Gretna 1	Montrose 1 Gretna 4
Montrose 2 Gretna 0	Stranraer 3 Gretna 2
Gretna 2 East Stirling 1	Gretna 3 Peterhead 2
Stranraer 1 Gretna 2	Queen's Park 1 Gretna 1

HAMILTON ACCIES

NICKNAME:	The Accies
COLOURS:	Red and white
GROUND:	New Douglas Park
TELEPHONE No:	01698 368650
FAX No:	01698 285422
CAPACITY:	5330
RECORD ATT:	28,690 (v Hearts, 1937)
RECORD VICTORY:	11-1 (v Chryston, 1885)
RECORD DEFEAT:	1-11 (v Hibs, 1965)
MANAGER:	Allan Maitland
CHAIRMAN:	Ronnie MacDonald
MOST LEAGUE GOALS (1 SEASON):	35, David Wilson, 1936-37

HONOURS

LEAGUE CHAMPIONS: First Division: 1985-86. B&Q Cup (2); 1991-92, 1992-93. Third Division: 2000-01.

LEAGUE RESULTS 2003-2004

Hamilton 1 Forfar 2
Berwick 3 Hamilton 1
Hamilton 2 Airdrie Utd 1
Arbroath 2 Hamilton 1
Hamilton 2 Stenhousemuir 0
Morton 1 Hamilton 1
Hamilton 2 East Fife 2
Hamilton 3 Alloa 4
Dumbarton 0 Hamilton 3
Hamilton 2 Berwick 2
Forfar 4 Hamilton 3
Stenhousemuir 0 Hamilton 3
Hamilton 2 Arbroath 0
Hamilton 1 Morton 2
East Fife 2 Hamilton 3
Alloa 1 Hamilton 3
Hamilton 2 Forfar 1
Morton 2 Hamilton 2

Hamilton 1 East Fife 0
Hamilton 0 Stenhousemuir 1
Arbroath 0 Hamilton 2
Dumbarton 2 Hamilton 0
Airdrie Utd 3 Hamilton 0
Berwick 2 Hamilton 4
Hamilton 2 Dumbarton 0
Hamilton 0 Airdrie Utd 1
Hamilton 0 Alloa 1
Hamilton 2 Arbroath 2
East Fife 2 Hamilton 3
Stenhousemuir 0 Hamilton 2
Hamilton 6 Morton 1
Hamilton 2 Dumbarton 1
Alloa 1 Hamilton 1
Airdrie Utd 1 Hamilton 1
Hamilton 2 Berwick 0
Forfar 0 Hamilton 4

HEART OF MIDLOTHIAN

NICKNAME:	The Jam Tarts
COLOURS:	Maroon and white
GROUND:	Tynecastle Park
TELEPHONE No:	0131 200 7200
FAX No:	0131 200 7222
WEBSITE:	heartsfc.co.uk
CAPACITY:	18,001
RECORD ATT:	53,396 (v Rangers, 1932)
RECORD VICTORY:	21-0 (v Anchor, 1880)
RECORD DEFEAT:	1-8 (v Vale of Leven, 1888)
MANAGER:	Craig Levein
CHAIRMAN:	George Foulkes
MOST LEAGUE	
GOALS (1 SEASON):	44, Barney Battles
GOALS (OVERALL):	214, John Robertson

HONOURS

LEAGUE CHAMPIONS: Division I (4) – 1894-95, 1896-97, 1957-58, 1959-60. First Division – 1979-80. **SCOTTISH CUP (6):** 1891, 1896, 1901, 1906, 1956, 1998. **LEAGUE CUP (4):** 1954-55, 1958-59, 1962-63.

LEAGUE RESULTS 2003-2004

Hearts 2 Aberdeen 0	Hearts 0 Celtic 1
Hibernian 1 Hearts 0	Hearts 2 Partick 0
Hearts 3 Dundee Utd 0	Hearts 1 Aberdeen 0
Hearts 1 Dunfermline 0	Hibernian 1 Hearts 1
Kilmarnock 0 Hearts 2	Hearts 3 Dundee Utd 1
Hearts 0 Rangers 4	Livingston 2 Hearts 3
Motherwell 1 Hearts 1	Dunfermline 0 Hearts 0
Hearts 2 Dundee 2	Kilmarnock 1 Hearts 1
Celtic 5 Hearts 0	Hearts 1 Rangers 1
Partick 1 Hearts 4	Hearts 3 Dundee 1
Hearts 3 Livingston 1	Celtic 2 Hearts 2
Aberdeen 0 Hearts 1	Motherwell 1 Hearts 1
Hearts 2 Hibernian 0	Partick 1 Hearts 0
Dundee Utd 2 Hearts 1	Hearts 1 Livingston 0
Dunfermline 2 Hearts 1	Hearts 1 Celtic 1
Hearts 2 Kilmarnock 1	Dundee Utd 0 Hearts 2
Rangers 2 Hearts 1	Hearts 2 Dunfermline 1
Hearts 0 Motherwell 0	Rangers 0 Hearts 1
Dundee 1 Hearts 2	Hearts 3 Motherwell 2

HIBERNIAN

NICKNAME:	The Hibees
COLOURS:	Green and white
GROUND:	Easter Road
TELEPHONE No:	0131 661 2159
FAX No:	0131 652 2202
WEBSITE:	hibs.org.uk
CAPACITY:	16,039
RECORD ATT:	65,860 (v Hearts, 1950)
RECORD VICTORY:	22-1 (v 42nd Highlanders, 1881)
RECORD DEFEAT:	0-10 (v Rangers, 1898)
MANAGER:	Tony Mowbray
CHAIRMAN:	Ken Lewandowski
MOST LEAGUE GOALS (1 SEASON):	42, Joe Baker
GOALS (OVERALL):	364, Gordon Smith

HONOURS

LEAGUE CHAMPIONS: Division I (4) – 1902-03, 1947-48, 1950-51,1951-52. Division II (3) – 1893-94, 1894-94, 1932-33. First Division (2) – 1980-81, 1998-99. SCOTTISH CUP (2): 1887, 1902. LEAGUE CUP (2): 1972-73, 1991-92.

LEAGUE RESULTS 2003-2004

Dundee Utd 1 Hibernian 2	Livingston 1 Hibernian 0
Hibernian 1 Hearts 0	Kilmarnock 0 Hibernian 2
Rangers 5 Hibernian 2	Hibernian 1 Dundee 1
Hibernian 1 Aberdeen 1	Dundee Utd 0 Hibernian 0
Hibernian 0 Motherwell 2	Hibernian 1 Hearts 1
Dunfermline 0 Hibernian 0	Rangers 3 Hibernian 0
Hibernian 1 Celtic 1	Hibernian 0 Aberdeen 1
Partick 0 Hibernian 1	Hibernian 0 Celtic 4
Hibernian 0 Livingston 2	Hibernian 3 Motherwell 3
Hibernian 3 Kilmarnock 1	Partick 1 Hibernian 1
Dundee 1 Hibernian 1	Hibernian 3 Livingston 1
Hibernian 2 Dundee Utd 2	Hibernian 3 Kilmarnock 1
Hearts 2 Hibernian 0	Dunfermline 1 Hibernian 1
Hibernian 0 Rangers 1	Dundee 2 Hibernian 2
Aberdeen 3 Hibernian 1	Kilmarnock 2 Hibernian 0
Motherwell 0 Hibernian 1	Hibernian 1 Dundee 0
Hibernian 1 Dunfermline 2	Hibernian 1 Partick 2
Celtic 6 Hibernian 0	Aberdeen 0 Hibernian 1
Hibernian 3 Partick 2	Livingston 4 Hibernian 1

INVERNESS CT

NICKNAME:	Caley Thistle
COLOURS:	Blue and red
GROUND:	Caledonian Stadium
TELEPHONE No:	01463 222880
FAX No:	01463 715816
WEBSITE:	caley-thistle.co.uk
CAPACITY:	6200
RECORD ATT:	5821 (v Dundee United, 1998)
RECORD VICTORY:	8-1 (v Annan Athletic, 1998)
RECORD DEFEAT:	0-6 (v Airdrie, 2001)
MANAGER:	John Robertson
CHAIRMAN:	Ken Mackie
MOST LEAGUE GOALS (1 SEASON):	27, Iain Stewart, 1996-97

HONOURS

LEAGUE CHAMPIONS: Third Division – 1996-97. First Division – 2003-04. BELL'S CUP – 2003-04.

LEAGUE RESULTS 2003-2004

Falkirk 2 Inverness CT 1
Inverness CT 0 Clyde 0
St Johnstone 1 Inverness CT 2
Ross County 1 Inverness CT 1
Inverness CT 1 Ayr 0
Brechin 0 Inverness CT 2
Inverness CT 2 St Mirren 0
Inverness CT 2 Raith 1
Queen of Sth 3 nverness CT 2
Inverness CT 1 Falkirk 2
Clyde 1 Inverness CT 0
Ayr 0 Inverness CT 3
Inverness CT 3 Ross County 3
St Mirren 0 Inverness CT 4
Inverness CT 5 Brechin 0
Inverness CT 4 Queen of Sth 1
Raith 1 Inverness CT 3
Inverness CT 1 St Johnstone 0

Ross County 1 Inverness CT 0
Inverness CT 2 Ayr 1
Brechin 2 Inverness CT 4
Inverness CT 1 St Mirren 1
Inverness CT 3 Raith 0
Queen of Sth 2 Inverness CT 1
Falkirk 2 Inverness CT 1
St Johnstone 3 Inverness CT 2
Inverness CT 3 Clyde 1
Ayr 1 nverness CT 1
Inverness CT 1 Ross County 0
St Mirren 0 Inverness CT 0
Inverness CT 1 Brechin 0
Inverness CT 4 Queen of Sth 1
Raith 0 Inverness CT 1
Inverness CT 0 Falkirk 0
Clyde 1 Inverness CT 2
Inverness CT 3 St Johnstone 1

KILMARNOCK

NICKNAME:	Killie
COLOURS:	Blue and white
GROUND:	Rugby Park
TELEPHONE No:	01563 545300
FAX No:	01563 522181
WEBSITE:	kilmarnockfc.co.uk
CAPACITY:	18,128
RECORD ATT:	35,995 (v Rangers, 1962)
RECORD VICTORY:	11-1 (v Paisley Academical, 1930)
RECORD DEFEAT:	1-9 (v Celtic, 1938)
MANAGER:	Jim Jefferies
CHAIRMAN:	Jamie Moffat
MOST LEAGUE	
GOALS (1 SEASON):	34, Harry Cunningham, 1927-28
GOALS (OVERALL):	148, W Culley, 1912-23

HONOURS

LEAGUE CHAMPIONS: Division I – 1964-65. Division II (2) – 1897-98, 1898-99. SCOTTISH CUP (3): 1920, 1929, 1997.

LEAGUE RESULTS 2003-2004

Rangers 4 Kilmarnock 0
Kilmarnock 2 Partick 1
Motherwell 2 Kilmarnock 1
Kilmarnock 1 Dundee 1
Kilmarnock 0 Hearts 3
Livingston 1 Kilmarnock 2
Dundee Utd 1 Kilmarnock 1
Kilmarnock 1 Aberdeen 3
Dunfermline 2 Kilmarnock 3
Hibernian 3 Kilmarnock 1
Kilmarnock 0 Celtic 5
Kilmarnock 2 Rangers 3
Partick 2 Kilmarnock 4
Kilmarnock 2 Motherwell 0
Dundee 1 Kilmarnock 2
Hearts 2 Kilmarnock 1
Kilmarnock 0 Livingston 3
Kilmarnock 0 Dundee Utd 2
Aberdeen 3 Kilmarnock 1

Kilmarnock 1 Dunfermline 1
Kilmarnock 0 Hibernian 2
Celtic 5 Kilmarnock 1
Rangers 2 Kilmarnock 0
Kilmarnock 2 Partick 1
Motherwell 1 Kilmarnock 0
Kilmarnock 4 Dundee 2
Kilmarnock 1 Hearts 1
Dundee Utd 4 Kilmarnock 1
Kilmarnock 3 Aberdeen 1
Dunfermline 2 Kilmarnock 1
Livingston 1 Kilmarnock 1
Hibernian 3 Kilmarnock 0
Kilmarnock 0 Celtic 1
Kilmarnock 2 Hibernian 0
Kilmarnock 4 Livingston 2
Dundee 2 Kilmarnock 0
Kilmarnock 4 Aberdeen 0
Partick 2 Kilmarnock 2

LIVINGSTON

NICKNAME:	Livi Lions
COLOURS:	Black and gold
GROUND:	The City Stadium
TELEPHONE No:	01506 417000
FAX No:	01506 418888
WEBSITE:	livingstonfc.co.uk
CAPACITY:	10,122
RECORD ATT:	10,112 (v Rangers, 2001)
RECORD VICTORY:	6-0 (v Raith Rovers, 1985)
RECORD DEFEAT:	0-8 (v Hamilton Accies, 1974)
MANAGER:	Allan Preston
CHAIRMAN:	Pearse Flynn
MOST LEAGUE GOALS (1 SEASON):	21, John McGachie, 1986-87

HONOURS

LEAGUE CHAMPIONS: Third Division – 1995-96. Second Division (2) – 1986-87, 1998-99. First Division – 2000-01.
LEAGUE CUP WINNERS – 2003-04.

LEAGUE RESULTS 2003-2004

Partick 1 Livingston 1	Livingston 1 Hibernian 0
Livingston 1 Motherwell 0	Rangers 1 Livingston 0
Dundee 2 Livingston 1	Partick 5 Livingston 1
Celtic 5 Livingston 1	Livingston 3 Motherwell 1
Livingston 0 Dundee Utd 0	Dundee 1 Livingston 0
Livingston 1 Kilmarnock 2	Livingston 2 Hearts 3
Aberdeen 0 Livingston 3	Celtic 5 Livingston 1
Livingston 0 Dunfermline 0	Aberdeen 1 Livingston 2
Hibernian 0 Livingston 2	Livingston 2 Dundee Utd 3
Livingston 0 Rangers 0	Livingston 0 Dunfermline 0
Hearts 3 Livingston 1	Hibernian 3 Livingston 1
Livingston 2 Partick 0	Livingston 1 Kilmarnock 1
Motherwell 1 Livingston 1	Livingston 1 Rangers 1
Livingston 1 Dundee 1	Hearts 1 Livingston 1
Livingston 0 eltic 2	Livingston 2 Aberdeen 0
Dundee Utd 2 Livingston 0	Kilmarnock 4 Livingston 2
Kilmarnock 0 Livingston 3	Livingston 2 Partick 2
Livingston 1 Aberdeen 1	Dundee 2 Livingston 0
Dunfermline 2 Livingston 2	Livingston 4 Hibernian 1

MONTROSE

NICKNAME:	The Gable Endies
COLOURS:	Blue and white
GROUND:	Links Park
TELEPHONE No:	01674 673200
FAX No:	01674 677311
WEBSITE:	montrosefc.co.uk
CAPACITY:	4338
RECORD ATT:	8983
	(v Dundee, 1973)
RECORD VICTORY:	12-0 (v Vale of
	Leithen, 1975)
RECORD DEFEAT:	0-13 (v Aberdeen, 1951)
MANAGER:	Henry Hall
CHAIRMAN:	John F Paton
MOST LEAGUE	
GOALS (1 SEASON)	28, Brian Third, 1972-73

HONOURS

LEAGUE CHAMPIONSHIP: Second Division – 1984-85

LEAGUE RESULTS 2003-2004

Montrose 0 Peterhead 1	Montrose 2 Peterhead 1
East Stirling 1 Montrose 1	Queen's Park 1 Montrose 1
Montrose 1 Cowdenbeath 3	Montrose 1 Stranraer 4
Montrose 3 Elgin City 3	Albion 3 Montrose 0
Albion 0 Montrose 1	Montrose 4 Elgin City 3
Queen's Park 1 Montrose 1	Montrose 1 Stirling 4
Montrose 2 Stranraer 4	Gretna 1 Montrose 2
Gretna 1 Montrose 1	East Stirling 1 Montrose 4
Stirling 3 Montrose 0	Montrose 1 Cowdenbeath 1
Montrose 2 Stirling 3	Montrose 3 Albion 1
Montrose 5 East Stirling 1	Elgin City 2 Montrose 1
Peterhead 0 Montrose 0	Stranraer 6 Montrose 0
Montrose 1 Albion 0	Montrose 1 Queen's Park 1
Elgin City 2 Montrose 3	Stirling 1 Montrose 1
Montrose 0 Queen's Park 0	Montrose 1 Gretna 4
Stranraer 2 Montrose 0	Cowdenbeath 0 Montrose 0
Montrose 2 Gretna 0	Montrose 1 East Stirling 0
Cowdenbeath 3 Montrose 3	Peterhead 1 Montrose 2

MORTON

NICKNAME:	The Ton
COLOURS:	Blue and white
GROUND:	Cappielow Park
TELEPHONE No:	01475 723571
FAX No:	01475 781084
WEBSITE:	gmfc.net
CAPACITY:	11,612
RECORD ATT:	23,500 (v Celtic, 1922)
RECORD VICTORY:	11-0 (v Carfin Shamrock, 1886)
RECORD DEFEAT:	1-10 (v Port Glasgow Athletic, 1894; v St Bernard's, 1933)
MANAGER:	John McCormack
CHAIRMAN:	Douglas Rae
MOST LEAGUE GOALS (1 SEASON):	58, Allan McGraw, 1963-64

HONOURS
LEAGUE CHAMPIONS: First Division (3) – 1977-78, 1983-84, 1986-87. Division II (3) – 1949-50, 1963-64, 1966-67. Second Division – 1994-95. Division Three – 2002-03 SCOTTISH CUP: 1922.

LEAGUE RESULTS 2003-2004

Morton 3 Airdrie Utd 1	Arbroath 2 Morton 2
Stenhousemuir 0 Morton 2	Forfar 2 Morton 1
Morton 2 Dumbarton 2	Morton 1 East Fife 1
Morton 2 East Fife 1	Alloa 3 Morton 3
Forfar 2 Morton 3	Stenhousemuir 0 Morton 1
Morton 1 Hamilton 1	Morton 1 Airdrie Utd 1
Arbroath 0 Morton 4	Morton 3 Dumbarton 2
Morton 1 Berwick 3	Morton 2 Berwick 1
Alloa 0 Morton 1	East Fife 1 Morton 0
Morton 5 Stenhousemuir 2	Morton 2 Alloa 2
Airdrie Utd 1 Morton 6	Morton 1 Arbroath 0
Morton 1 Forfar 1	Morton 1 Forfar 1
East Fife 0 Morton 0	Hamilton 6 Morton 1
Hamilton 1 Morton 2	Morton 2 Alloa 1
Morton 6 Arbroath 4	Berwick 2 Morton 0
Berwick 2 Morton 3	Dumbarton 3 Morton 0
Dumbarton 1 Morton 0	Morton 1 Stenhousemuir 4
Morton 2 Hamilton 2	Airdrie Utd 2 Morton 0

MOTHERWELL

NICKNAME:	The Well
COLOURS:	Claret and amber
GROUND:	Fir Park
TELEPHONE No:	01698 333333
FAX No:	01698 338001
WEBSITE:	motherwellfc.co.uk
CAPACITY:	13,742
RECORD ATT:	35,632 (v Rangers, 1952)
RECORD VICTORY:	12-1 (v Dundee United, 1954)
RECORD DEFEAT:	0-8 (v Aberdeen, 1979)
MANAGER:	Terry Butcher
CHAIRMAN:	Bill Dickie
MOST LEAGUE GOALS (1 SEASON):	52, William McFadyen, 1931-32
GOALS (OVERALL):	283, Hugh Ferguson, 1916-25

HONOURS

LEAGUE CHAMPIONSHIP: Division I – 1931-32. Division II (2) – 1953-54, 1968-69. First Division (2) – 1981-82, 1984-85. SCOTTISH CUP: (2) 1952, 1991. LEAGUE CUP: 1950-51.

LEAGUE RESULTS 2003-2004

Motherwell 0 Dundee 3
Livingston 1 Motherwell 0
Motherwell 2 Kilmarnock 1
Motherwell 2 Partick 2
Hibernian 0 Motherwell 2
Celtic 3 Motherwell 0
Motherwell 1 Hearts 1
Dundee Utd 0 Motherwell 2
Motherwell 1 Rangers 1
Aberdeen 0 Motherwell 3
Dundee 0 Motherwell 1
Motherwell 1 Livingston 1
Motherwell 2 Dunfermline 2
Kilmarnock 2 Motherwell 0
Partick 1 Motherwell 0
Motherwell 0 Hibernian 1
Motherwell 0 Celtic 2
Hearts 0 Motherwell 1
Motherwell 3 Dundee Utd 1

Rangers 1 Motherwell 0
Dunfermline 1 Motherwell 0
Motherwell 5 Dundee 3
Livingston 3 Motherwell 1
Motherwell 1 Kilmarnock 0
Motherwell 1 Aberdeen 0
Motherwell 3 Partick 0
Celtic 1 Motherwell 1
Hibernian 3 Motherwell 3
Dundee Utd 1 Motherwell 0
Motherwell 0 Rangers 1
Motherwell 1 Hearts 1
Motherwell 1 Dunfermline 0
Aberdeen 0 Motherwell 2
Dunfermline 3 Motherwell 0
Rangers 4 Motherwell 0
Motherwell 0 Dundee Utd 1
Motherwell 1 Celtic 1
Hearts 3 Motherwell 2

PARTICK THISTLE

NICKNAME:	The Jags
COLOURS:	Red and yellow
GROUND:	Firhill Park
TELEPHONE No:	0141 579 1971
FAX No:	0141 945 1525
WEBSITE:	ptfc.co.uk/v2/
CAPACITY:	13,300
RECORD ATT:	49,838
	(v Rangers, 1922)
RECORD VICTORY:	16-0 (v Royal Albert, 1931)
RECORD DEFEAT:	0-10 (v Queen's Park, 1881)
C0-MANAGERS:	Derek Whyte/Gerry Britton
CHAIRMAN:	Tom Hughes
MOST LEAGUE GOALS (1 SEASON):	41, Alex Hair, 1926-27

HONOURS

LEAGUE CHAMPIONS: Division II (3) – 1896-97, 1899-1900, 1970-71. First Division (2) – 1975-76, 2001-2002. Second Division – 2000-01. **SCOTTISH CUP:** 1921. **LEAGUE CUP:** 1971-72.

LEAGUE RESULTS 2003-2004

Partick 1 Livingston 1	Partick 1 Dundee 2
Kilmarnock 2 artick 1	Hearts 2 Partick 0
Partick 1 Celtic 2	Partick 0 Rangers 1
Motherwell 2 Partick 2	Partick 5 Livingston 2
Aberdeen 2 Partick 1	Kilmarnock 2 Partick 1
Partick 0 Dundee Utd 2	Partick 1 Celtic 4
Dunfermline 2 Partick 1	Motherwell 3 Partick 0
Partick 0 Hibernian 1	Aberdeen 0 Partick 0
Dundee 1 Partick 0	Partick 1 Dundee Utd 1
Partick 1 Hearts 4	Dunfermline 1 Partick 0
Rangers 3 Partick 1	Partick 1 Hibernian 1
Livingston 2 Partick 0	Dundee 2 Partick 1
Partick 2 Kilmarnock 4	Partick 1 Hearts 0
Celtic 3 Partick 1	Rangers 2 Partick 0
Partick 1 Motherwell 0	Partick 0 Dundee 1
Partick 0 Aberdeen 3	Partick 2 Aberdeen 0
Dundee Utd 0 Partick 0	Hibernian 1 Partick 2
Partick 4 Dunfermline 1	Livingston 2 Partick 2
Hibernian 3 Partick 2	Partick 2 Kilmarnock 2

PETERHEAD

NICKNAME:	The Blue Toon
COLOURS:	Blue and white
GROUND:	Balmoor Stadium
TELEPHONE:	01779 478256
FAX:	01779 490682
WEBSITE:	peterheadfc.org.uk
CAPACITY:	4500
RECORD ATT:	1500 (v Fraserburgh, 1999)
RECORD VICTORY:	17-1 (v Fort William, 1998)
MANAGER:	Iain Stewart
CHAIRMAN:	Roger Taylor
MOST LEAGUE GOALS (1 SEASON):	21, Iain Stewart, 2002-03

LEAGUE RESULTS 2003-2004

Montrose 0 Peterhead 1
Peterhead 2 Gretna 0
Elgin City 2 Peterhead 3
Peterhead 1 Stranraer 2
Stirling 3 Peterhead 1
Peterhead 2 East Stirling 0
Albion 2 Peterhead 0
Queen's Park 0 Peterhead 2
Peterhead 0 Cowdenbeath 1
Gretna 3 Peterhead 2
Peterhead 0 Montrose 0
Peterhead 2 Stirling 2
Stranraer 0 Peterhead 2
East Stirling 1 Peterhead 3
Peterhead 2 Albion 1
Cowdenbeath 2 Peterhead 0
Peterhead 5 Elgin City 1

Montrose 2 Peterhead 1
Peterhead 6 East Stirling 0
Stirling 0 Peterhead 2
Peterhead 2 Stranraer 0
Peterhead 0 Cowdenbeath 0
Queen's Park 1 Peterhead 0
Peterhead 2 Gretna 1
Elgin City 1 Peterhead 0
Albion 3 Peterhead 3
Peterhead 0 Stirling 0
Stranraer 1 Peterhead 1
Peterhead 5 Albion 0
East Stirling 0 Peterhead 3
Cowdenbeath 0 Peterhead 3
Peterhead 1 Queen's Park 1
Peterhead 3 Elgin City 1
Gretna 3 Peterhead 2
Peterhead 1 Montrose 2

QUEEN OF THE SOUTH

NICKNAME:	The Doonhamers
COLOURS:	Royal blue
GROUND:	Palmerston Park
TELEPHONE No:	01387 254853
FAX No:	01387 240470
WEBSITE:	qosfc.co.uk
CAPACITY:	6412
RECORD ATT:	24,500 (v Hearts, 1952)
RECORD VICTORY:	11-1 (v Stranraer, 1932)
RECORD DEFEAT:	2-10 (v Dundee, 1962)
MANAGER:	Iain Scott
CHAIRMAN:	David Rae
MOST LEAGUE GOALS (1 SEASON):	41, Jimmy Rutherford, 1931-32

HONOURS

LEAGUE CHAMPIONS: Division II – 1950-51. Second Division – 2001-02. Bell's Cup – 2002-03.

LEAGUE RESULTS 2003-2004

St Johnstone 4 Queen of Sth 1	Queen of Sth 2 Falkirk 0
Queen of Sth 1 Ross County 0	Ayr 1 Queen of Sth 1
Falkirk 0 Queen of Sth 0	Queen of Sth 1 Raith 1
Ayr 1 Queen of Sth 4	St Mirren 3 Queen of Sth 1
Queen of Sth 0 Raith 2	Brechin 2 Queen of Sth 1
St Mirren 1 Queen of Sth 2	Queen of Sth 2 Inverness CT 1
Queen of Sth 4 Clyde 1	Queen of Sth 1 Ross County 1
Brechin 0 Queen of Sth 1	Queen of Sth 1 Clyde 2
Queen of Sth 3 Inverness CT 2	Falkirk 0 Queen of Sth 2
Ross County 1 Queen of Sth 0	Raith 3 Queen of Sth 1
Queen of Sth 1 St Johnstone 1	Queen of Sth 0 Ayr 0
Raith 0 Queen of Sth 1	Clyde 2 Queen of Sth 0
Queen of Sth 1 Ayr 0	Queen of Sth 1 St Mirren 0
Clyde 3 Queen of Sth 1	Inverness CT 4 Queen of Sth 1
Queen of Sth 1 St Mirren 2	Queen of Sth 2 Brechin 2
Inverness CT 4 Queen of Sth 1	Queen of Sth 1 St Johnstone 1
Queen of Sth 1 Brechin 0	Ross County 1 Queen of Sth 2
St Johnstone 2 Queen of Sth 2	Queen of Sth 1 Falkirk 0

QUEEN'S PARK

NICKNAME:	The Spiders
COLOURS:	White and black
GROUND:	Hampden Park
TELEPHONE No:	0141 632 1275
FAX No:	0141 636 1612
WEBSITE:	queensparkfc.co.uk
CAPACITY:	52,046
RECORD ATT:	95,772 (v Rangers, 1930). 149,547 (for ground Scotland v England, 1937)
RECORD VICTORY:	16-0 (v St Peter's, 1885)
RECORD DEFEAT:	0-9 (v Motherwell, 1930)
MANAGER:	Kenny Brannigan
PRESIDENT:	David Gordon
MOST LEAGUE GOALS (1 SEASON):	30, William Martin, 1937-38

HONOURS

LEAGUE CHAMPIONSHIP: Division II – 1922-23. B Division – 1955-56. Second Division – 1980-81. Third Division – 1999-00.
SCOTTISH CUP (10): 1874, 1875, 1876, 1880, 1881, 1882, 1884, 1886, 1890, 1893.

LEAGUE RESULTS 2003-2004

Gretna 1 Queen's Park 1	Gretna 0 Queen's Park 1
Queen's Park 5 Elgin City 2	Queen's Park 1 Montrose 1
Albion 3 Queen's Park 1	Cowdenbeath 5 Queen's Pk 1
Queen's Park 0 Stirling 2	Queen's Park 1 Stirling 4
Cowdenbeath 0 Queen's Pk 1	Stranraer 3 Queen's Park 1
Queen's Park 1 Montrose 1	Queen's Park 1 Peterhead 0
East Stirling 1 Queen's Park 2	East Stirling 2 Queen's Park 4
Queen's Park 0 Peterhead 2	Queen's Park 4 Elgin City 0
Stranraer 1 Queen's Park 0	Albion 3 Queen's Park 1
Elgin City 2 Queen's Park 2	Queen's Pk 1 Cowdenbeath 2
Queen's Park 0 Gretna 1	Stirling 0 Queen's Park 0
Queen's Pk 0 Cowdenbeath 0	Queen's Park 1 East Stirling 0
Stirling 1 Queen's Park 0	Montrose 1 Queen's Park 1
Montrose 0 Queen's Park 0	Queen's Park 0 Stranraer 2
Queen's Park 3 East Stirling 0	Peterhead 1 Queen's Park 1
Peterhead 4 Queen's Park 1	Queen's Park 0 Albion 1
Queen's Park 1 Albion 1	Elgin City 1 Queen's Park 3
Queen's Park 0 Stranraer 4	Queen's Park 1 Gretna 1

RAITH ROVERS

NICKNAME: The Rovers
COLOURS: Navy blue and white
GROUND: Stark's Park
TELEPHONE No: 01592 263514
FAX No: 01592 642833
WEBSITE: raithroversfc.com
CAPACITY: 10,104
RECORD ATT: 31,306 (v Hearts, 1953)
RECORD VICTORY: 10-1 (v Coldstream, 1954)
RECORD DEFEAT: 2-11 (v Morton, 1936)
CHAIRMAN: Turnbull Hutton
MOST LEAGUE GOALS (1 SEASON): 38, Norman Haywood, 1937-38

HONOURS

LEAGUE CHAMPIONS: First Division (2) – 1992-93, 1994-95. Second Division – 2002-03. Division II (4) – 1907-08, 1909-10 (shared), 1937-38, 1948-49. LEAGUE CUP – 1994-95.

LEAGUE RESULTS 2003-2004

Raith 1 St Mirren 1
Brechin 0 Raith 3
Raith 1 Ayr 1
Raith 0 Falkirk 1
Queen of Sth 0 Raith 2
St Johnstone 0 Raith 1
Raith 1 Ross County 7
Inverness CT 2 Raith 1
Raith 0 Clyde 1
Raith 2 Brechin 1
St Mirren 2 Raith 1
Raith 0 Queen of Sth 1
Falkirk 3 Raith 2
Ross County 3 Raith 2
Raith 1 St Johnstone 4
Clyde 0 Raith 0
Raith 1 Inverness CT 3
Ayr 1 Raith 0

Raith 2 Falkirk 0
Queen of Sth 1 Raith 1
St Johnstone 5 Raith 2
Raith 0 Ross County 0
Inverness CT 3 Raith 0
Raith 0 Clyde 3
Raith 2 St Mirren 0
Brechin 1 Raith 1
Raith 2 Ayr 1
Raith 3 Queen of Sth 1
Falkirk 1 Raith 0
Ross County 1 Raith 1
Raith 1 St Johnstone 1
Clyde 4 Raith 1
Raith 0 Inverness CT 1
St Mirren 1 Raith 1
Raith 1 Brechin 1
Ayr 1 Raith 0

RANGERS

NICKNAME:	The Gers
COLOURS:	Blue, red and white
GROUND:	Ibrox Stadium
TELEPHONE No:	0870 600 1972
FAX No:	0870 600 1978
WEBSITE:	rangers.co.uk
CAPACITY:	50,467
RECORD ATT:	118,567
	(v Celtic, 1939)
RECORD VICTORY:	14-2
	(v Blairgowrie, 1934)
RECORD DEFEAT:	2-10 (v Airdrie, 1886)
MANAGER:	Alex McLeish
CHAIRMAN:	John McClelland
MOST LEAGUE	
GOALS (1 SEASON):	44, Sam English, 1931-32
GOALS (OVERALL):	250, Ally McCoist

HONOURS

LEAGUE CHAMPIONSHIP (50): 1890-91 (shared), 1898-99, 1899-1900, 1900-01, 1901-02, 1910-11, 1911-12, 1912-13, 1917-18, 1919-20, 1920-21, 1922-23, 1923-24, 1924-25, 1926-27, 1927-28, 1928-29, 1929-30, 1930-31, 1932-33, 1933-34, 1934-35, 1936-37, 1938-39, 1946-47, 1948-49, 1949-50, 1952-53, 1955-56, 1956-57, 1958-59, 1960-61, 1962-63, 1963-64, 1974-75, 1975-76, 1977-78, 1986-87, 1988-89, 1989-90, 1990-91, 1991-92, 1992-93, 1993-94, 1994-95, 1995-96, 1996-97, 1998-99, 1999-00, 2002-03.

SCOTTISH CUP (31): 1894, 1897, 1898, 1903, 1928, 1930, 1932, 1934, 1935, 1936, 1948, 1949, 1950, 1953, 1960, 1962, 1963, 1964, 1966, 1973, 1976, 1978, 1979, 1981, 1992, 1993, 1996, 1999, 2000, 2002, 2003.

LEAGUE CUP (23): 1946-47, 1948-49, 1960-61, 1961-62, 1963-64, 1964-65, 1970-71, 1975-76, 1977-78, 1978-79, 1981-82, 1983-84, 1984-85, 1986-87, 1987-88, 1988-89, 1990-91, 1992-93, 1993-94, 1996-97, 1998-99, 2001-02, 2002-03.

EUROPEAN CUP-WINNERS' CUP: 1971-72.

ALAN HUTTON

STEFAN KLOS

LEAGUE RESULTS 2003-2004

Rangers 4 Kilmarnock 0
Aberdeen 2 Rangers 3
Rangers 5 Hibernian 2
Dundee Utd 1 Rangers 3
Rangers 4 Dunfermline 0
Hearts 0 Rangers 4
Rangers 3 Dundee 1
Rangers 0 Celtic 1
Motherwell 1 Rangers 1
Livingston 0 Rangers 0
Rangers 3 Partick 1
Kilmarnock 2 Rangers 3
Rangers 3 Aberdeen 0
Hibernian 0 Rangers 1
Rangers 2 Dundee Utd 1
Dunfermline 2 Rangers 0
Rangers 2 Hearts 1
Dundee 0 Rangers 2
Celtic 3 Rangers 0

Rangers 1 Motherwell 0
Rangers 1 Livingston 0
Partick 0 Rangers 1
Rangers 2 Kilmarnock 0
Aberdeen 1 Rangers 1
Rangers 3 Hibernian 0
Dundee Utd 2 Rangers 0
Hearts 1 Rangers 1
Rangers 4 Dundee 0
Rangers 4 Dunfermline 1
Rangers 1 Celtic 2
Motherwell 0 Rangers 1
Livingston 1 Rangers 1
Rangers 2 Partick 0
Dundee Utd 3 Rangers 3
Rangers 4 Motherwell 0
Celtic 1 Rangers 0
Rangers 0 Hearts 1
Dunfermline 2 Rangers 3

ROSS COUNTY

NICKNAME:	The County
COLOURS:	Dark blue, white and red
GROUND:	Victoria Park
TELEPHONE No:	01349 860860
FAX No:	01349 866277
WEBSITE:	rosscountyfootball club.co.uk
CAPACITY:	6700
RECORD ATT:	8000 (v Rangers, 1966)
RECORD VICTORY:	11-0 (v St Cuthbert's Wanderers, 1993)
RECORD DEFEAT:	1-10 (v Inverness Thistle)
MANAGER:	Alex Smith
CHAIRMAN:	Roy McGregor
MOST LEAGUE GOALS (1 SEASON):	22, Derek Adams, 1997-98

LEAGUE RESULTS 2003-2004

Ross County 4 Brechin 0	St Mirren 1 Ross County 1
Queen of Sth 1 Ross County 0	Ross County 1 Inverness CT 0
Ross County 2 St Mirren 0	Falkirk 2 Ross County 0
Ross County 1 Inverness CT 1	Ross County 1 Ayr 1
Falkirk 0 Ross County 2	Raith 0 Ross County 0
Ross County 2 Ayr 2	Clyde 1 Ross County 2
Raith 1 Ross County 7	Ross County 2 St Johnstone 0
Clyde 2 Ross County 2	Queen of Sth 1 Ross County 1
Ross County 0 St Johnstone 3	Ross County 1 St Mirren 0
Ross County 1 Queen of Sth 0	Ross County 1 Falkirk 1
Brechin 4 Ross County 2	Inverness CT 1 Ross County 0
Ross County 1 Falkirk	Ross County 1 Raith 1
Inverness CT 3 Ross County 3	Ayr 1 Ross County 2
Ross County 3 Raith 2	St Johnstone 1 Ross County 1
Ayr 1 Ross County 3	Ross County 0 Clyde 0
St Johnstone 1 Ross County 1	Brechin 1 Ross County 0
Ross County 0 Clyde 1	Ross County 1 Queen of Sth 2
Ross County 2 Brechin 1	St Mirren 2 Ross County 0

ST JOHNSTONE

NICKNAME:	The Saints
COLOURS:	Blue and white
GROUND:	McDiarmid Park
TELEPHONE No:	01738 459090
FAX No:	01738 625771
WEBSITE:	stjohnstonefc.co.uk
CAPACITY:	10,673
RECORD ATT:	10,504
	(v Rangers, 1990)
RECORD VICTORY:	9-0 (v Albion Rovers, 1946)
RECORD DEFEAT:	1-10 (v Third Lanark, 1903)
MANAGER:	John Connolly
CHAIRMAN:	Geoffrey S Brown
MOST LEAGUE	
GOALS (1 SEASON):	36, Jimmy Benson, 1931-32
GOALS (OVERALL):	140, John Brogan, 1977-83

HONOURS

LEAGUE CHAMPIONSHIP: First Division (3) – 1982-83, 1989-90, 1996-97. Division II (3) – 1923-24, 1959-60, 1962-63.

LEAGUE RESULTS 2003-2004

St Johnstone 4 Queen of Sth 1	Inverness CT 1 St Johnstone 0
St Mirren 1 St Johnstone 1	St Johnstone 2 Brechin 2
St Johnstone 1 Inverness CT 2	St Johnstone 5 Raith 2
St Johnstone 3 Brechin 1	St Johnstone 3 Ayr 0
Clyde 2 St Johnstone 0	Ross County 2 St Johnstone 0
St Johnstone 0 Raith 1	Clyde 2 St Johnstone 3
Falkirk 0 St Johnstone 3	Falkirk 0 St Johnstone 1
St Johnstone 1 Ayr 1	St Johnstone 3 Inverness CT 2
Ross County 0 St Johnstone 3	St Mirren 1 St Johnstone 1
St Johnstone 1 St Mirren 0	St Johnstone 1 Clyde 3
Queen of Sth 1 St Johnstone 1	Brechin 0 St Johnstone 2
St Johnstone 3 Clyde 0	St Johnstone 2 Falkirk 1
Brechin 0 St Johnstone 1	Raith 1 St Johnstone 1
St Johnstone 0 Falkirk 4	St Johnstone 1 Ross County 1
Raith 1 St Johnstone 4	Ayr 1 St Johnstone 1
St Johnstone 1 Ross County 1	Queen of Sth 1 St Johnstone 1
Ayr 1 St Johnstone 1	St Johnstone 1 St Mirren 3
St Johnstone 2 Queen of Sth 2	Inverness CT 3 St Johnstone 1

ST MIRREN

NICKNAME: The Buddies
COLOURS: Black and white
GROUND: St Mirren Park
TELEPHONE No: 0141 889 2558
FAX No: 0141 848 6444
WEBSITE: saintmirren.net
CAPACITY: 10,722
RECORD ATT: 47,438 (v Celtic, 1925)
RECORD VICTORY: 15-0 (v Glasgow University, 1960)
RECORD DEFEAT: 0-9 (v Rangers, 1897)
MANAGER: Gus MacPherson
CHAIRMAN: Stewart Gilmour
MOST LEAGUE
GOALS (1 SEASON): 45, Dunky Walker, 1921-22
GOALS (OVERALL): 221, David McCrae

HONOURS
**LEAGUE CHAMPIONS: First Division (2) – 1976-77, 1999-00.
Division II – 1967-68. SCOTTISH CUP (3): 1926, 1959, 1987.**

LEAGUE RESULTS 2003-2004

Raith 1 St Mirren 1	St Mirren 2 Clyde 3
St Mirren 1 St Johnstone 1	Brechin 2 St Mirren 0
Ross County 2 St Mirren 0	St Mirren 3 Queen of Sth 1
St Mirren 2 Clyde 1	Inverness CT 1 St Mirren 1
Brechin 1 St Mirren 1	St Mirren 1 Falkirk 1
St Mirren 1 Queen of Sth 2	Ayr 2 St Mirren 0
Inverness CT 2 St Mirren 0	Raith 2 St Mirren 0
St Mirren 0 Falkirk 0	Ross County 1 St Mirren 0
Ayr 0 St Mirren 2	St Mirren 1 St Johnstone 1
St Johnstone 1 St Mirren 0	St Mirren 3 Brechin 3
St Mirren 2 Raith 1	Clyde 2 St Mirren 2
St Mirren 0 Brechin 2	St Mirren 0 Inverness CT 0
Clyde 2 St Mirren 0	Queen of Sth 1 St Mirren 0
St Mirren 0 Inverness CT 4	St Mirren 4 Ayr 1
Queen of Sth 1 St Mirren 2	Falkirk 1 St Mirren 0
St Mirren 3 Ayr 2	St Mirren 1 Raith 1
Falkirk 0 St Mirren 0	St Johnstone 1 St Mirren 3
St Mirren 1 Ross County 1	St Mirren 2 Ross County 0

STENHOUSEMUIR

NICKNAME:	The Warriors
COLOURS:	Maroon and white
GROUND:	Ochilview Park
TELEPHONE No:	01324 562992
FAX No:	01324 562980
WEBSITE:	stenhousemuirfc.com
CAPACITY:	2354
RECORD ATT:	12,500 (v East Fife, 1950)
RECORD VICTORY:	9-2 (v Dundee United, 1937)
RECORD DEFEAT:	2-11 (v Dunfermline, 1930)
CO-MANAGERS:	Tony Smith/Des McKeown
CHAIRMAN:	Mike Laing
MOST LEAGUE GOALS (1 SEASON):	32, Robert Taylor, 1995-96

HONOURS

LEAGUE CHALLENGE CUP: 1995-96.

LEAGUE RESULTS 2003-2004

East Fife 3 Stenhousemuir 2
Stenhousemuir 0 Morton 2
Alloa 2 Stenhousemuir 2
Stenhousemuir 2 Forfar 0
Hamilton 2 Stenhousemuir 0
Stenhousemuir 0 Berwick 3
Dumbarton 0 Stenhousemuir 1
Stenhousemuir 1 Arbroath 0
Airdrie Utd 2 Stenhousemuir 0
Morton 5 Stenhousemuir 2
Stenhousemuir 3 East Fife 0
Stenhousemuir 0 Hamilton 3
Forfar 2 Stenhousemuir 0
Berwick 2 Stenhousemuir 1
Stenhousemuir 1 Dumbarton 1
Arbroath 2 Stenhousemuir 1
Stenhousemuir 0 Airdrie Utd 1
Stenhousemuir 1 Alloa 3

East Fife 1 Stenhousemuir 0
Stenhousemuir 3 Berwick 1
Hamilton 0 Stenhousemuir 1
Stenhousemuir 0 Forfar 2
Airdrie Utd 4 Stenhousemuir 0
Stenhousemuir 0 Morton 1
Alloa 1 Stenhousemuir 0
Dumbarton 4 Stenhousemuir 0
Forfar 1 Stenhousemuir 1
Stenhousemuir 0 Arbroath 3
Stenhousemuir 1 Dumbarton 2
Stenhousemuir 0 Hamilton 2
Berwick 3 Stenhousemuir 0
Stenhousemuir 0 Airdrie Utd 3
Arbroath 1 Stenhousemuir 1
Stenhousemuir 0 Alloa 1
Morton 1 Stenhousemuir 4
Stenhousemuir 0 East Fife 1

STIRLING ALBION

NICKNAME:	The Binos
COLOURS:	Red and white
GROUND:	Forthbank Stadium
TELEPHONE No:	01786 450399
FAX No:	01786 448400
CAPACITY:	3808
RECORD ATT:	26,400 (v Celtic, 1959, at Annfield)
RECORD VICTORY:	20-0 (v Selkirk, 1984)
RECORD DEFEAT:	0-9 (v Dundee United, 1967)
MANAGER:	Allan Moore
CHAIRMAN:	Peter McKenzie
MOST LEAGUE GOALS (1 SEASON:)	27, Joe Hughes, 1969-70

HONOURS

LEAGUE CHAMPIONS: Division II (4) – 1952-53, 1957-58, 1960-61, 1964-65. Second Division (3) – 1976-77, 1990-91, 1995-96.

LEAGUE RESULTS 2003-2004

Stirling 0 Cowdenbeath 0	Stirling 1 Cowdenbeath 1
Stranraer 0 Stirling 1	Stirling 3 Albion 0
Stirling 5 East Stirling 1	Stirling 0 Peterhead 2
Queen's Park 0 Stirling 2	Queen's Park 1 Stirling 4
Stirling 3 eterhead 1	Montrose 1 Stirling 4
Stirling 2 Albion 1	Gretna 1 Stirling 0
Gretna 0 Stirling 1	Stranraer 1 Stirling 1
Stirling 3 Elgin City 0	Stirling 6 Elgin City 1
Stirling 3 Montrose 0	Stirling 6 East Stirling 1
Montrose 2 Stirling 3	Peterhead 0 Stirling 0
Stirling 1 Stranraer 0	Stirling 0 Queen's Park 0
Cowdenbeath 2 Stirling 0	Stirling 0 Gretna 1
Peterhead 2 Stirling 2	Albion 3 Stirling 5
Stirling 1 Queen's Park 0	Stirling 1 Montrose 1
Albion 0 Stirling 3	Elgin City 0 Stirling 1
Stirling 0 Gretna 1	East Stirling 0 Stirling 3
Elgin City 0 Stirling 2	Stirling 2 Stranraer 2
East Stirling 2 Stirling 4	Cowdenbeath 0 Stirling 5

STRANRAER

NICKNAME:	The Blues
COLOURS:	Blue and white
GROUND:	Stair Park
TELEPHONE No:	01776 703271
FAX No:	01776 702194
WEBSITE:	stranraerfc.co.uk
CAPACITY:	5600
RECORD ATT:	6500
	(v Rangers, 1948)
RECORD VICTORY:	7-0 (v Brechin, 1965)
RECORD DEFEAT:	1-11 (v Queen of the South, 1932)
MANAGER:	Neil Watt
CHIEF EXECUTIVE:	James Hannah
MOST LEAGUE	
GOALS (1 SEASON):	27, Derek Frye, 1997-98

HONOURS
LEAGUE CHAMPIONS: Second Division (2) – 1993-94, 1997-98.
Third Division – 2003-04. LEAGUE CHALLENGE CUP: 1996-97.

LEAGUE RESULTS 2003-2004

Albion 1 Stranraer 1
Stranraer 0 Stirling 1
Gretna 1 Stranraer 1
Peterhead 1 Stranraer 2
Stranraer 4 East Stirling 0
Stranraer 4 Elgin City 3
Montrose 2 Stranraer 4
Cowdenbeath 0 Stranraer 1
Stranraer 1 Queen's Park 0
Stirling 1 Stranraer 0
Stranraer 5 Albion 0
East Stirling 1 Stranraer 4
Stranraer 0 Peterhead 2
Elgin City 1 Stranraer 3
Stranraer 2 Montrose 0
Stranraer 2 Cowdenbeath 0
Stranraer 1 Gretna 2
Queen's Park 0 Stranraer 4

Stranraer 6 Elgin City 0
Montrose 1 Stranraer 4
Stranraer 7 East Stirling 1
Peterhead 2 Stranraer 0
Albion 1 Stranraer 4
Stranraer 3 Queen's Park 1
Stranraer 1 Stirling 1
Cowdenbeath 1 Stranraer 2
Gretna 0 Stranraer 0
East Stirling 1 Stranraer 2
Stranraer 1 Peterhead 1
Stranraer 6 Montrose 0
Elgin City 0 Stranraer 0
Queen's Park 0 Stranraer 2
Stranraer 1 Cowdenbeath 0
Stranraer 3 Gretna 2
Stirling 2 Stranraer 2
Stranraer 4 Albion 0

LEGS 'N' CO
lap top dancing!!

STAG NIGHTS • WORK NIGHTS OUT ETC

86 MAXWELL STREET, GLASGOW

Open From 6pm Sunday-Thursday, midday Friday & 2pm Sat.

Strict House Rules Apply

No Jeans, Trainers, etc

0141 221 4657

www.legsnco.com

WINNERS 2004

DEPARTING SWEDE Henrik Larsson and his son, Jordan, take in all the excitement of winning the SPL title for season 2003-2004.

STANDING FIRM: Rangers centre-half Craig Moore holds off Celtic's Henrik Larsson during the clubs' Scottish Cup quarter-final clash at Parkhead. Larsson netted the game's only goal.

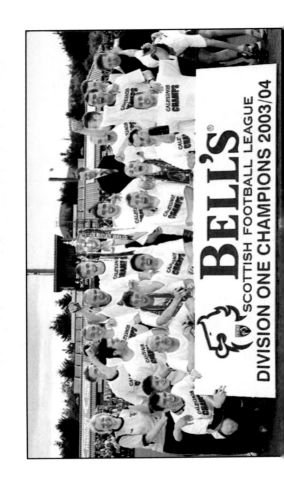

LIVINGSTON players enjoy their winning of the League Cup Final at Hampden

SECOND DIVISION champions Airdrie United get ready to start their title-winning party

BELL'S
SCOTTISH FOOTBALL LEAGUE
DIVISION THREE CHAMPIONS 2003/04

LEAGUE CHAMPIONS

YEAR	WINNERS
1890-91	RANGERS/DUMBARTON
1891-92	DUMBARTON
1892-93	CELTIC
1893-94	CELTIC
1894-95	HEARTS
1895-96	CELTIC
1896-97	HEARTS
1897-98	CELTIC
1898-99	RANGERS
1899-1900	RANGERS
1900-01	RANGERS
1901-02	RANGERS
1902-03	HIBERNIAN
1903-04	THIRD LANARK
1904-05	CELTIC
1905-06	CELTIC
1906-07	CELTIC
1907-08	CELTIC
1908-09	CELTIC
1909-10	CELTIC
1910-11	RANGERS
1911-12	RANGERS
1912-13	RANGERS
1913-14	CELTIC
1914-15	CELTIC
1915-16	CELTIC
1916-17	CELTIC
1917-18	RANGERS
1918-19	CELTIC
1919-20	RANGERS
1920-21	RANGERS
1921-22	CELTIC
1922-23	RANGERS
1923-24	RANGERS
1924-25	RANGERS
1925-26	CELTIC
1926-27	RANGERS
1927-28	RANGERS
1928-29	RANGERS

YEAR	WINNERS
1929-30	RANGERS
1930-31	RANGERS
1931-32	MOTHERWELL
1932-33	RANGERS
1933-34	RANGERS
1934-35	RANGERS
1935-36	CELTIC
1936-37	RANGERS
1937-38	CELTIC
1938-39	RANGERS
NO CHAMPIONSHIP	
1946-47	RANGERS
1947-48	HIBERNIAN
1948-49	RANGERS
1949-50	RANGERS
1950-51	HIBERNIAN
1951-52	HIBERNIAN
1952-53	RANGERS
1953-54	CELTIC
1954-55	ABERDEEN
1955-56	RANGERS
1956-57	RANGERS
1957-58	HEARTS
1958-59	RANGERS
1959-60	HEARTS
1960-61	RANGERS
1961-62	DUNDEE
1962-63	RANGERS
1963-64	RANGERS
1964-65	KILMARNOCK
1965-66	CELTIC
1966-67	CELTIC
1967-68	CELTIC
1968-69	CELTIC
1969-70	CELTIC
1970-71	CELTIC
1971-72	CELTIC
1972-73	CELTIC
1973-74	CELTIC
1974-75	RANGERS

PREMIER DIVISION

YEAR	WINNERS
1975-76	RANGERS
1976-77	CELTIC
1977-78	RANGERS
1978-79	CELTIC
1979-80	ABERDEEN
1980-81	CELTIC
1981-82	CELTIC
1982-83	DUNDEE UNITED
1983-84	ABERDEEN
1984-85	ABERDEEN
1985-86	CELTIC
1986-87	RANGERS
1987-88	CELTIC
1988-89	RANGERS

YEAR	WINNERS
1989-90	RANGERS
1990-91	RANGERS
1991-92	RANGERS
1992-93	RANGERS
1993-94	RANGERS
1994-95	RANGERS
1995-96	RANGERS
1996-97	RANGERS
1997-98	CELTIC
1998-99	RANGERS
1999-00	RANGERS
2000-01	CELTIC
2001-02	CELTIC
2002-03	RANGERS
2003-04	CELTIC

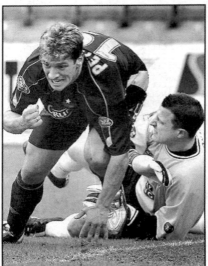

STAN'S THE MAN: Stilian Petrov turns away after netting the goal that clinched the SPL title for Celtic at Rugby Park

PROMOTION/RELEGATION

1921-1922	Promoted	Alloa
	Relegated	Dumbarton, Queen's Park, Clydebank
1922-23	Promoted	Queen's Park, Clydebank
	Relegated	Albion Rovers, Alloa
1923-24	Promoted	St Johnstone, Cowdenbeath
	Relegated	Clyde, Clydebank
1924-25	Promoted	Dundee Utd, Clydebank
	Relegated	Ayr United, Third Lanark
1925-26	Promoted	Dunfermline, Clyde
	Relegated	Raith Rovers, Clydebank
1926-27	Promoted	Bo'ness, Raith Rovers
	Relegated	Morton, Dundee United
1927-28	Promoted	Ayr United, Third Lanark
	Relegated	Bo'ness, Dunfermline
1928-29	Promoted	Dundee United, Morton
	Relegated	Third Lanark, Raith Rovers
1929-30	Promoted	Leith Ath, East Fife
	Relegated	Dundee United, St Johnstone
1930-31	Promoted	Third Lanark, Dundee United
	Relegated	Hibernian, East Fife
1931-32	Promoted	East Stirling, St Johnstone
	Relegated	Dundee United, Leith Ath
1932-33	Promoted	Hibernian, Queen of the South
	Relegated	Morton, East Stirling
1933-34	Promoted	Albion Rovers, Dunfermline
	Relegated	Third Lanark, Cowdenbeath
1934-35	Promoted	Third Lanark, Arbroath
	Relegated	St Mirren, Falkirk
1935-36	Promoted	Falkirk, St Mirren
	Relegated	Airdrie, Ayr United
1936-37	Promoted	Ayr United, Morton
	Relegated	Dunfermline, Albion Rovers
1937-38	Promoted	Raith Rovers, Albion Rovers
	Relegated	Dundee, Morton
1938-39	Promoted	Cowdenbeath, Alloa
	Relegated	Queen's Park, Raith Rovers
1946-47	Promoted	Dundee, Airdrie
	Relegated	Kilmarnock, Hamilton
1947-48	Promoted	East Fife, Albion Rovers
	Relegated	Airdrie, Queen's Park
1948-49	Promoted	Raith Rovers, Stirling Albion
	Relegated	Morton, Albion Rovers

1949-50	Promoted	Morton, Airdrie
	Relegated	Queen of the South, Stirling Alb
1950-51	Promoted	Queen of the South, Stirling Alb
	Relegated	Clyde, Falkirk
1951-52	Promoted	Clyde, Falkirk
	Relegated	Morton, Stirling Albion
1952-53	Promoted	Stirling Albion, Hamilton Accies
	Relegated	Motherwell, Third Lanark
1953-54	Promoted	Motherwell, Kilmarnock
	Relegated	Airdrie, Hamilton Accies
1954-55	Promoted	Airdrie, Dunfermline
	Relegated	Motherwell, Stirling Albion
1955-56	Promoted	Queen's Park, Ayr United
	Relegated	Clyde, Stirling Albion
1956-57	Promoted	Clyde, Third Lanark
	Relegated	Dunfermline, Ayr United
1957-58	Promoted	Stirling Albion, Dunfermline
	Relegated	East Fife, Queen's Park
1958-59	Promoted	Ayr United, Arbroath
	Relegated	Falkirk, Queen of the South
1959-60	Promoted	St Johnstone, Dundee United
	Relegated	Stirling Albion, Arbroath
1960-61	Promoted	Stirling Albion, Falkirk
	Relegated	Clyde, Ayr United
1961-62	Promoted	Clyde, Queen of the South
	Relegated	St Johnstone, Stirling Albion
1962-63	Promoted	St Johnstone, East Stirling
	Relegated	Clyde, Raith Rovers
1963-64	Promoted	Morton, Clyde
	Relegated	Queen of the South, East Stirling
1964-65	Promoted	Stirling Albion, Hamilton Accies
	Relegated	Airdrie, Third Lanark
1965-66	Promoted	Ayr United, Airdrie
	Relegated	Morton, Hamilton Accies
1966-67	Promoted	Morton, Raith Rovers
	Relegated	St Mirren, Ayr United
1967-68	Promoted	St Mirren, Arbroath
	Relegated	Motherwell, Stirling Albion
1968-69	Promoted	Motherwell, Ayr United
	Relegated	Falkirk, Arbroath
1969-70	Promoted	Falkirk, Cowdenbeath
	Relegated	Raith Rovers, Partick Thistle
1970-71	Promoted	Partick Thistle, East Fife
	Relegated	St Mirren, Cowdenbeath
1971-72	Promoted	Dumbarton, Arbroath
	Relegated	Clyde, Dunfermline
1972-73	Promoted	Clyde, Dunfermline
	Relegated	Kilmarnock, Airdrie

1973-74	**Promoted**	Airdrie, Kilmarnock
	Relegated	East Fife, Falkirk

1974-75 Leagues reformed into Premier, First and Second Divisions

1975-76	**Promoted to Premier** – Kilmarnock, Partick Th
	Relegated to First – Dundee, St Johnstone
	Promoted to First – Clydebank, Raith Rovers
	Relegated to Second – Clyde, Dunfermline
1976-77	**Promoted to Premier** – St Mirren, Clydebank
	Relegated to First – Hearts, Kilmarnock
	Promoted to First – Alloa, Stirling Albion
	Relegated to Second – Falkirk, Raith Rovers
1977-78	**Promoted to Premier** – Morton, Hearts
	Relegated to First – Ayr United, Clydebank
	Promoted to First – Clyde, Raith Rovers
	Relegated to Second – Alloa Athletic, East Fife
1978-79	**Promoted to Premier** – Dundee, Kilmarnock
	Relegated to First – Hearts, Motherwell
	Promoted to First – Berwick Ran, Dunfermline
	Relegated to Second – Montrose, QOS
1979-80	**Promoted to Premier** – Hearts, Airdrie
	Relegated to First – Dundee, Hibernian
	Promoted to First – East Stirling, Falkirk
	Relegated to Second – Arbroath, Clyde
1980-81	**Promoted to Premier** – Dundee, Hibernian
	Relegated to First – Hearts, Kilmarnock
	Promoted to First – Queen's Park, QOS
	Relegated to Second – Berwick R, Stirling Alb
1981-82	**Promoted to Premier** – Motherwell, Kilmarnock
	Relegated to First – Airdrie, Partick Thistle
	Promoted to First – Clyde, Alloa Athletic
	Relegated to Second – QOS, East Stirling
1982-83	**Promoted to Premier** – St Johnstone, Hearts
	Relegated to First – Kilmarnock, Morton
	Promoted to First – Brechin, Meadowbank
	Relegated to Second – Queen's Pk, Dunf'line
1983-84	**Promoted to Premier** — Dumbarton, Morton
	Relegated to First — Motherwell, St Johnstone
	Promoted to First — East Fife, Forfar
	Relegated to Second — Alloa, Raith Rovers
1984-85	**Promoted to Premier** — Motherwell, Clydebank
	Relegated to First — Dumbarton, Morton
	Promoted to First — Montrose, Alloa Athletic
	Relegated to Second — M'dowbank, St Johnstone
1985-86	**Promoted to Premier** – Hamilton Accies, Falkirk
	No relegation to First – league reorganisation
	Promoted to First – Dunfermline, QOS
	Relegated to Second – Ayr United, Alloa

1986-87	**Promoted to Premier** – Morton, Dunfermline Ath
	Relegated to First – Clydebank, Hamilton Accies
	Promoted to First – Meadowbank Th, Raith Rovers
	Relegated to Second – Brechin, Montrose
1987-88	**Promoted to Premier** – Hamilton Accies
	Relegated to First – Falkirk, Dunfermline, Morton
	Promoted to First – Ayr United, St Johnstone
	Relegated to Second – East Fife, Dumbarton
1988-89	**Promoted to Premier** – Dunfermline Ath
	Relegated to First – Hamilton Accies
	Promoted to First – Albion Rovers, Alloa Ath
	Relegated to Second – QOS, Kilmarnock
1989-90	**Promoted to Premier** – St Johnstone
	Relegated to First – Dundee
	Promoted to First – Brechin, Kilmarnock
	Relegated to Second – Alloa Ath, Albion Rovers
1990-91	**Promoted to Premier** – Falkirk, Airdrie
	No relegation to First
	Promoted to First – Stirling Albion, Montrose
	Relegated to Second – Brechin, Clyde
1991-92	**Promoted to Premier** – Dundee, Partick Thistle
	Relegated to First – Dunfermline Ath, St Mirren
	Promoted to First – Dumbarton, Cowdenbeath
	Relegated to Second – Montrose, Forfar
1992-93	**Promoted to Premier** – Raith Rov, Kilmarnock
	Relegated to First – Airdrie, Falkirk
	Promoted to First – Clyde, Brechin
	Relegated to Second – Cowdenbeath, Meadowb'k
1993-94	**Promoted to Premier** – Falkirk
	Relegated to First – St Johnstone, Raith Rovers, Dundee
	Promoted to First – Stranraer
	Relegated to Second – Dumbarton, Stirling Alb, Clyde, Morton, Brechin
	Relegated to Third – Alloa, Forfar East Stirling, Montrose, Queen's Park, Arbroath Albion Rovers, Cowdenbeath
	Leagues reformed into *Premier, First, Second and Third Divisions*
1994-95	**Promoted to Premier** — Raith Rovers
	Relegated to First — Dundee United
	Promoted to First — Morton, Dumbarton
	Relegated to Second — Ayr United, Stranraer
	Relegated to Third — Meadowbank, Brechin City
1995-96	**Promoted to Premier** — Dunfermline, Dundee Utd
	Relegated to First — Falkirk, Partick Thistle
	Promoted to First — Stirling Albion, East Fife
	Relegated to Second — Dumbarton, Hamilton
	Promoted to Second — Livingston, Brechin C
	Relegated to Third — Forfar, Montrose

1996-97	**Promoted to Premier** – St Johnstone
	Relegated to First – Raith Rovers
	Promoted to First – Ayr United, Hamilton Accies
	Relegated to Second –Clydebank, East Fife
	Promoted to Second – Inverness CT, Forfar
	Relegated to Third – Dumbarton, Berwick Rangers
1997-98	**Promoted to Premier** – Dundee
	Relegated to First – Hibs
	Promoted to First – Stranraer, Clydebank
	Relegated to Second –Partick Thistle, Stirling Alb
	Promoted to Second – Alloa, Arbroath
	Relegated to Third – Stenhousemuir, Brechin
1998-99	**Promoted to Premier** – Hibs
	Relegated to First – Dunfermline
	Promoted to First – Livingston, Inverness CT
	Relegated to Second – Hamilton, Stranraer
	Promoted to Second – Ross Co, Stenhousemuir
	Relegated to Third – East Fife, Forfar Athletic
1999-00	**Promoted to Premier** – St Mirren, Dunfermline
	Relegated to First – No relegation
	Promoted to First – Clyde, Alloa, Ross County
	Relegated to Second – Clydebank
	Promoted to Second – Queen's Pk, Berwick Forfar
	Relegated to Third – Hamilton Accies
	New league entrants – Elgin City, Peterhead
2000-01	**Promoted to Premier** – Livingston
	Relegated to First – St Mirren
	Promoted to First – Partick Thistle, Arbroath
	Relegated to Second – Morton, Alloa
	Promoted to Second – Hamilton, Cowdenbeath
	Relegated to Third – Queen's Park, Stirling Albion
2001-02	**Promoted to Premier** – Partick Thistle
	Relegated to First – St Johnstone
	Promoted to First – Queen of the South, Alloa
	Relegated to Second – Raith Rovers
	Promoted to Second – Brechin, Dumbarton
	Relegated to Third – Morton
2002-03	**Promoted to Premier** – No promotion
	Relegated to First – No relegation
	Promoted to First – Raith Rovers, Brechin City
	Relegated to Second – Alloa, Arbroath
	Promoted to Second – Morton, East Fife
	Relegated to Third – Stranraer, Cowdenbeath
2003-04	**Promoted to Premier** – Inverness Caley Thistle
	Relegated to First – Partick Thistle
	Promoted to First – Airdrie United, Hamilton Accies
	Relegated to Second – Brechin City, Ayr United
	Promoted to Second – Stranraer, Stirling Albion
	Relegated to Third – Stenhousemuir, East Fife

CIS INSURANCE LEAGUE CUP 2003-2004

FIRST ROUND: Arbroath 1 Raith Rovers 0, Ayr United 1 Dumbarton 2, Cowdenbeath 3 Alloa 0, East Fife 0 Airdrie United 2, East Stirling 1 Ross County 2, Elgin City 0 Brechin City 4, Forfar 1 Berwick 0, Gretna 1 Peterhead 2, Hamilton 3 Albion Rovers 2, Inverness CT 1 Queen's Park 2, Montrose 2 Stirling Albion 0, Morton 2 Stranraer 0, St Mirren 0 St Johnstone 2 (after extra time), Stenhousemuir 1 Queen of the South 2.

SECOND ROUND

Aberdeen	3	Dumbarton	1
Arbroath	3	Falkirk	4

(after extra time, 90 mins 2-2)

Brechin	1	Kilmarnock	0
Clyde	2	Airdrie United	1
Dundee United	3	Morton	1
Dunfermline	2	Cowdenbeath	0
Forfar	3	Motherwell	3

(after extra time, Forfar win 4-2 on penalties, 90 mins 0-0)

Hibernian	9	Montrose	0
Peterhead	2	Partick Thistle	2

(after extra time, Partick win 4-3 on penalties, 90 mins 1-1)

Queen's Park	1	Livingston	3
Ross County	0	Queen of the South	3
St Johnstone	3	Hamilton Accies	2

(after extra time, 90 mins 2-2)

THIRD ROUND

Aberdeen	5	Brechin	0
Clyde	2	Dundee	5
Dundee United	0	Livingston	1
Hearts	2	Falkirk	1
Hibernian	2	Queen of the South	1
Partick Thistle	0	Celtic	2
Rangers	6	Forfar	0
St Johnstone	3	Dunfermline	2

QUARTER-FINALS

Aberdeen	2	Livingston	3

(after extra time, 90 mins 2-2)

Dundee	1	Hearts	0

(after extra time, 90 mins 0-0)

Hibernian	2	Celtic	1
Rangers	3	St Johnstone	0

SEMI-FINALS

Dundee	0	Livingston	1
Hibernian	1	Rangers	1

(after extra time, Hibernian win 4-3 on penalties, 90 mins 1-1)

FINAL

Hibernian	0	Livingston	2

LEAGUE CUP WINNERS

1946-47	RANGERS	4	Aberdeen	0
1947-48	EAST FIFE	4	Falkirk	1

(after 0-0 draw)

1948-49	RANGERS	2	Raith Rovers	0
1949-50	EAST FIFE	3	Dunfermline	0
1950-51	MOTHERWELL	3	Hibernian	0
1951-52	DUNDEE	3	Rangers	2
1952-53	DUNDEE	2	Kilmarnock	0
1953-54	EAST FIFE	3	Partick Thistle	2
1954-55	HEARTS	4	Motherwell	2
1955-56	ABERDEEN	2	St Mirren	1
1956-57	CELTIC	3	Partick Thistle	0
1957-58	CELTIC	7	Rangers	1
1958-59	HEARTS	5	Partick Thistle	1
1959-60	HEARTS	2	Third Lanark	1
1960-61	RANGERS	2	Kilmarnock	0
1961-62	RANGERS	3	Hearts	1

(after 1-1 draw)

1962-63	HEARTS	1	Kilmarnock	0
1963-64	RANGERS	5	Morton	0
1964-65	RANGERS	2	Celtic	1
1965-66	CELTIC	2	Rangers	1
1966-67	CELTIC	1	Rangers	0
1967-68	CELTIC	5	Dundee	3
1968-69	CELTIC	6	Hibs	2
1969-70	CELTIC	1	St Johnstone	0
1970-71	RANGERS	1	Celtic	0
1971-72	PARTICK THISTLE	4	Celtic	1
1972-73	HIBS	2	Celtic	1
1973-74	DUNDEE	1	Celtic	0
1974-75	CELTIC	6	Hibs	3
1975-76	RANGERS	1	Celtic	0
1976-77	ABERDEEN	2	Celtic	1

(after extra time)

1977-78	Celtic	1	RANGERS	2

(after extra time)

1978-79	RANGERS	2	Aberdeen	1
1979-80	Aberdeen	0	DUNDEE UNITED	3

(after 0-0 draw)

1980-81	Dundee	0	DUNDEE UNITED	3
1981-82	RANGERS	2	Dundee United	1
1982-83	CELTIC	2	Rangers	1
1983-84	RANGERS	3	Celtic	2

(after extra time)

1984-85	Dundee United	0	RANGERS	1
1985-86	ABERDEEN	3	Hibernian	0
1986-87	Celtic	1	RANGERS	2
1987-88	RANGERS	3	Aberdeen	3

(after extra time, Rangers won 5-3 on penalties)

1988-89	Aberdeen	2	RANGERS	3
1989-90	ABERDEEN	2	Rangers	1

(after extra time)

1990-91	RANGERS	2	Celtic	1

(after extra time)

1991-92	HIBERNIAN	2	Dunfermline	0
1992-93	RANGERS	2	Aberdeen	1

(after extra time)

1993-94	RANGERS	2	Hibernian	1
1994-95	Celtic	2	RAITH ROVERS	2

(after extra time, Raith Rovers won 6-5 on penalties)

1995-96	ABERDEEN	2	Dundee	0
1996-97	RANGERS	4	Hearts	3
1997-98	CELTIC	3	Dundee United	0
1998-99	RANGERS	2	St Johnstone	1
1999-00	CELTIC	2	Aberdeen	0
2000-01	CELTIC	3	Kilmarnock	0
2001-02	Ayr United	0	RANGERS	4
2002-03	Celtic	1	RANGERS	2
2003-04	Hibernian	0	LIVINGSTON	2

CIS FINAL KEEPERS ... Daniel Andersson and Roddy McKenzie

THE BELL'S CUP 2003-2004

FIRST ROUND

Airdrie Utd	2	Montrose	0
Albion Rovers	1	East Fife	0
Alloa	1	Clyde	2
Ayr United	1	Stirling Albion	2

(after extra time)

Brechin	1	Falkirk	0
Cowdenbeath	1	Ross County	2
East Stirling	2	Raith Rovers	5
Forfar	4	Elgin	0
Gretna	0	Inverness CT	5
Hamilton	2	St Johnstone	3

(after extra time)

Morton	4	Arbroath	3
St Mirren	3	Queen's Park	2

(after extra time)

Stenhousemuir	0	Peterhead	3
Stranraer	2	Queen of South	1

SECOND ROUND

Brechin City	3	Stirling Albion	1
Clyde	0	St Johnstone	1
Forfar	4	Albion Rovers	2

(after extra time)

Morton	1	Airdrie United	2
Peterhead	2	Inverness CT	2
Raith Rovers	2	Stranraer	0
Ross County	5	Dumbarton	0
St Mirren	2	Berwick Rangers	1

QUARTER-FINALS

Forfar	0	Airdrie United	2
Inverness CT	1	Ross County	0
Raith Rovers	3	St Mirren	2
St Johnstone	1	Brechin City	2

SEMI-FINALS

Raith Rovers	0	Inverness CT	4
Brechin City	1	Airdrie United	2

(after extra time)

FINAL

Inverness CT	2	Airdrie United	0

TENNENT'S SCOTTISH CUP 2003-2004

FIRST ROUND: Albion Rovers 1 Montrose 3 (after 1-1 draw), Clachnacuddin 0 Stranraer 2, Cowdenbeath 5 Edinburgh City 2, East Fife 3 Forfar 3 (after extra time, East Fife win 4-1 on penalties, 90 mins 2-2; after 1-1 draw), Elgin City 1 Peterhead 2, Gretna 2 Dumbarton 0, Montrose 1 Albion Rovers 1, Spartans 6 Buckie Thistle 1, Stirling Albion 3 Queen's Park 1.

SECOND ROUND: Berwick 4 Huntly 2, East Stirling 0 Cowdenbeath 5, Gretna 5 Stenhousemuir 1, Inverurie Locos 1 Airdrie United 5, Montrose 1 Threave Rovers 0, Morton 4 Vale of Leithen 0, Peterhead 0 East Fife 2, Spartans 5 Alloa 3 (after 3-3 draw), Stranraer 0 Hamilton 1, Stirling Albion 1 Arbroath 2.

THIRD ROUND

Arbroath	1	Spartans	4
Ayr United	1	Falkirk	2
Celtic	2	Ross County	0
Clyde	3	Gretna	0
Dundee	2	Aberdeen	3

(after 0-0 draw)

Dunfermline	3	Dundee United	1
East Fife	0	Queen of the South	1
Hamilton	2	Cowdenbeath	0
Hearts	2	Berwick	0
Hibernian	0	Rangers	1
Inverness CT	1	Brechin	1
Livingston	1	Montrose	0
Morton	0	Partick Thistle	3
Raith Rovers	1	Kilmarnock	3
St Johnstone	0	Motherwell	4
St Mirren	2	Airdrie United	0

FOURTH ROUND

Clyde	0	Dunfermline	3
Falkirk	0	Aberdeen	2
Hearts	0	Celtic	3
Kilmarnock	0	Rangers	2
Motherwell	3	Queen of the South	2
Partick Thistle	5	Hamilton	1
Spartans	0	Livingston	4
St Mirren	0	Inverness CT	1

QUARTER-FINALS

Celtic	1	Rangers	0
Livingston	1	Aberdeen	0

(after 1-1 draw)

Motherwell	0	Inverness CT	1
Partick Thistle	0	Dunfermline	3

SEMI-FINALS

Dunfermline	3	Inverness CT	2

(after 1-1 draw)

Livingston	1	Celtic	3

FINAL

Celtic	3	Dunfermline	1

PREVIOUS WINNERS

1873-74	QUEEN'S PARK......2	Clydesdale 0
1874-75	QUEEN'S PARK......3	Renton 0
1875-76	QUEEN'S PARK......2	3rd Lanark Rifles 0

(after 1-1 draw)

1876-77	VALE OF LEVEN ...3	Rangers 2

(After two replays 0-0, 1-1)

1877-78	VALE OF LEVEN 1	3rd Lanark Rifles 0
1878-79	VALE OF LEVEN 1	Rangers 1

(Vale of Leven awarded cup, Rangers failed to appear)

1879-80	QUEEN'S PARK......3	Thornliebank.......................0
1880-81	QUEEN'S PARK......3	Dumbarton 1

(after Dumbarton protested first game)

1881-82	QUEEN'S PARK......4	Dumbarton 1

(after 2-2 draw)

1882-83	DUMBARTON 2	Vale of Leven 1

(after 2-2 draw)

1883-84	QUEEN'S PARK ..wo	Vale of Leven

(Queen's Park awarded cup, Vale of Leven failed to appear.)

884-85	RENTON 3	Vale of Leven 1

(after 0-0 draw)

1885-86	QUEEN'S PARK......3	Renton 1
1886-87	HIBERNIAN 2	Dumbarton 1
1887-88	RENTON 6	Cambuslang 1
1888-89	THIRD LANARK 2	Celtic 1

(after replay by order of Scottish FA because of playing conditions in first match)

1889-90	QUEEN'S PARK......2	Vale of Leven 1

(after 1-1 draw)

1890-91	HEARTS 1	Dumbarton 0
1891-92	CELTIC....................5	Queen's Park 1

(after mutually-protested first game)

1892-93	QUEEN'S PARK......2	Celtic 1

(after 0-0 draw)

1893-94	RANGERS 3	Celtic 1
1894-95	ST BERNARD'S 2	Renton 1
1895-96	HEARTS 3	Hibernian 1
1896-97	RANGERS 5	Dumbarton 1
1897-98	RANGERS 2	Kilmarnock 0
1898-99	CELTIC....................2	Rangers 0
1899-00	CELTIC....................4	Queen's Park 3
1900-01	HEARTS 4	Celtic 3
1901-02	HIBS......................1	CELTIC.................................0
1902-03	RANGERS 2	Hearts 0

(after two replays, 1-1, 0-0)

1903-04	CELTIC	3	Rangers	2
1904-05	THIRD LANARK	3	Rangers	1
	(after 0-0 draw)			
1905-06	HEARTS	1	Third Lanark	0
1906-07	CELTIC	3	Hearts	0
1907-08	CELTIC	5	St Mirren	1
1908-09	Celtic	–	Rangers	–
(owing to riot, cup was withheld after two drawn games)				
1909-10	DUNDEE	2	Clyde	1
	(after two draws, 2-2, 0-0)			
1910-11	CELTIC	2	Hamilton Accies	0
	(after 0-0 draw)			
1911-12	CELTIC	2	Clyde	0
1912-13	FALKIRK	2	Raith Rovers	0
1913-14	CELTIC	4	HIBS	1
	(after 0-0 draw)			
1919-20	KILMARNOCK	3	Albion Rovers	2
1920-21	PARTICK THISTLE	1	Rangers	0
1921-22	MORTON	1	Rangers	0
1922-23	CELTIC	1	Hibernian	0
1923-24	AIRDRIE	2	Hibernian	0
1924-25	CELTIC	2	Dundee	1
1925-26	ST MIRREN	2	Celtic	0
1926-27	CELTIC	3	East Fife	1
1927-28	RANGERS	4	Celtic	0
1928-29	KILMARNOCK	2	Rangers	0
1929-30	RANGERS	2	Partick Thistle	1
	(after 0-0 draw)			
1930-31	CELTIC	4	Motherwell	2
	(after 2-2 draw)			
1931-32	RANGERS	3	Kilmarnock	0
	(after 1-1 draw)			
1932-33	CELTIC	1	Motherwell	0
1933-34	RANGERS	5	St Mirren	0
1934-35	RANGERS	2	Hamilton Accies	1
1935-36	RANGERS	1	Third Lanark	0
1936-37	CELTIC	2	Aberdeen	1
1937-38	EAST FIFE	4	Kilmarnock	2
	(after 1-1 draw)			
1938-39	CLYDE	4	Motherwell	0
1946-47	ABERDEEN	2	Hibernian	1
1947-48	RANGERS	1	Morton	1
	(after extra time; after 1-1 draw)			
1948-49	RANGERS	4	Clyde	1
1949-50	RANGERS	3	East Fife	0

1950-51	CELTIC	1	Motherwell	0
1951-52	MOTHERWELL	4	Dundee	0
1952-53	RANGERS	1	Aberdeen	0

(after 1-1 draw)

1953-54	CELTIC	2	Aberdeen	1
1954-55	CLYDE	1	Celtic	0

(after 1-1 draw)

1955-56	HEARTS	3	Celtic	1
1956-57	FALKIRK	2	Kilmarnock	1

(after extra time; after 1-1 draw)

1957-58	CLYDE	1	Hibernian	0
1958-59	ST MIRREN	3	Aberdeen	1
1959-60	RANGERS	2	Kilmarnock	0
1960-61	DUNFERMLINE	2	Celtic	0

(after 0-0 draw)

1961-62	RANGERS	2	St Mirren	0
1962-63	RANGERS	3	Celtic	0

(after 1-1 draw)

1963-64	RANGERS	3	Dundee	1
1964-65	CELTIC	3	Dunfermline Athletic	2
1965-66	RANGERS	1	Celtic	0

(after 0-0 draw)

1966-67	CELTIC	2	Aberdeen	0
1967-68	DUNFERMLINE	3	Hearts	1
1968-69	CELTIC	4	Rangers	0
1969-70	ABERDEEN	3	Celtic	1
1970-71	CELTIC	2	Rangers	1

(after 1-1 draw)

1971-72	CELTIC	6	Hibernian	1
1972-73	RANGERS	3	Celtic	2
1973-74	CELTIC	3	Dundee United	0
1974-75	CELTIC	3	Airdrie	1
1975-76	RANGERS	3	Hearts	1
1976-77	CELTIC	1	Rangers	0
1977-78	RANGERS	2	Aberdeen	1
1978-79	RANGERS	3	Hibernian	2

(after two 0-0 draws, and extra time)

1979-80	CELTIC	1	Rangers	0

(after extra time)

1980-81	RANGERS	4	Dundee United	1

(after 0-0 draw)

1981-82	ABERDEEN	4	Rangers	1

(after extra time)

1982-83	ABERDEEN	1	Rangers	0

(after extra time)

1983-84	ABERDEEN 2	Celtic 1	

(after extra time)

1984-85	CELTIC 2	Dundee United 1
1985-86	ABERDEEN 3	Hearts 0
1986-87	ST MIRREN 1	Dundee United 0

(after extra time)

1987-88	CELTIC 2	Dundee United 1
1988-89	CELTIC 1	Rangers 0
1989-90	ABERDEEN 0	Celtic 0

(after extra time, Aberdeen won 9-8 on penalties)

1990-91	MOTHERWELL 4	Dundee United 3

(after extra time)

1991-92	RANGERS 2	Airdrie 1
1992-93	RANGERS 2	Aberdeen 1
1993-94	DUNDEE UTD 1	Rangers 0
1994-95	CELTIC 1	Airdrie 0
1995-96	RANGERS 5	Hearts 1
1996-97	KILMARNOCK 1	Falkirk 0
1997-98	HEARTS 2	Rangers 1
1998-99	RANGERS 1	Celtic 0
1999-00	RANGERS 4	Aberdeen 0
2000-01	CELTIC 3	Hibernian 0
2001-02	RANGERS 3	Celtic 2
2002-03	RANGERS 1	Dundee 0
2003-04	CELTIC 3	Dunfermline 1

Jackie McNamara and Barry Nicholson led Celtic and Dunfermline out on cup final day at Hampden

TAKE A FRESH LOOK
AT SATURDAY

**Glasgow's liveliest lifestyle
magazine free with the**

weekend times

SCOTTISH CUP-WINNING TEAMS

1976-77 – CELTIC: Latchford, McGrain, Lynch, Stanton, McDonald, Aitken, Dalglish, Edvaldsson, Craig, Conn, Wilson.

1977-78 – RANGERS: McCloy, Jardine, Greig, Forsyth, Jackson, MacDonald, McLean, Russell, Johnstone, Smith, Cooper.

1978-79 – RANGERS: McCloy, Jardine, Dawson, Johnstone, Jackson, Watson, McLean, Russell, Parlane, McDonald, Cooper.

1979-80 – CELTIC: Latchford, Sneddon, McGrain, Aitken, Conroy, MacLeod, Provan, Doyle, McCluskey, Burns, McGarvey.

1980-81 – RANGERS: Stewart, Jardine, Dawson, Stevens, Forsyth, Bett, Cooper, Russell, D. Johnstone, Redford, MacDonald.

1981-82 – ABERDEEN: Leighton, Kennedy, Rougvie, McMaster, McLeish, Miller, Strachan, Cooper, McGhee, Simpson, Hewitt.

1982-83 – ABERDEEN: Leighton, Rougvie, McMaster, Cooper, McLeish, Miller, Strachan, Simpson, McGhee, Black, Weir.

1983-84 – ABERDEEN: Leighton, McKimmie, Rougvie, Cooper, McLeish, Miller, Strachan, Simpson, McGhee, Black, Weir.

1984-85 – CELTIC: Bonner, W. McStay, McGrain, Aitken, McAdam, MacLeod, Provan, P. McStay, Johnston, Burns, McGarvey.

1985-86 – ABERDEEN: Leighton, McKimmie, McQueen, McMaster, McLeish, Miller, Hewitt, Cooper, McDougall, Bett, Weir.

1986-87 – ST MIRREN: Money, Wilson, D. Hamilton, Abercromby, Winnie, Cooper, Ferguson, McGarvey, McDowall, B. Hamilton, Lambert.

1987-88 – CELTIC: McKnight, Morris, Rogan, Aitken, McCarthy, Whyte, Miller, McStay, McAvennie, Walker, Burns.

1988-89 – CELTIC: Bonner, Morris, Rogan, Aitken, McCarthy, Whyte, Grant, McStay, Miller, McGhee, Burns.

1989-90 – ABERDEEN: Snelders, McKimmie, Robertson, Grant, McLeish, Irvine, Nicholas, Bett, Mason, Connor, Gillhaus.

1990-91 – MOTHERWELL: Maxwell, Nijholt, Boyd, Griffin, Paterson, McCart, Arnott, Angus, Ferguson (Kirk), O'Donnell, Cooper (O'Neill).

1991-92 – RANGERS: Goram, Stevens, Robertson, Gough, Spackman, Brown, McCall, McCoist, Hateley, Mikhailitchenko, Durrant. Subs: Gordon, Rideout.

1992-93 – RANGERS: Goram, McPherson, Gough, Brown, Robertson, Murray, Ferguson, McCall, Durrant, Hateley, Huistra. Subs: Pressley, McSwegan.

1993-94 – DUNDEE UNITED: Van De Kamp, Cleland, Malpas, McInally, Petric, Welsh, Bowman, Hannah, McLaren, Brewster, Dailly. Subs: Nixon, Bollan.

1994-95 – CELTIC: Bonner, Boyd, McKinlay, Vata, McNally, Grant, McLaughlin, McStay, Van Hooijdonk (Falconer), Donnelly (O'Donnell), Collins.

1995-96 – RANGERS: Goram, Cleland, Robertson, Gough, McLaren, Brown, Durie, Gascoigne, Ferguson (Durrant), McCal Laudrup. Subs (not used): Petric, Andersen.

1996-97 – KILMARNOCK: Lekovic, MacPherson, Kerr, Montgomerie McGowne, Reilly, Bagan (Mitchell), Holt, Wright (Henry), McIntyr (Brown), Burke.

1997-98 – HEARTS: Rousett, McPherson, Naysmith, Weir, Salvatore Ritchie, McCann, Fulton, Adam (Hamilton), Cameron, Flogel.

1998-99 – RANGERS: Klos, Porrini (Kanchelskis), Vidma Amoruso, Hendry, McCann (I Ferguson), McInnes, Wallace, va Bronckhorst, Amato (Wilson), Albertz.

1999-00 – RANGERS: Klos, Reyna, Moore (Porrini), Vidma Numan, Kanchelskis, Ferguson, Albertz, van Bronckhorst (Tugay Wallace (McCann), Dodds

2000-01 – CELTIC: Douglas, Mjallby, Vega, Valgaeren, Agathe Lennon, Lambert (Boyd) Moravcik (McNamara) Thompso (Johnson), Larsson, Sutton.

2001-02 – RANGERS: Klos, Ross, Moore, Amoruso, Numan, Rickse de Boer, Ferguson, Lovenkrands, McCann, Caniggia (Arveladze).

2002-03 – RANGERS: Klos, Malcolm, Moore, Amoruso, Numa (Muscat), Ricksen, Ferguson, de Boer, McCann, Arveladz (Thompson), Mols (Ross).

2003-04 – CELTIC: Marshall, Varga, Balde, McNamara, Agathe Lennon, Petrov, Pearson (Wallace), Thompson, Larsson, Sutton.

STUART DOUGAL took charge of the 2004 Tennent's Scottish Cup Final

PLAYER OF THE YEAR

*AWARDED BY THE SCOTTISH FOOTBALL
WRITERS' ASSOCIATION.*

1965	BILLY McNEILL (Celtic)
1966	JOHN GREIG (Rangers)
1967	RONNIE SIMPSON (Celtic)
1968	GORDON WALLACE (Raith Rovers)
1969	BOBBY MURDOCH (Celtic)
1970	PAT STANTON (Hibernian)
1971	MARTIN BUCHAN (Aberdeen)
1972	DAVE SMITH (Rangers)
1973	GEORGE CONNELLY (Celtic)
1974	WORLD CUP SQUAD
1975	SANDY JARDINE (Rangers)
1976	JOHN GREIG (Rangers)
1977	DANNY McGRAIN (Celtic)
1978	DEREK JOHNSTONE (Rangers)
1979	ANDY RITCHIE (Morton)
1980	GORDON STRACHAN (Aberdeen)
1981	ALAN ROUGH (Partick Thistle)
1982	PAUL STURROCK (Dundee United)
1983	CHARLIE NICHOLAS (Celtic)
1984	WILLIE MILLER (Aberdeen)
1985	HAMISH McALPINE (Dundee United)
1986	SANDY JARDINE (Hearts)
1987	BRIAN McCLAIR (Celtic)
1988	PAUL McSTAY (Celtic)
1989	RICHARD GOUGH (Rangers)
1990	ALEX McLEISH (Aberdeen)
1991	MAURICE MALPAS (Dundee United)
1992	ALLY McCOIST (Rangers)
1993	ANDY GORAM (Rangers)
1994	MARK HATELEY (Rangers)
1995	BRIAN LAUDRUP (Rangers)
1996	PAUL GASCOIGNE (Rangers)
1997	BRIAN LAUDRUP (Rangers)
1998	CRAIG BURLEY (Celtic)
1999	HENRIK LARSSON (Celtic)
2000	BARRY FERGUSON (Rangers)
2001	HENRIK LARSSON (Celtic)
2002	PAUL LAMBERT (Celtic)
2003	BARRY FERGUSON (Rangers)
2004	JACKIE McNAMARA (Celtic)

PLAYER OF THE YEAR

*AWARDED BY THE SCOTTISH PROFESSIONAL
FOOTBALLERS' ASSOCIATION*

1977-78
Premier Division ....Derek Johnstone (Rangers)
First Division ....Billy Pirie (Dundee)
Second Division ....Dave Smith (Berwick Rangers)
Young Player ....Graeme Payne (Dundee United)

1978-79
Premier Division ....Paul Hegarty (Dundee United)
First Division...Brian McLaughlin (Ayr United)
Second Division.....................Michael Leonard (Dunfermline Ath)
Young Player.........................Raymond Stewart (Dundee United)

1979-80
Premier Division...Davie Provan (Celtic)
First Division...Sandy Clark (Airdrie)
Second Division..Paul Leetion (Falkirk)
Young Player...John MacDonald (Rangers)

1980-81
Premier Division...Mark McGhee (Aberdeen)
First Division...Eric Sinclair (Dundee)
Second Division ....Jimmy Robertson (Queen of the South)
Young Player..Charlie Nicholas (Celtic)

1981-82
Premier Division...Sandy Clark (Airdrie)
First Division...Brian McLaughlin (Motherwell)
Second Division ....Pat Nevin (Clyde)
Young Player ....Frank McAvennie (St Mirren)

1982-83
Premier Division...Charlie Nicholas (Celtic)
First Division.....................................Gerry McCabe (Clydebank)
Second Division ....John Colquhoun (Stirling Albion)
Young Player ....Paul McStay (Celtic)

1983-84
Premier Division...Willie Miller (Aberdeen)
First Division.......................................Gerry McCabe (Clydebank)
Second Division ....Jim Liddle (Forfar Athletic)
Young Player ....John Robertson (Hearts)

1984-85
Premier Division...Jim Duffy (Morton)
First Division.......................................Gerry McCabe (Clydebank)
Second Division ....Bernie Slaven (Albion Rovers)
Young Player ....Craig Levein (Hearts)

1985-86
Premier Division...........................Richard Gough (Dundee United)
First Division...John Brogan (Hamilton)
Second Division ....Mark Smith (Queen's Park)
Young Player ....Craig Levein (Hearts)

1986-87

Premier Division ....Brian McClair (Celtic)
First Division ....Jim Holmes (Morton)
Second Division ....John Sludden (Ayr United)
Young Player ....Robert Fleck (Rangers)

1987-88

Premier Division ....Paul McStay (Celtic)
First Division...............................Alex Taylor (Hamilton)
Second Division ....Henry Templeton (Ayr United)
Young Player ....John Collins (Hibernian)

1988-89

Premier Division ....Theo Snelders (Aberdeen)
First Division ....Ross Jack (Dunfermline)
Second Division ....Paul Hunter (East Fife)
Young Player ....Billy McKinlay (Dundee United)

1989-90

Premier Division ....Jim Bett (Aberdeen)
First Division ....Ken Eadie (Clydebank)
Second Division ....Willie Watters (Kilmarnock)
Young Player ....Scott Crabbe (Hearts)

1990-91

Premier Division ....Paul Elliott (Celtic)
First Division ....Simon Stainrod (Falkirk)
Second Division ....Kevin Todd (Berwick Rangers)
Young Player .... Eoin Jess (Aberdeen)

1991-92

Premier Division ....Ally McCoist (Rangers)
First Division ....Gordon Dalziel (Raith Rovers)
Second Division ....Andy Thomson (Queen of the South)
Young Player ....Phil O'Donnell (Motherwell)

1992-93

Premier Division ....Andy Goram (Rangers)
First Division ....Gordon Dalziel (Raith Rovers)
Second Division ....Sandy Ross (Brechin City)
Young Player .... Eoin Jess (Aberdeen)

1993-94

Premier Division ....Mark Hateley (Rangers)
First Division...............................Richard Cadette (Falkirk)
Second Division ....Andy Thomson (Queen of the South)
Young Player ....Phil O'Donnell (Motherwell)

1994-95

Premier Division ....Brian Laudrup (Rangers)
First Division...............................Stephen Crawford (Raith Rovers)
Second Division ....Derek McInnes (Morton)
Third Division...............................David Bingham (Forfar Ath.)
Young Player ....Charlie Miller (Rangers)

1995-96

Premier Division ....Paul Gascoigne (Rangers)
First Division...............................George O'Boyle (St Johnstone)
Second Division ....Steven McCormick (Stirling A.)
Third Division ....Jason Young (Livingston)
Young Player ....Jackie McNamara (Celtic)

1996-97

Premier Division	Paolo di Canio (Celtic
First Division	Roddy Grant (St Johnstone
Second Division	Paul Ritchie (Hamilton
Third Division	Ian Stewart (Inverness CT
Young Player	Robbie Winters (Dundee United

1997-98

Premier Division	Jackie McNamara (Celtic
First Division	James Grady (Dundee
Second Division	Paul Lovering (Clydebank
Third Division	Willie Irvine (Alloa
Young Player	Gary Naysmith (Hearts

1998-99

Premier Division	Henrik Larsson (Celtic
First Division	Russell Latapy (Hibs
Second Division	David Bingham (Livingston
Third Division	Neil Tarrant (Ross County
Young Player	Barry Ferguson (Rangers

1999-2000

Premier Division	Mark Viduka (Celtic
First Division	Stevie Crawford (Dunfermline
Second Division	Brian Carrigan (Clyde
Third Division	Stevie Milne (Forfar
Young Player	Kenny Miller (Hibs

2000-2001

Premier Division	Henrik Larsson (Celtic
First Division	David Bingham (Livingston
Second Division	Scott McLean (Partick Thistle
Third Division	Steve Hislop (East Stirling
Young Player	Stilian Petrov (Celtic

2001-2002

Premier Division	Lorenzo Amoruso (Rangers
First Division	Owen Coyle (Airdrie
Second Division	John O'Neill (Queen of the South
Third Division	Paul McManus (East Fife
Young Player	Kevin McNaughton (Aberdeen

2002-2003

Premier Division	Barry Ferguson (Rangers
First Division	Dennis Wyness (Inverness Caley Thistle
Second Division	Chris Templeman (Brechin
Third Division	Alex Williams (Morton
Young Player	James McFadden (Motherwell

2003-2004

Premier Division	Chris Sutton (Celtic
First Division	Ian Harty (Clyde
Second Division	Paul Tosh (Forfar
Third Division	Michael Moore (Stranraer
Young Player	Stephen Pearson (Celtic

ENGLISH PLAYER OF THE YEAR

AWARDED BY THE ENGLISH FOOTBALL WRITERS' ASSOCIATION

1948 **Stanley Matthews** (Blackpool)
1949 **Johnny Carey** (Man U)
1950 **Joe Mercer** (Arsenal)
1951 **Harry Johnston** (Blackpool)
1952 **Billy Wright** (Wolves)
1953 **Nat Lofthouse** (Bolton W.)
1954 **Tom Finney** (Preston NE)
1955 **Don Revie** (Man City)
1956 **Bert Trautmann** (Man City)
1957 **Tom Finney** (Preston NE)
1958 **Danny Blanchflower** (Spurs)
1959 **Syd Owen** (Luton Town)
1960 **Bill Slater** (Wolves)
1961 **Danny Blanchflower** (Spurs)
1962 **Jimmy Adamson** (Burnley)
1963 **Stanley Matthews** (Stoke C)
1964 **Bobby Moore** (West Ham)
1965 **Bobby Collins** (Leeds U)
1966 **Bobby Charlton** (Man U)
1967 **Jackie Charlton** (Leeds U)
1968 **George Best** (Man U)
1969 **Dave Mackay** (Derby)/
     Tony Book (Man City)
1970 **Billy Bremner** (Leeds U)
1971 **Frank McLintock** (Arsenal)
1972 **Gordon Banks** (Stoke City)
1973 **Pat Jennings** (Spurs)
1974 **Ian Callaghan** (Liverpool)
1975 **Alan Mullery** (Fulham)

1976 **Kevin Keegan** (Liverpool)
1977 **Emlyn Hughes** (Liverpool)
1978 **Kenny Burns** (Notts Fores
1979 **Kenny Dalglish** (Liverpool)
1980 **Terry McDermott** (Liverpoo
1981 **Frans Thijssen** (Ipswich T)
1982 **Steve Perryman** (Spurs)
1983 **Kenny Dalglish** Liverpool)
1984 **Ian Rush** (Liverpool)
1985 **Neville Southall** (Everton)
1986 **Gary Lineker** (Everton)
1987 **Clive Allen** (Tottenham H.)
1988 **John Barnes** (Liverpool)
1989 **Steve Nicol** (Liverpool)
1990 **John Barnes** (Liverpool)
1991 **Gordon Strachan** (Leeds U
1992 **Gary Lineker** (Spurs)
1993 **Chris Waddle** (Sheffield W)
1994 **Alan Shearer** (Blackburn R
1995 **Jurgen Klinsmann** (Spurs)
1996 **Eric Cantona** (Man U)
1997 **Gianfranco Zola** (Chelsea)
1998 **Dennis Bergkamp** (Arsena
1999 **David Ginola** (Spurs)
2000 **Roy Keane** (Man U)
2001 **Teddy Sheringham** (Man U
2002 **Robert Pires** (Arsenal)
2003 **Thierry Henry** (Arsenal)
2004 **Thierry Henry** (Arsenal)

THIERRY HENRY
shows off his
player of the
year award

EUROPEAN FOOTBALLER OF THE YEAR

1956	STANLEY MATTHEWS (Blackpool
1957	ALFREDO DI STEFANO (Real Madrid
1958	RAYMOND KOPA (Real Madrid
1959	ALFREDO DI STEFANO (Real Madrid
1960	LUIS SUAREZ (Barcelona
1961	OMAR SIVORI (Juventus
1962	JOSEF MASOPUST (Dukla Prague
1963	LEV YASHIN (Moscow Dynamo
1964	DENIS LAW (Manchester United
1965	EUSEBIO (Benfica
1966	BOBBY CHARLTON (Manchester United
1967	FLORIAN ALBERT (Ferencvaros
1968	GEORGE BEST (Manchester United
1969	GIANNI RIVERA (AC Milan
1970	GERD MULLER (Bayern Munich
1971	JOHAN CRUYFF (Ajax Amsterdam
1972	FRANZ BECKENBAUER (Bayern Munich
1973	JOHAN CRUYFF (Barcelona
1974	JOHAN CRUYFF (Barcelona
1975	OLEG BLOKHIN (Dynamo Kiev
1976	FRANZ BECKENBAUER (Bayern Munich
1977	ALLAN SIMONSEN (Borussia Moenchengladbach
1978	KEVIN KEEGAN (SV Hamburg
1979	KEVIN KEEGAN (SV Hamburg
1980	KARL-HEINZ RUMMENIGGE (Bayern Munich
1981	KARL-HEINZ RUMMENIGGE (Bayern Munich
1982	PAOLO ROSSI (Juventus
1983	MICHEL PLATINI (Juventus
1984	MICHEL PLATINI (Juventus
1985	MICHEL PLATINI (Juventus
1986	IGOR BELANOV (Dynamo Kiev
1987	RUUD GULLIT (AC Milan
1988	MARCO VAN BASTEN (AC Milan
1989	MARCO VAN BASTEN (AC Milan
1990	LOTHAR MATTHAUS
	(West Germany World Cup-winning captain
1991	JEAN-PIERRE PAPIN (Marseilles
1992	MARCO VAN BASTEN (AC Milan
1993	ROBERTO BAGGIO (Juventus
1994	HIRSTO STOICHKOV (Barcelona
1995	GEORGE WEAH (AC Milan
1996	MATTHIAS SAMMER (Borussia Dortmund
1997	RONALDO (Inter Milan
1998	ZINEDINE ZIDANE (Juventus
1999	RIVALDO (Barcelona
2000	LUIS FIGO (Real Madrid
2001	MICHAEL OWEN (Liverpool
2002	RONALDO (Real Madrid
2003	PAVEL NEDVED (Juventus

SCOTLAND'S INTERNATIONAL RECORD

v ENGLAND (Scotland scores first)

The year refers to the season, i.e. 1873 is season 1872-73

1873	0-0	Partick		1913	0-1	Chelsea
1873	2-4	The Oval		1914	3-1	Hampden
1874	2-1	Partick		1920	4-5	Sheffield
1875	2-2	The Oval		1921	3-0	Hampden
1876	3-0	Partick		1922	1-0	Aston Villa
1877	3-1	The Oval		1923	2-2	Hampden
1878	7-2	Hampden		1924	1-1	Wembley
1879	4-5	The Oval		1925	2-0	Hampden
1880	5-4	Hampden		1926	1-0	Manchester
1881	6-1	The Oval		1927	1-2	Hampden
1882	5-1	Hampden		1928	5-1	Wembley
1883	3-2	Sheffield		1929	1-0	Hampden
1884	1-0	Cathkin		1930	2-5	Wembley
1885	1-1	The Oval		1931	2-0	Hampden
1886	1-1	Hampden		1932	0-3	Wembley
1887	3-2	Blackburn		1933	2-1	Hampden
1888	0-5	Hampden		1934	0-3	Wembley
1889	3-2	The Oval		1935	2-0	Hampden
1890	1-1	Hampden		1936	1-1	Wembley
1891	1-2	Blackburn		1937	3-1	Hampden
1892	1-4	Ibrox		1938	1-0	Wembley
1893	2-5	Richmond		1939	1-2	Hampden
1894	2-2	Celtic Park		1947	1-1	Wembley
1895	0-3	Everton		1948	0-2	Hampden
1896	2-1	Celtic Park		1949	3-1	Wembley
1897	2-1	Crystal Pal		1950	0-1	Hampden
1898	1-3	Celtic Park		1951	3-2	Wembley
1899	1-2	Birmingham		1952	1-2	Hampden
1900	4-1	Celtic Park		1953	2-2	Wembley
1901	2-2	Crystal Pal		1954	2-4	Hampden
1902	2-2	Birmingham		1955	2-7	Wembley
1903	2-1	Sheffield		1956	1-1	Hampden
1904	0-1	Celtic Park		1957	1-2	Wembley
1905	0-1	Crystal Pal		1958	0-4	Hampden
1906	2-1	Hampden		1959	0-1	Wembley
1907	1-1	Newcastle		1960	1-1	Hampden
1908	1-1	Hampden		1961	3-9	Wembley
1909	0-2	Crystal Pal		1962	2-0	Hampden
1910	2-0	Hampden		1963	2-1	Wembley
1911	1-1	Liverpool		1964	1-0	Hampden
1912	1-1	Hampden		1965	2-2	Wembley

1966	3-4	Hampden
1967	3-2	Wembley
1968	1-1	Hampden
1969	1-4	Wembley
1970	0-0	Hampden
1971	1-3	Wembley
1972	0-1	Hampden
1973	0-5	Hampden
1973	0-1	Wembley
1974	2-0	Hampden
1975	1-5	Wembley
1976	2-1	Hampden
1977	2-1	Wembley
1978	0-1	Hampden
1979	1-3	Wembley
1980	0-2	Hampden
1981	1-0	Wembley
1982	0-1	Hampden
1983	0-2	Wembley

1984	1-1	Hampd

SIR STANLEY ROUS CUP

1985	1-0	Hampd
1986	1-2	Wembl

BECAME A THREE-NATIO COMPETITION

1987	0-0	Hampd

(Scotland 0 Brazil 2. England Brazil 1; Winners – Brazil)

1988	0-1	Wembl

(Scotland 0 Colombia 0; England Colombia 1. Winners: England

1989	0-2	Hampd

(Scotland 2 Chile 0; England Chile 0. Winners – England

1996	0-2	Wembl
1999	0-2	Hampd
1999	1-0	Wembl

JOHN ROBERTSON celebrates Scotland's 1-0 win over England in the 1981 Home Internationals at Wembley

v NORTHERN IRELAND
(Scotland scores first)

1884	5-0	Belfast	1932	3-1	Glasgow
1885	8-2	Glasgow	1933	4-0	Belfast
1886	7-2	Belfast	1934	1-2	Glasgow
1887	4-1	Glasgow	1935	1-2	Belfast
1888	10-2	Belfast	1936	2-1	Edinburgh
1889	7-0	Glasgow	1937	3-1	Belfast
1890	4-1	Belfast	1938	1-1	Aberdeen
1891	2-1	Glasgow	1939	2-0	Belfast
1892	3-2	Belfast	1947	0-0	Glasgow
1893	6-1	Glasgow	1948	0-2	Belfast
1894	2-1	Belfast	1949	3-2	Glasgow
1895	3-1	Glasgow	1950	8-2	Belfast
1896	3-3	Belfast	1951	6-1	Glasgow
1897	5-1	Glasgow	1952	3-0	Belfast
1898	3-0	Belfast	1953	1-1	Glasgow
1899	9-1	Glasgow	1954	3-1	Belfast
1900	3-0	Belfast	1955	2-2	Glasgow
1901	11-0	Glasgow	1956	1-2	Belfast
1902	5-1	Belfast	1957	1-0	Glasgow
1903	0-2	Glasgow	1958	1-1	Belfast
1904	1-1	Dublin	1959	2-2	Glasgow
1905	4-0	Glasgow	1960	4-0	Belfast
1906	1-0	Dublin	1961	5-2	Glasgow
1907	3-0	Glasgow	1962	6-1	Belfast
1908	5-0	Dublin	1963	5-1	Glasgow
1909	5-0	Glasgow	1964	1-2	Belfast
1910	0-1	Belfast	1965	3-2	Glasgow
1911	2-0	Glasgow	1966	2-3	Belfast
1912	4-1	Belfast	1967	2-1	Glasgow
1913	2-1	Dublin	1968	0-1	Belfast
1914	1-1	Belfast	1969	1-1	Glasgow
1920	3-0	Glasgow	1970	1-0	Belfast
1921	2-0	Belfast	1971	0-1	Glasgow
1922	2-1	Glasgow	1972	2-0	Glasgow
1923	1-0	Belfast	1973	1-2	Glasgow
1924	2-0	Glasgow	1974	0-1	Glasgow
1925	3-0	Belfast	1975	3-0	Glasgow
1926	4-0	Glasgow	1976	3-0	Glasgow
1927	2-0	Belfast	1977	3-0	Glasgow
1928	0-1	Glasgow	1978	1-1	Glasgow
1929	7-3	Belfast	1979	1-0	Glasgow
1930	3-1	Glasgow	1980	0-1	Belfast
1931	0-0	Belfast	1981	1-1	Glasgow

1981	2-0	Glasgow	1983	0-0	Glasgow
1982	0-0	Belfast	1984	0-2	Belfast
1982	1-1	Belfast	1992	1-0	Glasgow

v WALES
(Scotland scores first)

1876	4-0	Glasgow	1914	0-0	Glasgow
1877	2-0	Wrexham	1920	1-1	Cardiff
1878	9-0	Glasgow	1921	2-1	Aberdeen
1879	3-0	Wrexham	1922	1-2	Wrexham
1880	5-1	Glasgow	1923	2-0	Paisley
1881	5-1	Wrexham	1924	0-2	Cardiff
1882	5-0	Glasgow	1925	3-1	Edinburgh
1883	4-1	Wrexham	1926	3-0	Cardiff
1884	4-1	Glasgow	1927	3-0	Glasgow
1885	8-1	Wrexham	1928	2-2	Wrexham
1886	4-1	Glasgow	1929	4-2	Glasgow
1887	2-0	Wrexham	1930	4-2	Cardiff
1888	5-1	Edinburgh	1931	1-1	Glasgow
1889	0-0	Wrexham	1932	3-2	Wrexham
1890	5-0	Paisley	1933	2-5	Edinburgh
1891	4-3	Wrexham	1934	2-3	Cardiff
1892	6-1	Edinburgh	1935	3-2	Aberdeen
1893	8-0	Wrexham	1936	1-1	Cardiff
1894	5-2	Kilmarnock	1937	1-2	Dundee
1895	2-2	Wrexham	1938	1-2	Cardiff
1896	4-0	Dundee	1939	3-2	Edinburgh
1897	2-2	Wrexham	1946	1-3	Wrexham
1898	5-2	Motherwell	1947	1-2	Glasgow
1899	6-0	Wrexham	1948	3-1	Cardiff
1900	5-2	Aberdeen	1949	2-0	Glasgow
1901	1-1	Wrexham	1950	3-1	Cardiff
1902	5-1	Greenock	1951	0-1	Glasgow
1903	1-0	Cardiff	1952	2-1	Cardiff
1904	1-1	Dundee	1953	3-3	Glasgow
1905	1-3	Wrexham	1954	1-0	Cardiff
1906	0-2	Edinburgh	1955	2-0	Glasgow
1907	0-1	Wrexham	1956	2-2	Cardiff
1908	2-1	Dundee	1957	1-1	Glasgow
1909	2-3	Wrexham	1958	3-0	Cardiff
1910	1-0	Kilmarnock	1959	1-1	Glasgow
1911	2-2	Cardiff	1960	0-2	Cardiff
1912	1-0	Edinburgh	1961	2-0	Glasgow
1913	0-0	Wrexham	1962	3-2	Cardiff

1963	2-1	Glasgow
1964	2-3	Cardiff
1965	4-1	Glasgow
1966	1-1	Cardiff
1967	3-2	Glasgow
1969	5-3	Wrexham
1970	0-0	Glasgow
1971	0-0	Cardiff
1972	1-0	Glasgow
1973	2-0	Wrexham
1974	2-0	Glasgow
1975	2-2	Cardiff
1976	3-1	Glasgow
1977	1-0	Glasgow
1977	0-0	Wrexham

1978	2-0	Liverpool
(Wales' home game in World Cup qualifier)		
1978	1-1	Glasgow
1979	0-3	Cardiff
1980	1-0	Glasgow
1981	0-2	Swansea
1982	1-0	Glasgow
1983	2-0	Cardiff
1984	2-1	Glasgow
1985	0-1	Glasgow
1986	1-1	Cardiff
1997	0-1	Kilmarnock
2004	0-4	Cardiff

ROBERT EARNSHAW netted a hat-trick against Scotland in the 4-0 defeat at the Millennium Stadium in Cardiff

ARGENTINA
(Scotland scores first)

977	1-1	Buenos Aires	1990	1-0 .... Glasgow
979	1-3	Glasgow		

AUSTRALIA
(Scotland scores first)

986	2-2	Glasgow	1996	1-0 .... Glasgow
986	0-0	Melbourne	2000	0-2 .... Glasgow

AUSTRIA
(Scotland scores first)

931	0-5	Vienna	*(Referee abandoned match ....*
934	2-2	Glasgow	*after 79 minutes)*
937	1-1	Vienna	1969	2-1 .... Glasgow
951	0-1	Glasgow	1970	0-2 .... Vienna
951	0-4	Vienna	1979	2-3 .... Vienna
954	0-1	Zurich	1980	1-1 .... Glasgow
955	4-1	Vienna	1994	2-1 .... Vienna
956	1-1	Glasgow	1997	0-0 .... Vienna
960	1-4	Vienna	1997	2-0 .... Glasgow
963	4-1	Glasgow	2003	0-2 .... Glasgow

BELARUS
(Scotland scores first)

1997	1-0	Minsk	1998	4-1 .... Aberdeen

BELGIUM
(Scotland scores first)

1946	2-2	Glasgow	1980	1-3 .... Glasgow
1947	1-2	Brussels	1983	2-3 .... Brussels
1948	2-0	Glasgow	1984	1-1 .... Glasgow
1951	5-0	Brussels	1987	1-4 .... Brussels
1971	0-3	Liege	1988	2-0 .... Glasgow
1972	1-0	Aberdeen	2001	2-2 .... Glasgow
1974	1-2	Brussels	2001	0-2 .... Brussels
1980	0-2	Brussels		

BOSNIA
(Scotland scores first)

1999 2-1 ....Sarajevo	1999 1-0 ....Glasgow

BRAZIL
(Scotland scores first)

1966 1-1 ....Glasgow	1982 1-4 ....Seville
1972 0-1 ....Rio	1987 0-2 ....Glasgow
1973 0-1 ....Glasgow	1990 0-1 ....Turin
1974 0-0 ....Frankfurt	1998 1-2 ....Paris
1977 0-2 ....Rio	

BULGARIA
(Scotland scores first)

1978 2-1 ....Glasgow	1991 1-1 ....Sofia
1987 0-0 ....Glasgow	1991 1-1 ....Glasgow
1988 1-0 ....Sofia	

CANADA
(Scotland scores first)

1983 2-0 ....Vancouver	1992 3-1 ....Toronto
1983 3-0 ....Edmonton	2003 3-1 ....Edinburgh
1983 2-0 ....Toronto	

CHILE
(Scotland scores first)

1977 4-2 ....Santiago	1989 2-0 ....Glasgow

C.I.S.
(Scotland score first)

1992 3-0 ....Sweden

COLOMBIA
(Scotland scores first)

1988 0-0 ....Glasgow	1998 2-2 ....New Jersey
1996 0-1 ....Miami	

COSTA RICA
(Scotland score first)

1990 0-1 ....Genoa

CROATIA
(Scotland score first)

2001 1-1.....................Zagreb | 2002 0-0...................Glasgow

CYPRUS
(Scotland scores first)

1969 5-0 ....Nicosia	1989 3-2 ....Limassol
1969 8-0 ....Glasgow	1989 2-1 ....Glasgow

CZECHOSLOVAKIA
(Scotland scores first)

1937 3-1 ....Prague	1972 0-0 ....Porto Alegre
1938 5-0 ....Glasgow	1974 2-1 ....Glasgow
1961 0-4 ....Bratislava	1974 0-1 ....Bratislava
1962 3-2 ....Glasgow	1977 0-2 ....Prague
1962 2-4 ....Brussels	1978 3-1 ....Glasgow

CZECH REPUBLIC
(Scotland scores first)

1999 1-2 ....Glasgow | 1999 2-3.....................Prague

DENMARK
(Scotland scores first)

1951 3-1 ....Glasgow	1976 1-0 ....Copenhagen
1952 2-1 ....Copenhagen	1976 3-1 ....Glasgow
1969 1-0 ....Copenhagen	1986 0-1 ....Neza
1971 1-0 ....Glasgow	1996 0-2 ....Copenhagen
1971 0-1 ....Copenhagen	1998 0-1 ....Glasgow
1973 4-1 ....Copenhagen	2003 0-1 ....Glasgow
1973 2-0 ....Glasgow	2004 0-1 ....Copenhagen

EAST GERMANY
(Scotland scores first)

1975 3-0 ....Glasgow	1984 1-2 ....Halle
1978 0-1 ....East Berlin	1986 0-0 ....Glasgow
1983 2-0 ....Glasgow	1990 0-1 ....Glasgow

ECUADOR
(Scotland score first)

1995 2-1 ....Toyama

EGYPT
(Scotland score first)

1990   1-3 ....Aberdeen

ESTONIA
(Scotland scores first)

1993 3-0 ....Tallinn	1997 0-0 ....Monaco
1993 3-1 ....Aberdeen	1997 2-0 ....Kilmarnock
1997 0-0 ....Tallinn	1998 3-2 ....Tynecastle
(abandoned after 3 seconds,	1999 0-0 ....Tallinn
replay ordered in Monaco)	2004 1-0 ....Tallinn

FAROE ISLANDS
(Scotland scores first)

1995 5-1 ....Glasgow	1999 1-1 ....Toftir
1995 2-0 ....Torshavn	2003 2-2 ....Toftir
1998 2-1.................Aberdeen	2004 3-1 ....Glasgow

FINLAND
(Scotland scores first)

1954 2-1 ....Helsinki	1992 1-1 ....Glasgow
1965 3-1 ....Glasgow	1995 2-0 ....Helsinki
1965 2-1 ....Helsinki	1996 1-0 ....Glasgow
1977 6-0 ....Glasgow	1998 1-1 ....Edinburgh

FRANCE
(Scotland scores first)

1930 2-0 ....Paris	1958 1-2 ....Obrero
1932 3-1 ....Paris	1984 0-2 ....Marseilles
1948 0-3 ....Paris	1989 2-0 ....Glasgow
1949 2-0 ....Glasgow	1990 0-3 ....Paris
1950 1-0 ....Paris	1998 1-2 ....St Etienne
1951 1-0 ....Glasgow	2000 0-2 ....Glasgow
	2002 0-5 ....Paris

GERMANY
(Scotland scores first)

1929 1-1 ....Berlin	1999 1-0 ....Bremen
1937 2-0 ....Glasgow	2003 1-1 ....Glasgow
1992 0-2...................Sweden	2004 1-2 ....Dortmund
1993 0-1 ....Glasgow	

GREECE
(Scotland scores first)

1995 0-1 ....Athens	1996 1-0 ....Glasgow

HOLLAND
(Scotland scores first)

1929 2-0 ....Amsterdam	1986 0-0 ....Eindhoven
1938 3-1 ....Amsterdam	1992 0-1 ....Sweden
1959 2-1 ....Amsterdam	1994 0-1 ....Glasgow
1966 0-3 ....Glasgow	1994 1-3 ....Utrecht
1968 0-0 ....Amsterdam	1996 0-0...........Birmingham
1972 1-2 ....Amsterdam	2000 0-0 ....Arnhem
1978 3-2.................Argentina	2004 1-0 ....Glasgow
1982 2-1 ....Glasgow	2004 0-6 ....Amsterdam

HONG KONG
(Scotland scores first)

2002 4-0 ....Hong Kong	

JAMES McFADDEN has starred for Scotland of late, netting against Holland at Hampden

HUNGARY
(Scotland scores first)

1939	3-1	Glasgow	1960	3-3	Budapest
1955	2-4	Glasgow	1980	1-3	Budapest
1955	1-3	Budapest	1988	2-0	Glasgow
1958	1-1	Glasgow			

ICELAND
(Scotland scores first)

1985	3-0	Glasgow	2003	2-0	Reykjavik
1985	1-0	Reykjavik	2003	2-1	Glasgow

IRAN
(Scotland score first)

1978	1-1	Cordoba

ISRAEL
(Scotland scores first)

1981	1-0	Tel Aviv	1986	1-0	Tel Aviv
1981	3-1	Glasgow			

ITALY
(Scotland scores first)

1931	0-3	Rome	1989	0-2	Perugia
1965	1-0	Glasgow	1993	0-0	Ibrox
1965	0-3	Naples	1994	1-3	Rome

JAPAN
(Scotland score first)

1995	0-0	Hiroshima

LATVIA
(Scotland scores first)

1997	2-0	Riga	2000	1-0	Riga
1998	2-0	Celtic Park	2001	2-1	Glasgow

LITHUANIA
(Scotland scores first)

1998	0-0	Vilnius	2003	0-1	Kaunas
1999	3-0	Glasgow	2004	1-0	Glasgow

THE KING OF DIAMONDS

N.C.P.

GORDON STREET

MITCHELL ST

GYLE STREET

BUCHANAN ST

Frasers

Princes Square

John Macintyre & Son
THE KING OF DIAMONDS
14 Mitchell Lane, Glasgow G1 3NU
Tel: 0141 221 2164

Opening hours: Mon, Tue, Wed, Fri 9.00am-5.30pm
Thu 9.00am-6.30pm. Sat 9.00am-5.30pm
Sun 12.00pm-4.00pm

LUXEMBOURG
(Scotland scores first)

| 1947 | 6-0 | Luxembourg | 1988 | 0-0 | Luxembourg |
| 1987 | 3-0 | Glasgow | | | |

MALTA
(Scotland scores first)

1988	1-1	Valetta	1994	2-0	Valetta
1990	2-1	Valetta	1997	3-2	Valetta
1993	3-0	Glasgow			

MOROCCO
(Scotland score first)

| 1998 | 0-3 | St Etienne |

NEW ZEALAND
(Scotland score first)

| 1982 | 5-2 | Malaga | 2003 | 1-1 | Edinburgh |

NIGERIA
(Scotland score first)

| 2002 | 1-2 | Aberdeen |

NORWAY
(Scotland scores first)

1929	7-3	Bergen	1979	4-0	Oslo
1954	1-0	Glasgow	1989	2-1	Oslo
1954	1-1	Oslo	1990	1-1	Glasgow
1963	3-4	Bergen	1992	0-0	Oslo
1964	6-1	Glasgow	1998	1-1	Bordeaux
1974	2-1	Oslo	2004	0-0	Oslo
1979	3-2	Glasgow			

PARAGUAY
(Scotland score first)

| 1958 | 2-3 | Norrkoping |

PERU
(Scotland scores first)

| 1972 | 2-0 | Glasgow | 1980 | 1-1 | Glasgow |
| 1978 | 1-3 | Cordoba | | | |

POLAND
(Scotland scores first)

1958	2-1	Warsaw	1980	0-1	Poznan
1960	2-3	Glasgow	1990	1-1	Glasgow
1965	1-1	Chorzow	2001	1-1	Bydgoszcz
1966	1-2	Glasgow			

PORTUGAL
(Scotland score first)

1950	2-2	Lisbon	1979	1-0	Lisbon
1955	3-0	Glasgow	1980	4-1	Glasgow
1959	0-1	Lisbon	1981	0-0	Glasgow
1966	0-1	Glasgow	1982	1-2	Lisbon
1971	0-2	Lisbon	1993	0-0	Glasgow
1972	2-1	Glasgow	1993	0-5	Lisbon
1975	1-0	Glasgow	2003	0-2	Braga

REPUBLIC OF IRELAND
(Scotland scores first)

1961	4-1	Glasgow	1987	0-0	Dublin
1961	3-0	Dublin	1987	0-1	Glasgow
1963	0-1	Dublin	2000	2-1	Dublin
1970	1-1	Dublin	2003	0-2	Glasgow

ROMANIA
(Scotland scores first)

1975	1-1	Bucharest	1991	2-1	Glasgow
1976	1-1	Glasgow	1992	0-1	Bucharest
1986	3-0	Glasgow	2004	1-2	Glasgow

RUSSIA
(Scotland scores first)

995	1-1	Glasgow	1995	0-0	Moscow

SAN MARINO
(Scotland scores first)

1991	2-0	Serravalle	1996	5-0	Glasgow
1992	4-0	Glasgow	2000	2-0	Serravalle
1995	2-0	Serravalle	2001	4-0	Glasgow

SAUDI ARABIA
(Scotland score first)

1988 2-2 ....Riyadh |

SOUTH AFRICA
(Scotland score first)

2002 0-2 ....Hong Kong |

SOUTH KOREA
(Scotland score first)

2002 1-4 ....Busan |

SOVIET UNION
(Scotland scores first)

1967	0-2 ....Glasgow	1982	2-2 ....Malaga
1971	0-1 ....Moscow	1991	0-1 ....Glasgow

SPAIN
(Scotland scores first)

1957	4-2 ....Glasgow	1975	1-1..................Valencia
1957	1-4......................Madrid	1982	0-3..................Valencia
1963	6-2......................Madrid	1985	3-1 ....Glasgow
1965	0-0 ....Glasgow	1985	0-1 ....Seville
1975	1-2 ....Glasgow	1988	0-0...................Madrid

SWEDEN
(Scotland scores first)

1952	1-3................Stockholm	1982	2-0 ....Glasgow
1953	1-2 ....Glasgow	1990	2-1 ....Genoa
1975	1-1................Gothenburg	1996	0-2................Stockholm
1977	3-1 ....Glasgow	1997	1-0 ....Glasgow
1981	1-0................Stockholm	1997	1-2.............Gothenburg

SWITZERLAND
(Scotland scores first)

1931	3-2 ....Geneva	1983	0-2......................Berne
1946	3-1 ....Glasgow	1983	2-2 ....Glasgow
1948	1-2 ....Berne	1991	2-1 ....Glasgow
1950	3-1 ....Glasgow	1992	2-2......................Berne
1957	2-1 ....Basel	1993	1-3......................Berne
1958	3-2 ....Glasgow	1994	1-1................Aberdeen
1973	0-1 ....Berne	1996	1-0.............Birmingham
1976	1-0 ....Glasgow		

TRINIDAD & TOBAGO
(Scotland score first)

2004 4-1 ....Edinburgh

TURKEY
(Scotland score first)

1960 2-4 ....Ankara

URUGUAY
(Scotland scores first)

1954 0-7 ....Switzerland	1984 2-0 ....Glasgow
1962 2-3 ....Glasgow	1986 0-0 ....Neza

USA
(Scotland scores first)

1952 6-0 ....Glasgow	1996 1-2 ....Hartford
1992 1-0.....................Denver	1998 0-0 ....Washington

WEST GERMANY
(Scotland scores first)

1957 3-1 ....Stuttgart	1970 2-3 ....Hamburg
1959 3-2...................Glasgow	1974 1-1 ....Glasgow
1964 2-2...................Hanover	1974 1-2 ....Frankfurt
1969 1-1 ....Glasgow	1986 1-2 ....Queretaro

YUGOSLAVIA
(Scotland scores first)

1955 2-2 ....Belgrade	1974 1-1 ....Frankfurt
1957 2-0...................Glasgow	1985 6-1 ....Glasgow
1958 1-1 ....Vaasteras	1989 1-1 ....Glasgow
1972 2-2 ....Belo Horizonte	1990 1-3.....................Zagreb

ZAIRE
(Scotland score first)

1974 2-0 ....Dortmund

LIST OF
PLAYERS
HONOURED

This is a list of full international appearances by Scots in matches against the Home Countries and against foreign nations.

The code for countries is as follows

A, Austria; Arg, Argentina; Aus, Australia; Bel, Belgium; Blr, Belarus; Bos, Bosnia; Br, Brazil; Bul, Bulgaria; Ca, Canada; Ch, Chile; CIS Commonwealth of Independent States; Co, Colombia; Cr, Costa Rica; Cro, Croatia; Cy, Cyprus; Cz, Czechoslovakia; CzR, Czech Republic; D, Denmark; E, England; Ec, Ecuador; EG, East Germany; Eg, Egypt; Est, Estonia; Fr, France; Fin, Finland; Fi, Faroe Islands; G, Germany; Gr, Greece; H, Hungary; Holl, Holland; HK, Hong Kong; I, Italy; Ice, Iceland; Ir, Iran; Is, Israel; J, Japan; L, Luxembourg; La, Latvia; Lth, Lithuania; M, Morocco; Ma, Malta; Nig, Nigeria; N, Norway; Ni, Northern Ireland; Nz, New Zealand; Por, Portugal; Pe, Peru; Pol, Poland; Ei, Republic of Ireland; R, Romania; Ru, Russia; SAr, Saudi Arabia; Se, Sweden; Sm, San Marino; SA, South Africa; Skor, South Korea; Sp, Spain; Sw, Switzerland; Trin, Trinidad & Tobago; T, Turkey; U, Uruguay; US, United States of America; USSR, Soviet Union; W, Wales; WG, West Germany; Y, Yugoslavia; Z, Zaire.

The year refers to the season. For example, 1989 is the 1988-89 season

ADAMS, J. (Hearts) (3): 1889 v Ni; 1892 v W; 1893 v Ni.

AGNEW, W. B. (Kilmarnock) (3): 1907 v Ni; 1908 v W, Ni.

AIRD, J. (Burnley) (4): 1954 v N (2); A, U.

AITKEN A. (Newcastle Utd, Middlesbrough, Leicester Fosse) (14):
1901 v E; 1902 v E; 1903 v E, W; 1904 v E; 1905 v E, W; 1906 v E;
1907 v E, W; 1908 v E; 1910 v E; 1911 v E, Ni.

AITKEN, G, G. (East Fife, Sunderland) (8): 1949 v E, Fr; 1950 v W,
Ni, Sw; 1953 v W, Ni; 1954 v E.

AITKEN, R. (Dumbarton) (2): 1886 v E: 1888 v Ni.

AITKEN, R. (Celtic, Newcastle Utd, St Mirren) (57): 1980 v Pe, Be,
W, E, Pol; 1983 v Bel, Ca (2); 1984 v Bel, Ni, W; 1985 v E, Ice; 1986
v W, EG, Aus (2), Is, R, E, D, WG, U; 1987 v Bul, Ei (2), L, Bel, E, Br;
1988 v H, Bel, Bul, L, S.Ar., Ma, Sp, Co, E; 1989 v N, Y, I, Cy, (2), Fr,
E, Ch; 1990 v Y, Fr, N, Arg, Pol, Ma, Cr, Se, Br; 1992 v E.

AITKENHEAD, W. A. C. (Blackburn R.) (1): 1912 v Ni.

ALBISTON, A. (Manchester Utd) (14): 1982 v Ni; 1984 v U, Bel, EG,
W, E; 1985 v Y, Ice, Sp (2), W; 1986 v EG, Holl, U.

ALEXANDER, D. (East Stirlingshire) (2): 1894 v W, Ni.

ALEXANDER, G. (Preston) (14): 2002 v Nig, Skor, SA, HK; 2003
D, Fi, Can, Por, Ei, Ice, Lth, Nz; 2004 v Lth; 2004 v R.

ALLAN, D. S. (Queen's Park) (3): 1885 v E, W; 1886 v W.

ALLAN, G. (Liverpool) (1): 1897 v E.

ALLAN, H. (Hearts) (1): 1902 v W.

ALLAN, J. (Queen's Park) (2): 1887 v E, W.

ALLAN, T. (Dundee) (2): 1974 v WG, N.

ANCELL, R. F. D. (Newcastle Utd) (1): 1937 v W, Ni.

ANDERSON, A. (Hearts) (23): 1933 v E; 1934 v A, E, W, Ni; 1935
E, W, Ni; 1936 v E, W, Ni; 1937 v G, E, W, Ni, A; 1938 v E, W, Ni, Cz,
Holl; 1939 v W, H.

ANDERSON, F. (Clydesdale) (1): 1874 v E.

ANDERSON, G. (Kilmarnock) (1): 1901 v Ni.

ANDERSON, H. A. (Raith Rovers) (1): 1914 v W.

ANDERSON, J. (Leicester City) (1): 1954 v Fin.

ANDERSON, K. (Queen's Park) (3): 1896 v E; 1898 v E, Ni.

ANDERSON, R. (Aberdeen) (4): 2003 v Ice, Can, Por, Ei.

ANDERSON, W. (Queen's Park) (6): 1882 v E: 1883 v E, W; 1884 v
E; 1885 v E, W.

ANDREWS, P. (Eastern) (1): 1875 v E.

ARCHIBALD, A. (Rangers) (8): 1921 v W; 1922 v E; 1923 v N;
1924 v E, W; 1931 v E; 1932 v E.

ARCHIBALD, S. (Aberdeen, Tottenham H., Barcelona) (27): 1980
Por, Ni, Pol, H; 1981 v Se, Is (2), Ni (2), E; 1982 v Ni, Por, Sp, Holl,
Nz, Br, USSR; 1983 v EG, Sw, Bel; 1984 v EG, E, Fr; 1985 v Sp, E,
Ice; 1986 v WG.

ARMSTRONG, M. W. (Aberdeen) (3): 1936 v W, Ni; 1937 v G.

ARNOTT, W. (Queen's Park) (14): 1883 v W; 1884 v E, Ni; 1885 v E,

W; 1886 v E; 1887 v E, W; 1888 v E; 1889 v E; 1890 v E; 1891 v E; 1892 v E; 1893 v E.

AULD, J. R. (Third Lanark) (3): 1887 v E, W; 1889 v W.

AULD, R. (Celtic) (3): 1959 v H, Por; 1960 v W.

BAIRD, A. (Queen's Park) (2): 1892 v Ni; 1894 v W.

BAIRD, D. (Hearts) (3): 1890 v Ni; 1891 v E; 1892 v W.

BAIRD, H. (Airdrie) (1): 1956 v A.

BAIRD, J. C. (Vale of Leven) (3): 1876 v E; 1878 v W; 1880 v E.

BAIRD, S. (Rangers) (7): 1957 v Y, Sp (2), Sw, WG: 1958 v Fr, Ni.

BAIRD, W. U. (St Bernard's) (1): 1897 v Ni.

BANNON, E. (Dundee Utd) (11): 1980 v Bel; 1983 v Ni, W, E, Ca; 1984 v EG; 1986 v Is, R, E, D, WG.

BARBOUR, A. (Renton) (1): 1885 v Ni.

BARKER, J. B. (Rangers) (2): 1893 v W: 1894 v W.

BARRETT, F. (Dundee) (2): 1894 v Ni; 1895 v W.

BATTLES, B. (Celtic) (3): 1901 v E, W, Ni.

BATTLES, B. (Hearts) (1): 1931 v W.

BAULD, W. (Hearts) (3): 1950 v E, Sw, Por.

BAXTER, J. C. (Rangers, Sunderland) (34): 1961 v Ni, Ei (2), Cz; 1962 v Ni, W, E, Cz (2), U; 1963 v W, Ni, E, A, N, Ei, Sp; 1964 v W, E, N, WG; 1965 v W, Ni, Fin; 1966 v Por, Br, Ni, W, E, I; 1967 v E, USSR; 1968 v W.

BAXTER, R. D. (Middlesbrough) (3): 1939 v E, W, H.

BEATTIE, A. (Preston NE) (7): 1937 v E, A, Cz; 1938 v E; 1939 v W, Ni, H.

BEATTIE, R. (Preston NE) (1): 1939 v W.

BEGBIE, I. (Hearts) (4): 1890 v Ni; 1891 v E; 1892 v W; 1894 v E.

BELL, A. (Manchester Utd) (1): 1912 v W.

BELL, J. (Dumbarton, Everton, Celtic) (10): 1890 v Ni; 1892 v E; 1896 v E; 1897 v E; 1898 v E; 1899 v E, W, Ni; 1900 v E, W.

BELL, M. (Hearts) (1): 1901 v W.

BELL, W. J. (Leeds Utd) (2): 1966 v Por, Br.

BENNETT, A. (Celtic, Rangers) (11): 1904 v W; 1907 v Ni; 1908 v W: 1909 v W, Ni, E; 1910 v E, W; 1911 E, W; 1913 v Ni.

BENNIE, R. (Airdrie) (3): 1925 v W, Ni; 1926 v Ni.

BERNARD, P. (Oldham Ath.) (2): 1995 v J, Ec.

BERRY, D. (Queen's Park) (3): 1894 v W; 1899 v W, Ni.

BERRY, W. H. (Queen's Park) (4): 1888 v E; 1889 v E; 1890 v E; 1891 v E.

BETT, J. (Rangers, Lokeren, Aberdeen) (25): 1982 v Holl; 1983 v Bel; 1984 v Bel, W, E, Fr; 1985 v Y, Ice, (2), Sp (2), W, E; 1986 v W, Is, Holl; 1987 v Bel; 1988 v E; 1989 v Y; 1990 v Fr, N, Arg, Ma, Cr.

BEVERIDGE, W. W. (Glasgow University) (3): 1879 v E; 1880 v W.

BLACK, A (Hearts) (3): 1938 v Cz, Holl; 1939 v H.

BLACK, D. (Hurlford) (1): 1889 v Ni.

BLACK, E. (Metz) (2): 1988 v H, L.

BLACK, I. H. (Southampton) (1): 1948 v E.

BLACKBURN, J. E. (Royal Engineers) (1): 1873 v E.

BLACKLAW, A. S. (Burnley) (3): 1963 v N, Sp; 1966 v I.

BLACKLEY, J. (Hibernian) (7): 1974 v Cz, E, Bel, Z; 1976 v Sw; 1977 v W, Se.

BLAIR, D. (Clyde, Aston Villa) (8): 1929 v W, Ni; 1931 v E, A, I; 1932 v W, Ni; 1933 v W.

BLAIR, J. (Sheffield W., Cardiff City) (8): 1920 v E, Ni; 1921 v E; 1922 v E; 1923 v E, W, Ni; 1924 v W.

BLAIR, J. (Motherwell) (1): 1934 v W.

BLAIR, J. A. (Blackpool) (1): 1947 v W.

BLAIR, W. (Third Lanark) (1): 1896 v W.

BLESSINGTON, J. (Celtic) (4): 1894 v E, Ni; 1896 v E, Ni.

BLYTH, J. A. (Coventry City) (2): 1978 v Bul, W.

BONE, J. (Norwich City) (2): 1972 v Y; 1973 v D.

BOOTH, S. (Aberdeen, Utrecht) (19): 1993 v G, Est (2); 1994 v Sw, Ma; 1995 v Fi, Ru; 1996 v Fin, Sm, Aus, US, Holl, Sw; 1998 v D, Fin, Co, M; 2001 v Pol; 2002 Cro, Bel, La.

BOWIE, J. (Rangers) (2): 1920 v E, Ni.

BOWIE, W. (Linthouse) (1): 1891 v Ni.

BOWMAN, D. (Dundee United) (6): 1992 v Fin, US; 1993 v G, Est; 1994 v Sw, I.

BOWMAN, G. A. (Montrose) (1): 1892 v Ni.

BOYD, J. M. (Newcastle Utd) (1): 1934 v Ni.

BOYD, R. (Mossend Swifts) (2): 1889 v Ni; 1891 v W.

BOYD, T. (Motherwell, Chelsea, Celtic) (72): 1991 v R (2), Sw, Bul, USSR; 1992 Sw, Fin, Ca, CIS; 1993 v Sw, Por, I, Ma, G, Est (2); 1994 v I, Ma, Holl, A; 1995 v Fin, Fi, Ru (2), Gr, Sm. 1996 v Gr, Fin, Se, Sm, Aus, D, US, U, Holl, E, Sw; 1997 v A (2), La, Se (2), Est (2), W, Ma, Blr; 1998 v Blr, La, Fr, D, Fin, Co, US, Br, N, M. 1999 v Lth, Est, Fi, CzR (2), Fi; 2001 v La, Cro, Aus, Bel, Sm, Pol; 2002 v Bel.

BOYD, W. G. (Clyde) (2): 1931 v I, Sw, Fin.

BRACKENBRIDGE, T. (Hearts) (1): 1888 v Ni.

BRADSHAW, T. (Bury) (1): 1928 v E.

BRAND, R. (Rangers) (8): 1961 v Ni, Cz, Ei. (2); 1962 v Ni, W, Cz, U.

BRANDEN, T. (Blackburn R.) (1): 1896 v E.

BRAZIL, A. (Ipswich Town) (13): 1980 v Pol, H; 1982 v Sp, Holl, Ni, W, E, Nz, USSR; 1983 v EG, Sw, W, E.

BREMNER, D. (Hibernian) (1): 1976 v Sw.

BREMNER, W. J. (Leeds Utd) (54): 1965 v Sp; 1966 v E, Pol, P, Br, (2); 1967 v W, Ni, E; 1968 v W, E; 1969 v W, E, Ni, D, A, WG, Cy (2) 1970 v Ei, WG, A; 1971 v W, E; 1972 v Por, Bel, Holl, Ni, W, E, Y, Cz Br; 1973 v D (2), E (2), Ni, Sw, Br; 1974 v Cz, WG, Ni, W, E, Bel, N Z, Br, Y; 1975 v Sp (2); 1976 v D.

BRENNAN, F. (Newcastle Utd) (7): 1947 v W, Ni; 1953 v W, Ni, E 1954 v Ni, E.

BRESLIN, B. (Hibernian) (1): 1897 v W.

BREWSTER, G. (Everton) (1): 1921 v E.

BROGAN, J. (Celtic) (4): 1971 v W, Ni, Por, E.

BROWN, A. (Middlesbrough) (1): 1904 v E.

BROWN, A. (St Mirren) (2): 1890 v W; 1891 v W.

BROWN, A. D. (East Fife, Blackpool) (14): 1950 v Sw, Por, Fr; 1952 v USA, D, Se; 1953 v W; 1954 v W, E, N (2), Fin, A, U.

BROWN, G. C. P. (Rangers) (19): 1931 v W; 1932 v E, W, Ni; 1933 v E; 1935 v A, E, W; 1936 v E, W; 1937 v G, E, W, Ni, Cz; 1938 v E, W, Cz, Holl.

BROWN, H. (Partick Th.) (3): 1947 v W, Bel, L.

BROWN, J. (Cambuslang) (1): 1890 v W.

BROWN, J. B. (Clyde) (1): 1939 v W.

BROWN, J. G. (Sheffield U.) (1): 1975 v R.

BROWN, R. (Dumbarton) (2): 1884 v W, Ni.

BROWN, R. (Rangers) (3): 1947 v Ni; 1949 v Ni; 1952 v E.

BROWN, R. (Dumbarton) (1): 1885 v W.

BROWN, W. D. F. (Dundee, Tottenham H.) (28): 1958 v Fr; 1959 v E, W, Ni; 1960 v W, Ni, Pol, A, H, T; 1962 v Ni, W, E, Cz; 1963 v W, Ni, E, A; 1964 v W, Ni, W, N; 1965 v E, Fin, Pol, Sp; 1966 v Ni, Pol, I.

BROWNING, J. (Celtic) (1): 1914 v W.

BROWNLIE, J. (Hibernian) (7): 1971 v USSR; 1972 v Pe, Ni, E; 1973 v D (2); 1976 v R.

BROWNLIE, J. (Third Lanark) (16): 1909 v E, Ni; 1910 v E, W, Ni; 1911 v W, Ni; 1912 v W, Ni, E; 1913 v W, Ni, E; 1914 v W, Ni, E.

BRUCE, D. (Vale of Leven) (1): 1890 v W.

BRUCE, R. F. (Middlesbrough) (1): 1934 v A.

BUCHAN, M. M. (Aberdeen, Manchester Utd.) (34): 1972 v Por, Bel, W, Y, Cz, Br; 1973 v D (2), E; 1974 v WG, Ni, W, N, Br, Y; 1975 v EG, Sp, Por; 1976 v D, R; 1977 v Fin, Cz, Ch, Arg, Br; 1978 v EG, W, Ni, Pe, Ir, Holl; 1979 v A, N, Por.

BUCHANAN, J. (Cambuslang) (1): 1889 v Ni.

BUCHANAN, J. (Rangers) (2): 1929 v E; 1930 v E.

BUCHANAN, P. S. (Chelsea) (1): 1938 v Cz.

BUCHANAN, R. (Abercorn) (1): 1891 v W.

BUCKLEY, P. (Aberdeen) (3): 1954 v N; 1955 v W, Ni.

BUICK, A. (Hearts) (2): 1902 v W, Ni.

BURCHILL, M. (Celtic) (6): 2000 v Bos, Lth, E (2), Fr, Holl.

BURLEY C. (Chelsea, Celtic, Derby) (46): 1995 v J, Ec, Fi. 1996 v Gr, Se, Aus, D, US, Co, Ho, E, Sw; 1997 v A (2), La, Se (2), Est, Ma, Blr 1998 v Blr, La, Fr, Co, US, Br, N, M. 1999 v Fi, CzR. 2000 v Bos (2), Est, Lth, E (2), Holl, Ei; 2001 v Cro, Aus, Bel, Sm; 2002 v Cro, Bel, La; 2003 v A.

BURLEY, G. (Ipswich Town) (11): 1979 v W, Ni, E, Arg, N; 1980 v Por, Ni, E, Pol; 1982 v W, E.

BURNS, F. (Manchester Utd) (1): 1970 v A.

BURNS, K. (Birmingham City, Nottingham F.) (20): 1974 v WG; 1975

v EG, Sp (2); 1977 v Cz, W, (2), Se; 1978 v Ni, W, E, Pe, Ir; 1979 v
N; 1980 v Pe, A, Bel; 1981 v Is, Ni, W.
BURNS, T. (Celtic) (8): 1981 v Ni; 1982 v Holl, W; 1983 v Bel, Ni, Ca
(2); 1988 v E.
BUSBY, M. W. (Manchester City) (1): 1934 v W.

CAIRNS, T. (Rangers) (8): 1920 v W; 1922 v E; 1923 v E, W; 1924 v
Ni; 1925 v W, E, Ni.
CALDERHEAD, D. (Q.O.S. Wanderers) (1): 1889 v Ni.
CALDERWOOD, C. (Tottenham Hotspur, Aston Villa) (36): 1995 v
Ru, Sm, J, Ec, Fi. 1996 v Gr, Fin, Se, Sm, US, U, Holl, E, Sw; 1997 v
A (2), La, Se (2), Est (2); 1998 v Blr, La, Fr, D, Fin, Co, US, Br, N. 1999
v Lth, Est, Fi, CzR. 2000 v Bos (2).
CALDERWOOD, R. (Cartvale) (3): 1885 v Ni, E, W.
CALDOW, E. (Rangers) (40): 1957 Sp (2), Sw, WG, E; 1958 v Ni, W,
Sw, Par, H, Pol, Y, Fr; 1959 v E, W, Ni, WG, Holl, Por; 1960 v E, W,
Ni, A, H, T; 1961 v E, W, Ni, Ei (2), Cz; 1962 v Ni, W, E, Cz (2), U;
1963 v W, Ni, E.
CALDWELL, G. (Newcastle, Hibernian) (9): 2002 v Fr, Nig, Skor, SA,
HK; 2004 v R, D, Est, Trin.
CALDWELL, S. (Newcastle) (4): 2001 v Pol; 2003 v Ei; 2004 v W,
Trin.
CALLAGHAN, P. (Hibernian) (1): 1900 v Ni.
CALLAGHAN, W. C. Dunfermline Ath.) (2): 1970 v Ei, W.
CAMERON, C. (Hearts, Wolves) (26): 1999 v G, Fi; 2000 v Lth, Fr,
Ei; 2001 v La, Sm, Cro, Aus, Sm, Pol; 2002 v Cro, Bel, La, Fr; 2003
v Ei, A, Lth, G; 2004 v N, Fi, G, Lth, W, R, D.
CAMERON, J. (Rangers) (1): 1886 v NI.
CAMERON, J. (Queen's Park) (1): 1896 v Ni.
CAMERON, J. (St Mirren, Chelsea) (2): 1904 v Ni; 1909 v E.
CAMPBELL, C. (Queen's Park) (13): 1874 v E; 1876 v W; 1877 v E,
W; 1878 v E; 1879 v E; 1880 v E; 1881 v E; 1882 v E, W; 1884 v E;
1885 v E; 1886 v E.
CAMPBELL, H. (Renton) (1): 1889 v W.
CAMPBELL, J. (Sheffield W.) (1): 1913 v W.
CAMPBELL, J. (South Western) (1): 1880 v W.
CAMPBELL, J. (Kilmarnock) (2): 1891 v Ni; 1892 v W.
CAMPBELL, J. (Celtic) (12): 1893 v E, Ni; 1898 v E, Ni; 1900 v E,
Ni; 1901 v E, W, Ni; 1902 v W, Ni; 1903 v W.
CAMPBELL, J. (Rangers) (4): 1899 v E, W, Ni; 1901 v Ni.
CAMPBELL, K. (Liverpool, Partick Th.) (8): 1920 v E, W, Ni; 1921 v
W, Ni; 1922 v W. Ni, E.
CAMPBELL, P. (Rangers) (2): 1878 v E; 1879 v W.
CAMPBELL, P. (Morton) (1): 1898 v W.
CAMPBELL, R. (Falkirk, Chelsea) (5): 1947 v Bel, L; 1950 v Sw, Por, Fr.
CAMPBELL, W. (Morton) (5): 1947 v Ni; 1948 v E, Bel, Sw, Fr.
CANERO, P. (Leicester) (1): 2004 v D.

CARABINE, J. (Third Lanark) (3): 1938 v Holl; 1939 v E, Ni.

CARR, W. M. (Coventry City) (6): 1970 v Ni, W, E; 1971 v D; 1972 v Pe; 1973 v D.

CASSIDY, J. (Celtic) (4): 1921 v W, Ni; 1923 v Ni; 1924 v W.

CHALMERS, S. (Celtic) (5): 1965 v W, Fin; 1966 v Por, Br; 1967 v Ni.

CHALMERS, W. (Rangers) (1): 1885 v Ni.

CHALMERS, W. S. (Queen's Park) (1): 1929 v Ni.

CHAMBERS, T. (Hearts) (1): 1894 v W.

CHAPLIN, G. D. (Dundee) (1): 1908 v W.

CHEYNE, A. G. (Aberdeen) (5): 1929 v E, N, G, Holl; 1930 v Fr.

CHRISTIE, A. J. (Queen's Park) (3): 1898 v W; 1899 v E, Ni.

CHRISTIE, R. M. (Queen's Park) (1): 1884 v E.

CLARK, J. (Celtic) (4): 1966 v Br; 1967 v W, Ni, USSR.

CLARK, R. B. (Aberdeen) (17): 1968 v W, Holl; 1970 v Ni; 1971 v W, Ni, E, D, Por, USSR; 1972 v Bel, Ni, W, E, Cz, Br; 1973 v D, E.

CLARKE, S. (Chelsea) (6): 1988 v H, Bel, Bul, S.Ar, Ma; 1984 v Holl.

CLELAND, J. (Royal Albert) (1): 1891 v Ni.

CLEMENTS, R. (Leith Ath.) (1): 1891 v Ni.

CLUNAS, W. L. (Sunderland) (2): 1924 v E; 1926 v W.

COLLIER, W. (Raith R.) (1): 1922 v W.

COLLINS, J. (Hibs, Celtic, Monaco, Everton) (58): 1988 v S.Ar; 1990 v EG, Pol, Ma; 1991 v Sw, Bul, Ni, Fin; 1993 v Por (2), Ma, G, Est (2); 1994 v Sw, Holl (2), A; 1995 v Fin, Fi (2), Ru (2), Gr, Sm. 1996 v Gr, Fin, Se, Sm, Aus, D, US, U, Holl, E, Sw; 1997 v A (2), La, Se (2), Est, Ma; 1998 v Blr, La, Fr, Fin, Co, US, Br, M, N. 1999 v Lth. 2000 v Bos (2), Est, E (2).

COLLINS, R. Y. (Celtic, Everton, Leeds Utd) (31): 1951 v W, Ni, A; 1955 v Y, A, H; 1956 v Ni, W; 1957 v E, W, Sp (2), Sw, WG; 1958 v Ni, W, Sw, H, Pol, Y, Fr, Par; 1959 v E, W, Ni, WG, Holl, Por; 1965 v E, Pol, Sp.

COLLINS, T. (Hearts) (1): 1909 v W.

COLMAN, D. (Aberdeen) (4): 1911 v E, W, Ni; 1913 v Ni.

COLQUHOUN, E. P. (Sheffield Utd) (9): 1972 v Por, Holl, Pe, Y, Cz; 1973 v D (2), E.

COLQUHOUN, J. (Hearts) (2): 1988 v S.Ar, Malta.

COMBE, J. R. (Hibernian) (3): 1948 v E, Bel, Sw.

CONN, A. (Hearts) (1): 1956 v A.

CONN, A. (Tottenham H.) (2): 1975 v Ni, E.

CONNACHAN, E. D. (Dunfermline Ath.) (2): 1962 v Cz, U.

CONNELLY, G. (Celtic) (2): 1974 v Cz, WG.

CONNOLLY, J. (Everton) (1): 1973 v Sw.

CONNOR, J. (Airdrie) (1): 1886 v Ni.

CONNOR, J. (Sunderland) (4): 1930 v Fr; 1932 v Ni; 1934 v E; 1935 v Ni.

CONNOR, R. (Dundee, Aberdeen) (4): 1986 v Holl; 1988 v S.Ar; 1989 v E; 1991 v R.

COOK, W. L. (Bolton W.) (3): 1934 v E; 1935 v W, Ni.

COOKE, C. (Dundee, Chelsea) (16): 1966 v W, I, Por, Br; 1968 v E, Holl; 1969 v W, Ni, A, WG, Cy (2); 1970 v A; 1971 v Bel; 1975 v Sp, Por.

COOPER, D. (Rangers, Motherwell) (22): 1980 v Pe, A; 1984 v W, E; 1985 v Y, Ice, Sp (2), W; 1986 v W, EG, Aus (2), Holl, WG, U; 1987 v Bul, L, Ei, Br; 1990 v N, Eg.

CORMACK, P. B. (Hibernian, Nottingham F.) (9): 1966 v Br; 1969 v D; 1970 v Ei, WG; 1971 v D, W, Por, E; 1972 v Holl.

COWAN, J. (Aston Villa) (3): 1896 v E; 1897 v E; 1898 v E.

COWAN, J. (Morton) (25): 1948 v Bel, Sw, Fr; 1949 v E, W, Fr; 1950 v E, W, Ni, Sw, Por, Fr; 1951 v E, W, Ni, A (2), D, Fr, Bel; 1952 v Ni, W, USA, D, Se.

COWAN, W. D. (Newcastle Utd) (1): 1924 v E.

COWIE, D. (Dundee) (20): 1953 v E, Se; 1954 v Ni, W, Fin, N, A, U; 1955 v Ni, A, H; 1956 v W, A; 1957 v Ni, W; 1958 v H, Pol, Y, Par.

COX, S. (Rangers) (25): 1948 v E; 1949 v E, Fr; 1950 v E, Fr, W, Ni, Sw, Por; 1951 v E, D, Fr, Bel, A; 1952 v Ni, W, USA, D, Se; 1953 v W, Ni, E; 1954 v W, Ni, E.

CRAIG, A. (Motherwell) (3): 1929 v Ni, Holl; 1932 v E.

CRAIG, J. (Celtic) (1): 1977 v Se.

CRAIG, J. P. (Celtic) (1): 1968 v W.

CRAIG, T. (Rangers) (8): 1927 v Ni; 1928 v Ni; 1929 v N, G, Holl; 1930 v Ni, E, W.

CRAIG, T. B. (Newcastle Utd) (1): 1976 v Sw.

CRAINEY, S (Celtic, Southampton) (6): 2002 v Fr, Nig; 2003 v D, Fi; 2004 v R, D.

CRAPNELL, J. (Airdrie) (9): 1929 v E, N, G; 1930 v Fr; 1931 v Ni, Sw; 1932 v E, Fr; 1933 v Ni.

CRAWFORD, D. (St Mirren) (3): 1894 v W, Ni; 1900 v Ni.

CRAWFORD, J. (Queen's Park) (5): 1932 v Fr, Ni; 1933 v E, W, Ni.

CRAWFORD, S. (Raith Rovers, Dunfermline) (20): 1995 v Ec; 2001 v Pol; 2002 v Fr; 2003 v Fi, Ice (2), Can, Por, Ei, A, Lth, Nz, G; 2004 v N, Fi, Lth, Holl, R, Est, Trin.

CRERAND, P. T. (Celtic, Manchester Utd) (16): 1961 v Ei (2), Cz; 1962 v Ni, W, E, Cz (2), U; 1963 v W, Ni; 1964 v Ni; 1965 v E, Pol, Fin; 1966 v Pol.

CRINGAN, W. (Celtic) (5): 1920 v W; 1922 v E, Ni; 1923 v W, E.

CROSBIE, J. A. (Ayr Utd, Birmingham C) (2): 1920 v W; 1922 v E.

CROAL, J. A. (Falkirk) (3): 1913 v Ni; 1914 v E, W.

CROPLEY, A. J. (Hibernian) (2): 1972 v Por, Bel.

CROSS, J. H. (Third Lanark) (1): 1903 v Ni.

CRUICKSHANK, J. (Hearts) (6): 1964 v WG; 1970 v W, E; 1971 v D, Bel; 1976 v R.

CRUM, J. (Celtic) (2): 1936 v E; 1939 v Ni.

CULLEN, M. J. (Luton Town) (1): 1956 v A.

CUMMING, D. S. (Middlesbrough) (1): 1938 v E.

CUMMING, J. (Hearts) (9): 1955 v E, H, Por, Y; 1960 v E, Pol, A, H, T.

CUMMINGS, G. (Partick Th., Aston Villa) (9): 1935 v E; 1936 v W, Ni, E; 1937 v G; 1938 v W, Ni, Cz; 1939 v E.

CUMMINGS, W. (WBA) (1): 2002 v HK.

CUNNINGHAM, A. N. (Rangers) (12): 1920 v Ni; 1921 v W, E; 1922 v Ni; 1923 v E, W; 1924 v E, Ni; 1926 v E, Ni; 1927 v E, W.

CUNNINGHAM, W. C. (Preston NE) (8): 1954 v N (2), U, Fin, A; 1955 v W, E, H.

CURRAN, H. P. (Wolves) (5): 1970 v A; 1971 v Ni, E, D, USSR.

DAILLY, C. (Derby, Blackburn, West Ham) (54): 1997 v N, Ma, Blr; 1998 v Blr, La, Fr, D, Fin, Co, US, Br, N, M. 1999 v Lth. 2000 v Bos (2), Est, Lth, E (2), Fr, Holl, Ei; 2001 v La, Sm, Aus, Pol; 2002 v Cro, Bel, La, F, Nig, Skor, SA, HK; 2003 v D, Fi, Ice (2), Can, Por, Ei, A, Lth, Nz, G; 2004 v N, G, Lth, Holl (2), W, R, D.

DALGLISH, K. (Celtic, Liverpool) (102): 1972 v Bel, Holl; 1973 v D (2), E (2), W, Ni, Sw, Br; 1974 v Cz (2), WG (2), Ni, W, E, Bel, N, Z, Br, Y; 1975 v EG, Sp (2), Se, Por, W, Ni, E, R; 1976 v D (2), R, Sw, Ni, E; 1977 v Fin, Cz, W (2), Se, Ni, E, Ch, Arg, Br; 1978 v EG, Cz, W, Bul, Ni, W, E, Pe, Ir, Holl; 1979 v A, N, Por, W, Ni, E, Arg, N; 1980 v Pe, A, Bel (2), Por, Ni, W, E, Pol, H; 1981 v Se, Por, Is; 1982 v Se, Ni, Por, Sp, Holl, Ni, W, E, Nz, Br; 1983 v Bel, Sw; 1984 v U, Bel, EG; 1985 v Y, Ice, Sp, W; 1986 v EG, Aus, R; 1987 v Bul, L.

DAVIDSON, C. (Blackburn Rovers, Leicester) (17): 1999 v Lth, Est, Fi, CzR (2), G, Fi; 2000 v Est, Bos, Lth, E, Fr; 2001 v La, Pol; 2002, La; 2003 v Ice, Can.

DAVIDSON, D. (Queen's Park) (5): 1878 v W; 1879 v W; 1880 v W; 1881 v E, W.

DAVIDSON, J. A. (Partick Th.) (8): 1954 v N (2), A, U; 1955 v W, Ni, E, H.

DAVIDSON, S. (Middlesbrough) (1): 1921 v E.

DAWSON, A. (Rangers) (5): 1980 v Pol, H; 1983 v Ni, Ca (2).

DAWSON, J. (Rangers) (14): 1935 v W; 1936 v E; 1937 v G, E, W, Ni, A, Cz; 1938 v W, Holl, Ni; 1939 v E, Ni, H.

DEANS, J. (Celtic) (2): 1975 v EG, Sp.

DELANEY, J. (Celtic, Manchester Utd) (13): 1936 v W, Ni; 1937 v G, E, A, Cz; 1938 v Ni; 1939 v W, Ni; 1947 v E; 1948 v E, W, Ni.

DEVINE, A. (Falkirk) (1): 1910 v W.

DEVLIN, P. (Birmingham City) (11): 2003 v Can, Por, Ei, A, Ice, Lth, Nz, G; 2004 v N, Fi.

DEWAR, G. (Dumbarton) (2): 1888 v Ni; 1889 v E.

DEWAR, N. (Third Lanark) (3): 1932 v E, Fr; 1933 v W.

DICK, J. (West Ham Utd) (1): 1959 v E.

DICKIE, M. (Rangers) (3): 1897 v Ni; 1899 v Ni; 1900 v W.

DICKOV, P. (Manchester City, Leicester) (8): 2001 v Sm, Cro, Aus; 2003 v Fi; 2004 v Fi, Holl (2), W.

DICKSON, W. (Dumbarton) (1): 1888 v Ni.

DICKSON, W. (Kilmarnock) (5): 1970 v Ni, W, E; 1971 v D, USSR.
DIVERS, J. (Celtic) (1): 1895 v W.
DIVERS, J. (Celtic) (1): 1939 v Ni.
DOBIE, S. (WBA) (6): 2002 v Skor, SA, HK; 2003 v D, Fi, Por.
DOCHERTY, T. H. (Preston NE, Arsenal) (25): 1952 v W; 1953 v E, Se; 1954 v N (2), A, U; 1955 v W E, H (2), A; 1957 v E, Y, Sp (2), Sw, WG; 1958 v Ni, W, E, Sw; 1959 v W, E, Ni.
DODDS, D. (Dundee Utd) (2): 1984 v U, Ni.
DODDS, J. (Celtic) (3): 1914 v E, W, Ni.
DODDS, W. (Aberdeen, Dundee Utd, Rangers) (26): 1997 v La, W, Blr; 1998 v Blr. 1999 v Est, Fi, G, Fi, CzR. 2000 v Bos (2), Est, Lth, E (2), Fr, Holl, Ei; 2001 v La, Sm (2), Aus, Bel, Pol; 2002 v Cro, Bel.
DOIG, J. E. (Arbroath, Sunderland) (5): 1887 v Ni; 1889 v Ni; 1896 v E; 1899 v E; 1903 v E.
DONACHIE, W. (Manchester City) (35): 1972 v Pe, Ni, E, Y, Cz, Br; 1973 v D, E, W, Ni; 1974 v Ni; 1976 v R, Ni, W, E,; 1977 v Fin, Cz, W (2), Se, Ni, E, Ch, Arg, Br; 1978 v EG, W (2), Bul, E, Ir, Holl; 1979 v A, N, Por.
DONALDSON, A. (Bolton) (6): 1914 v E, Ni, W; 1920 v E, Ni; 1922 v Ni.
DONNACHIE, J. (Oldham Ath.) (3): 1913 v E; 1914 v E, Ni.
DONNELLY, S. (Celtic) (10): 1997 v W, Ma; 1998 La, Fr, D, Fin, Co, US. 1999 v Est. Fi.
DOUGALL, C. (Birmingham City) (1): 1947 v W.
DOUGALL, J. (Preston NE) (1): 1939 v E.
DOUGAN, R. (Hearts) (1): 1950 v Sw.
DOUGLAS, A. (Chelsea) (1): 1911 v Ni.
DOUGLAS, J, (Renfrew) (1): 1880 v W.
DOUGLAS, R. (Celtic) (16): 2002 v Nig, SA, HK; 2003 v D, Fi, Ice (2), Por, Nz, G; 2004 v N, Fi, G, Lth, Holl (2), W.
DOWDS, P. (Celtic) (1): 1892 v Ni.
DOWNIE, R. (Third Lanark) (1): 1892 v W.
DOYLE, D. (Celtic) (8): 1892 v E; 1893 v W; 1894 v E; 1895 v E, Ni; 1897 v E; 1898 v E, Ni.
DOYLE, J. (Ayr Utd) (1): 1976 v R.
DRUMMOND, J. (Falkirk, Rangers) (14): 1892 v Ni; 1894 v Ni; 1895 v Ni, E; 1896 v E, Ni; 1897 v Ni; 1898 v E; 1900 v E; 1901 v E; 1902 v E, W, Ni; 1903 v Ni.
DUNBAR, M. (Cartvale) (1): 1886 v Ni.
DUNCAN, A. (Hibernian) (6): 1975 v Por, W, Ni, E, R; 1976 v D.
DUNCAN, D. (Derby Co.) (14): 1933 v E, W; 1934 v A, W; 1935 v E, W; 1936 v E, W, Ni; 1937 v G, E, W, Ni; 1938 v W.
DUNCAN, D. M. (East Fife) (3): 1948 v Bel, Sw, Fr.
DUNCAN, J. (Alexandra Ath.) (2): 1878 v W; 1882 v W.
DUNCAN, J. (Leicester City) (1): 1926 v W.
DUNCANSON, J. (Rangers) (1): 1947 v Ni.
DUNLOP, J. (St Mirren) (1): 1890 v W.

FLEMING, C. (East Fife) (1): 1954 v Ni.
FLEMING, J. W. (Rangers) (3): 1929 v G, Holl; 1930 v E.
FLEMING, R. (Morton): 1886 v Ni.
FLETCHER, D. (Manchester Utd) (8): 2004 v N, Lth, Holl (2), W, Est, Trin.
FORBES, A. R. (Sheffield Utd, Arsenal) (14): 1947 v Bel, L, E; 194 v W, Ni; 1950 v E, Por, Fr; 1951 v W, Ni, A; 1952 v W, D, Se.
FORBES, J. (Vale of Leven) (5): 1884 v E, W, Ni; 1887 v W, E.
FORD, D. (Hearts) (3): 1974 v Cz, WG, W.
FORREST, J. (Rangers, Aberdeen) (5): 1966 v W, I; 1971 v Bel, USSR.
FORREST, J. (Motherwell) (1): 1958 v E.
FORSYTH, A. (Partick Th., Manchester Utd) (10): 1972 v Y, Cz, E 1973 v D, E; 1975 v Sp, Ni, R, EG; 1976 v D.
FORSYTH, A. (Kilmarnock) (4): 1964 v E; 1965 v W, Ni, Fin.
FORSYTH, T. (Motherwell, Rangers) (22): 1971 v D; 1974 v Cz; 197 v Sw, Ni, W, E; 1977 v Fin, Se, W, Ni, E, Ch, Arg, Br; 1978 v Cz, Ni, W, E, Pe, Ir, Holl.
FOYERS, R. (St Bernard's) (2): 1893 v W; 1894 v W.
FRASER, D. M. (WBA) (2): 1968 v Holl; 1969 v Cy.
FRASER, J. (Moffat) (1): 1891 v Ni.
FRASER, M. J. E. (Queen's Park) (5): 1880 v W; 1882 v W, E; 188 v W, E.
FRASER, J. (Dundee) (1): 1907 v Ni.
FRASER, W. (Sunderland) (2): 1955 v W, Ni.
FREEDMAN, D. (Crystal Palace) (2): 2002 v L1, Fr.
FULTON, W. (Abercorn) (1): 1884 v Ni.
FYFE, J. H. (Third Lanark) (1): 1895 v W.

GABRIEL, J. (Everton) (2): 1961 v W; 1964 v N.
GALLACHER, K. W. (Dundee Utd, Coventry, Blackburn Ro Newcastle) (53): 1988 v Co, E; 1989 v N; I; 1991 v Sm (2); 1992 v Ni, N, Holl, G, CIS; 1993 v Sw, Por (2), Est (2); 1994 v I, Ma; 1996 Aus, D, U, Holl; 1997 v Se (2), Est (2), A, W, Ma, Blr; 1998 v Blr, L, Fr, Fin, US, Br, N, M. 1999 v Lth, Est, Fi, CzR. 2000 v Bos (2), Lt E, Fr, Ei; 2001 v Sm (2), Cro, Bel.
GALLACHER, P. (Sunderland) (1): 1935 v Ni.
GALLACHER, P. (Dundee United) (8): 2002 v HK; 2003 v Can, E A, Lth, R, D, Est.
GALLACHER, H. K. (Airdrie, Newcastle Utd, Chelsea, Derby C (20): 1924 v Ni; 1925 v E, W, Ni; 1926 v W, E, Ni; 1927 v E, W, N 1928 v E, W; 1929 v E, W, Ni; 1930 v W, Ni, Fr; 1934 v E; 1935 v N
GALLOWAY, M. (Celtic) (1): 1992 v N.
GALLAGHER, P. (Blackburn Rov) (1): 2004 v W.
GALT, J. H. (Rangers) (2): 1908 v W, Ni.
GARDINER, I. (Motherwell) (1): 1958 v W.
GARDNER, D. R. (Third Lanark) (1): 1897 v W.

ARDNER, R. (Queen's Park, Clydesdale) (5): 1872 v E; 1873 v E; 374 v E; 1875 v E; 1878 v E.

EMMELL, T. (St Mirren) (2): 1955 v Por, Y.

EMMELL, T. (Celtic) (18): 1966 v E; 1967 v W, Ni, E, USSR; 1968 Ni, E; 1969 v W, Ni, E, D, A, WG, Cy; 1970 v E, Ei, WG; 1971 v Bel.

EMMILL, A. (Derby Co., Nottingham F., Birmingham City) (43): 371 v Bel; 1972 v Por, Holl, Pe, Ni, W, E; 1976 v D, R, Ni, W, E; 377 v Fin, Cz, W (2), Ni, E, Ch, Arg, Br; 1978 v EG, Bul, Ni, W, E, , Ir, Holl; 1979 v A, N. Por, N; 1980 v A, Por, Ni, W, E, H; 1981 v , Por, Is, Ni.

EMMILL, S. (Nottingham F, Everton) (25): 1995 v J, Ec, Fi; 1996 v n, D, US; 1997 v Est, Se, W, Ma, Blr; 1998 v D, Fin; 1999 v G, Fi; 301 v Sm; 2002 v Cro, Fr, Nig, Skor, SA, HK; 2003 v Can, Ei, A.

IBB, W. (Clydesdale) (1): 1873 v E.

IBSON, D. W. (Leicester City) (7): 1963 v A, N, Ei, Sp; 1964 v Ni; 365 v W, Fin.

IBSON, J. D. (Partick Th., Aston Villa) (8): 1926 v E; 1927 v E, W, ; 1928 v E, W; 1930 v W. Ni.

IBSON, N. (Rangers, Partick Th.) (14): 1895 v E, Ni; 1896 v E, Ni; 397 v E, Ni; 1898 v E; 1899 v E, W, Ni; 1900 v E, Ni; 1901 v W; 1905 Ni.

ILCHRIST, J. E. (Celtic) (1): 1922 v E.

ILHOOLEY, M. (Hull City) (1): 1922 v W.

ILLESPIE, G. (Rangers, Queen's Park) (7): 1880 v E, W; 1882 v E; 386 v W; 1890 v W; 1891 v Ni.

ILLESPIE, G. T. (Liverpool) (13): 1988 v Bel, Bul, Sp; 1989 v N, Fr, h; 1990 v Y, EG, Eg, Pol, Ma, Br; 1991 v Bul.

ILLESPIE, Jas. (Third Lanark) (1): 1898 v W.

ILLESPIE, John (Queen's Park) (1): 1896 v W.

ILLESPIE, R. (Queen's Park) (4): 1927 v W; 1931 v W; 1932 v Fr; 333 v E.

ILLICK, T. (Everton) (5): 1937 v A, Cz; 1939 v W, Ni, H.

ILMOUR, J. (Dundee) (1): 1931 v W.

ILZEAN, A. J. (Dundee, Tottenham H.) (22): 1964 v W, E, N, WG; 365 v Ni, Sp; 1966 v Ni, W, Pol, I; 1968 v W; 1969 v W, E, WG, Cy), A; 1970 v Ni, E, WG, A; 1971 v Por.

LAVIN, R. (Celtic) (1): 1977 v Se.

LASS S. (Aberdeen) (1): 1999 v Fi.

LEN, A. (Aberdeen) (2): 1956 v E, Ni.

LEN, R. (Renton, Hibernian) (3): 1895 v W; 1896 v W; 1900 v Ni.

ORAM, A. L. (Oldham, Hibs, Rangers) (42): 1986 v EG, R, Holl; 387 v Br; 1989 v Y, I; 1990 v EG, Pol, Ma; 1991 v R (2), Sw, Bul (2), SSR, Sm (2); 1992 v Sw, Fin, Holl, G, CIS; 1993 v Sw, Por (2), Ma; 1994 v Holl; 1995 v Fin, Fi, Ru, Gr; 1996 v Se, D, Holl, Sw, E; 397 A, La, Est; 1998 v D

ORDON, C. (Hearts) (1): 2004 v Trin.

GORDON, J. E. (Rangers) (10): 1912 v E, Ni; 1913 v E, Ni, W; 191
v E, Ni; 1920 v W, E, Ni, U.

GOSSLAND, J. (Rangers) (1): 1884 v Ni.

GOUDLE, J. (Abercorn) (1): 1884 v Ni.

GOUGH, C. R. (Dundee Utd, Tottenham H., Rangers) (61): 1983
Sw, Ni, W, E, Ca (3); 1984 v U, Bel, EG, Ni, W, E, Fr; 1985 v Sp,
Ice; 1986 v W, EG, Aus, Is, R, E, D, WG, U; 1987 v Bul, L, Ei (2), Be
E, Br; 1988 v H, S.Ar, Sp, Co, E; 1989 v Y, I, Cy (2), Fr; 1990 v F
Arg, EG, Pol, Ma, Cr; 1991 v USSR, Bul; 1992 v Sm, Ni, Ca, N, Ho
G, CIS; 1993 v Sw, Por.

GOULD, J. (Celtic) (2): 2000 v Lth; 2001 v Aus.

GOURLAY, J. (Cambuslang) (2): 1886 v Ni; 1888 v W.

GOVAN, J. (Hibernian) (6): 1948 v E, W, Bel, Sw, Fr; 1949 v Ni.

GOW, D. R. (Rangers) (1): 1888 v E.

GOW, J. J. (Queen's Park) (1): 1885 v E.

GOW, J. R. (Rangers) (1): 1888 v Ni.

GRAHAM, A. (Leeds Utd) (10): 1978 v EG; 1979 v A, N, W, Ni, I
Arg, N; 1980 v J; 1981 v W.

GRAHAM, G. (Arsenal, Manchester Utd) (13): 1972 v Por, Sw, Ho
Ni, Y, Cz, Br; 1973 v D (2), E, W, Ni, Br.

GRAHAM, J. (Annbank) (1): 1884 v Ni.

GRAHAM, J. A. (Arsenal) (1): 1921 v Ni.

GRANT, J. (Hibernian) (2): 1959 v W, Ni.

GRANT, P. (Celtic) (2): 1989 v E, Ch.

GRAY, A, (Hibernian) (1): 1903 v Ni.

GRAY, A. (Bradford) (2): 2003 v Lth, Nz.

GRAY, A. M. (Aston Villa, Wolverhampton W., Everton) (20): 1976
R, Sw; 1977 v Fin, Cz; 1979 v A, N; 1980 v Por, E; 1981 v Se, Po
Is, Ni; 1982 v Se, Ni; 1983 v Ni, W, E, Ca (2); 1985 v Ice.

GRAY, D. (Rangers) (10): 1929 v W, Ni, G, Holl; 1930 v W, E, Ni; 193
v W; 1933 v W, Ni.

GRAY, E. (Leeds Utd) (12): 1969 v E, Cy; 1970 v WG, A; 1971 v W
Ni; 1972 v Bel, Holl; 1976 v W, E; 1977 v Fin, W.

GRAY, F. T. (Leeds Utd, Nottingham F.) (32): 1976 v Sw; 1979 v N
Por, W, Ni, E, Arg; 1980 v Bel; 1981 v Se, Por, Is (2), Ni, (2), W, E
1982 v Se, Ni, Por, Sp, Holl, W, Nz, Br, USSR; 1983 v EG, Sw, (2
Bel, W, E, Ca.

GRAY, W. (Pollokshields Ath.) (1): 1886 v Ni.

GREEN, A. (Blackpool) (6): 1971 v Bel, Por, Ni, E; 1972 v W, E.

GREIG, J. (Rangers) (44): 1964 v E, WG; 1965 v W, Ni, E, Fin (2), Sp
Pol; 1966 v Ni, W, E, Pol, I (2), Por, Holl, Br; 1967 v W, Ni, E; 1968
Ni, W, Holl; 1969 v Ni, E, D, A, WG, Cy (2); 1970 v W, E, E
WG, A; 1971 v D, Bel, W, Ni, E; 1976 v D.

GROVES, W. (Hibernian, Celtic) (3): 1888 v W; 1889 Ni; 1890 v E.

GUILLILAND, W. (Queen's Park) (4): 1891 v W; 1892 v Ni; 1894
E; 1895 v E.

GUNN, B. (Norwich City) (6): 1990 v Eg; 1993 v Est (2); 1994 v Sw, Holl.

HADDOCK, H. (Clyde) (6): 1955 v E, H (2), Por, Y; 1958 v E.

HADDOW, D. (Rangers) (1): 1894 v E.

HAFFEY, F. (Celtic) (2): 1960 v E; 1961 v E.

HAMILTON, A. (Queen's Park) (4): 1885 v E, W; 1886 v E; 1888 v E.

HAMILTON, A. W. (Dundee) (24): 1962 v Cz, U, W, E; 1963 v W, Ni, A, N, Ei; 1964 v Ni, W, E, N, WG; 1965 v Ni, W, E, Fin (2), Pol, Sp; 1966 v Pol, Ni.

HAMILTON, G. (Aberdeen) (5): 1947 v Ni; 1951 v Bel, A; 1954 v N (2).

HAMILTON, G. (Port Glasgow Ath.) (1): 1906 v Ni.

HAMILTON, J. (Queen's Park) (3): 1892 v W; 1893 v E, Ni.

HAMILTON, J. (St Mirren) (1): 1924 v Ni.

HAMILTON, R. C. (Rangers, Dundee) (11): 1899 v E, W, Ni; 1900 v W; 1901 v E, Ni; 1902 v W, Ni; 1903 v E; 1904 v Ni; 1911 v W.

HAMILTON, T. (Hurlford) (1): 1891 v Ni.

HAMILTON, T. (Rangers) (1): 1932 v E.

HAMILTON, W. M. (Hibernian) (1): 1965 v Fin.

HANNAH, A. B., (Renton) (1): 1888 v W.

HANNAH, J. (Third Lanark) (1): 1889 v W.

HANSEN, A. D. (Liverpool) (26): 1979 v W, Arg; 1980 v Bel, Por; 1981 v Se, Por, Is; 1982 v Se, Ni (2), Por, Sp, W, E, Nz, Br, USSR; 1983 v EG, Sw (2), Bel; 1985 v W; 1986 v R; 1987 v Ei (2), L.

HANSEN, J. (Partick Th.) (2): 1972 v Bel, Y.

HARKNESS, J. D. (Queen's Park, Hearts) (12): 1927 v E, Ni; 1928 v E; 1929 v E, W, Ni; 1930 v E, W; 1932 v W, Fr; 1934 v Ni, W.

HARPER, J. M. (Aberdeen, Hibernian) (4): 1973 v D (2); 1976 v D; 1978 v Ir.

HARPER, W. (Hibernian, Arsenal) (11): 1923 v E, Ni, W; 1924 v E, Ni, W; 1925 v E, Ni, W; 1926 v E, Ni.

HARRIS, J. (Partick Th.) (2): 1921 v W, Ni.

HARRIS, N. (Newcastle Utd) (1): 1924 v E.

HARROWER, W. (Queen's Park) (3): 1882 v E; 1884 v Ni; 1886 v W.

HARTFORD, R. A. (WBA, Manchester City, Everton) (50): 1972 v Pe, V, E, Y, Cz, Br; 1976 v D, R, Ni; 1977 v Cz, W, (2), Se, Ni, E, Ch, Arg, Br; 1978 v EG, Cz, W (2), Bul, E, Pe, Ir, Holl; 1979 v A, N, Por, W, Ni, Arg, N; 1980 v Pe, Bel; 1981 v Ni (2), Is, W, E; 1982 v Se, Ni (2), Por, Sp, W, E, Br.

HARVEY, D. (Leeds Utd.) (16): 1973 v D; 1974 v Cz, WG, Ni, W, E, Bel, Z, Br, Y; 1975 v EG, Sp (2); 1976 v D (2); 1977 v Fin.

HASTINGS, A. C. (Sunderland) (2): 1936 v Ni; 1938 v Ni.

HAUGHNEY, M. (Celtic) (1): 1954 v E.

HAY, D. (Celtic) (27): 1970 v Ni, W, E; 1971 v D, Bel, W, Por, Ni; 1972 v Por, Bel, Holl; 1973 v W, Ni, E, Sw, Br; 1974 v Cz (2), WG, Ni, W, Bel, N, Z, Br.

HAY, J. (Celtic, Newcastle Utd) (11): 1905 v Ni; 1909 v Ni; 1910 W, Ni, E; 1911 v Ni, E; 1912 v E, W; 1914 v E, Ni.

HEGARTY, P. (Dundee Utd.) (8): 1979 v W, Ni, E, Arg, N; 1980 v W, E; 1983 v Ni.

HEGGIE, C. (Rangers) (1): 1886 v Ni.

HENDERSON, G. H. (Rangers) (1): 1904 v Ni.

HENDERSON, J. G. (Portsmouth, Arsenal) (7): 1953 v Se; 1954 Ni, E, N; 1956 v W; 1959 v W, Ni.

HENDERSON, W. (Rangers) (30): 1963 v W, Ni, E, A, N, Ei, Sp; 196- v W, Ni, E, N, WG; 1965 v Fin, Pol, E, Sp; 1966 v Ni, W, Pol, I, Hol 1967 v W, Ni; 1968 v Holl; 1969 v Ni, E, Cy; 1970 v Ei; 1971 v Por

HENDRY, C. (Blackburn R., Rangers, Bolton) (51): 1993 v Est (2) 1994 v Ma, Holl (2), A; 1995 v Fin, Fi, Gr, Ru, Sm; 1996 v Fin, Se Sm, Aus, D, US, U, Holl, E, Sw; 1997 v A (2), Se (2), Est (2); 1998 La D, Fin, Co, US, Br, N, M. 1999 v Lth, Est, Fi, G. 2000 v Bos (2), Est E (2), Fr; 2001 v La, Sm (2), Cro, Aus, Bel.

HEPBURN, J. (Alloa Ath.) (1) 1891 v W.

HEPBURN, R. (Ayr Utd) (1): 1932 v Ni.

HERD, A. C. (Hearts): (1): 1935 v Ni.

HERD, D. G. (Arsenal): (5): 1959 v E, W, Ni; 1961 v E, Cz.

HERD, G. (Clyde) (5): 1958 v E; 1960 v H, T; 1961 v W, Ni.

HERRIOT, J. (Birmingham City) (8): 1969 v Ni, E, D, Cy (2), W; 197 v Ei, WG.

HEWIE, J. D. (Charlton Ath.) (19): 1956 v E, A; 1957 v E, Ni, W, Y, Sp (2), Sw, WG; 1958 v H, Pol, Y, Fr; 1959 v Holl, Por; 1960 v Ni, W, Pol

HIGGINS, A. (Kilmarnock) (1): 1885 v Ni.

HIGGINS, A. (Newcastle Utd) (4): 1910 v E, Ni; 1911 v E, Ni.

HIGHET, T. C. (Queen's Park) (4): 1875 v E; 1876 v E, W; 1878 v E.

HILL, D. (Rangers) (3): 1881 v E, W; 1882 v W.

HILL, D. A. (Third Lanark) (1): 1906 v Ni.

HILL, F. R. (Aberdeen) (3): 1930 v Fr; 1931 v W, Ni.

HILL, J. (Hearts) (2): 1891 v E; 1892 v E.

HOGG, G. (Hearts) (2): 1896 v E, Ni.

HOGG, J. (Ayr Utd.) (1): 1922 v Ni.

HOGG, R. M. (Celtic) (1): 1937 v Cz.

HOLM, A. H. (Queen's Park) (3): 1882 v W; 1883 v E, W.

HOLT, D. D. (Hearts) (5): 1963 v A, N, Ei, Sp; 1964 v WG.

HOLT, G. (Kilmarnock, Norwich) (6): 2001 v La, Cro; 2002 v Fr; 2004 v W, Est, Trin.

HOLTON, J. A. (Manchester Utd.) (15): 1973 v W, Ni, E, Sw, Br; 1974 v Cz, WG, Ni, W, E, N, Z, Br, Y; 1975 v EG.

HOPE, R. (WBA) (2): 1968 v Holl; 1969 v D.

HOPKIN, D. (Crystal Palace, Leeds) (7): 1997 v Ma, Blr; 1998 v Blr La; 1999 v CzR. 2000 v Bos (2).

HOULISTON, W. (Queen of the South) (3): 1949 v E, Ni, Fr.

HOUSTON, S. M. (Manchester Utd.) (1): 1976 v D.

HOWDEN, W. (Partick Th.) (1): 1905 v Ni.

HOWE, R. (Hamilton Accies) (2): 1929 v N, Holl.

HOWIE, J. (Newcastle Utd.) (3): 1905 v E; 1906 v E; 1908 v E.

HOWIE, H. (Hibernian) (1): 1949 v W.

HOWIESON, J. (St Mirren) (1): 1927 v Ni.

HUGHES, J. (Celtic) (8): 1965 v Pol, Sp; 1966 v Ni, I (2); 1968 v E; 1969 v A; 1970 v Ei.

HUGHES, R. (Portsmouth) (2): 2004 v Est, Trin.

HUGHES, W. (Sunderland) (1): 1975 v Se.

HUMPHRIES, W. (Motherwell) (1): 1952 v Se.

HUNTER, A. (Kilmarnock, Celtic) (4): 1972 v Pe, Y; 1973 v E; 1974 v Cz.

HUNTER, J. (Dundee) (1): 1909 v W.

HUNTER, J. (Third Lanark, Eastern) (4): 1874 v E, 1875 v E, 1876 v E, 1877 v W.

HUNTER, R. (St Mirren) (1): 1890 v Ni.

HUNTER, W. (Motherwell) (3): 1960 v H, T; 1961 v W.

HUSBAND, J. (Partick Th.) (1): 1947 v W.

HUTCHISON, D. (Everton, Sunderland, West Ham) (26): 1999 v CzR, S; 2000 v Bos, Est, Lth, E (2), Fr, Holl, Ei; 2001 v La, Sm (2), Cro, Aus, el; 2002 v Cro, Bel, La; 2003 v Ei, A, Ice, Lth; 2004 v N, Lth, Holl.

HUTCHISON, T. (Coventry City) (17): 1974 v Cz (2), WG (2), Ni, W, el, N, Z, Y; 1975 v EG, Sp (2), Por, E, R; 1976 v D.

HUTTON, J. (Aberdeen, Blackburn R.) (10): 1923 v E, W, Ni; 1924 v i; 1926 v E, Ni; 1927 v Ni; 1928 v W, Ni.

HUTTON, J. (St Bernard's) (1): 1887 v Ni.

HYSLOP, T. (Stoke City, Rangers) (2): 1896 v E; 1897 v E.

IMLACH, J. J. S. (Nottingham F.) (4): 1958 v H, Pol, Y. Fr.

IMRIE, W. N. (St Johnstone) (2): 1929 v N, G.

INGLIS, J. (Kilmarnock Ath.) (1): 1884 v Ni.

INGLIS, J. (Rangers) (2): 1883 v E, W.

IRONS, J. H. (Queen's Park) (1): 1900 v W.

IRVINE, B. (Aberdeen) (9): 1991 v R; 1993 v G, Est (2); 1994 v Sw, Ma, A, Holl.

JACKSON, A. (Cambuslang) (2): 1886 v W, 1888 v Ni.

JACKSON, A. (Aberdeen, Huddersfield Town) (17): 1925 v E, W, Ni; 1926 v E, W, Ni; 1927 v W, Ni; 1928 v E, W; 1929 v E, W, Ni; 1930 v E, W, Ni, Fr.

JACKSON, C. (Rangers) (8): 1975 v Se, Por, W; 1976 v D, R, Ni, W, E.

JACKSON D. (Hibs, Celtic) (28): 1995 v Ru, Sm, J, Ec, Fi. 1996 v r, Fin, Se, Sm, Aus, D, US; 1997 v La, Se (2), Est, A, W, Ma, Blr; 998 v D, Fin, Co, US, Br, N. 1999 v Lth, Est.

JACKSON, J. (Partick Th., Chelsea) (8): 1931 v A, I, Sw; 1933 v E; 934 v E; 1935 v E; 1936 v W, Ni.

JACKSON, T. A. (St Mirren) (6): 1904 v W, E, Ni; 1905 v W; 1907 v V, Ni.

JAMES, A. (Preston NE, Arsenal) (8): 1926 v W; 1928 v E; 1929 v E, Ni; 1930 v E, W, Ni; 1933 v W.

JARDINE, A. (Rangers) (38): 1971 v D; 1972 v Por, Bel, Holl; 1973 v E, Sw, Br; 1974 v Cz (2), WG (2), Ni, W, E, Bel, N, Z, Br, Y; 1975 v EG, Sp (2), Se, Por, W, Ni, E; 1977 v Se, Ch, Br; 1978 v Cz, W, Ni, Ir; 1980 v Pe, A. Bel (2).

JARVIE, A. (Airdrie) (3): 1971 v Por, Ni, E.

JESS, E. (Aberdeen) (18): 1993 v I, Ma; 1994 v Sw, I, Holl (2), A; 1995 v Fin; 1996 v Se, Sm, US, U, E; 1998 v D; 1999 v CzR (2), G, Fi.

JENKINSON, T. (Hearts) (1): 1887 v Ni.

JOHNSTON, A. (Sunderland, Rangers, Middlesbrough) (18): 1999 v Est, Fi, CzR (2), G, Fi; 2000 v Est, Fr, Ei; 2001 v Sm (2), Cro; 2002 v Nig, Skor, SA, HK; 2003 v D, Fi.

JOHNSTON, L. H. (Clyde) (2): 1948 v Bel, Sw.

JOHNSTON, M. (Watford, Celtic, Nantes, Rangers) (38): 1984 v W, E, Fr; 1985 v Y, Ice, Sp (2); W; 1986 v EG; 1987 v Bul, Ei (2), L; 1988 v H, Bel, L. S.Ar, Sp, Co, E; 1989 v N, Y, I, Cy (2), Fr, E, Ch; 1990 v Fr, N, EG, Pol, Ma, Cr, Se, Br; 1992 v Sw, Sm.

JOHNSTON, R. (Sunderland) (1): 1938 v Cz.

JOHNSTON, W. (Rangers, WBA) (22): 1966 v W, E, Pol, Holl; 1968 v W, E; 1969 v Ni; 1970 v Ni; 1971 v D; 1977 v Se, W, Ni, E, Ch, Arg, Br; 1978 v EG, Cz, W (2), E, Pe.

JOHNSTONE, D. (Rangers) (14): 1973 v W, Ni, E, Sw, Br; 1975 v EG, Se; 1976 v Sw, Ni, E; 1978 v Bul, Ni, W; 1980 v Bel.

JOHNSTONE, J. (Abercorn) (1): 1888 v W.

JOHNSTONE, J. (Celtic) (23): 1965 v W, Fin; 1966 v E; 1967 v W, USSR; 1968 v W; 1969 v A, WG; 1970 v E, WG; 1971 v D, E; 1972 v Por, Bel, Holl, Ni, E; 1974 v W, E, Bel, N; 1975 v EG, Sp.

JOHNSTONE, JAS. (Kilmarnock) (1): 1894 v W.

JOHNSTONE, J. A. (Hearts) (3): 1930 v W; 1933 v W, Ni.

JOHNSTONE, R. (Hibernian, Manchester City) (17): 1951 v E, D, Fr; 1952 v Ni, E; 1953 v E, Se; 1954 v W, E, N, Fin; 1955 v Ni, H, E; 1956 v E, Ni, W.

JOHNSTONE, W. (Third Lanark) (3): 1887 v Ni; 1889 v W; 1890 v E.

JORDAN, J. (Leeds Utd, Manchester Utd, AC Milan) (52): 1973 v E, Sw, Br; 1974 v Cz (2), WG, Ni, W, E, Bel, N, Z, Br, Y; 1975 v EG, Sp (2); 1976 v Ni, W, E; 1977 v Cz, W, Ni, E; 1978 v EG, Cz, W, Bul, Ni, E, Pe, Ir, Holl; 1979 v A, Por, W, Ni, E, N; 1980 v Bel, Ni, W, E, Pol; 1981 v Is, W, E; 1982 v Se, Holl, W, E, USSR.

KAY, J. L. (Queen's Park) (6): 1880 v E; 1882 v E, W; 1883 v E, W; 1884 v W.

KEILLOR, A. (Montrose, Dundee) (6): 1891 v W; 1892 v Ni; 1894 v Ni; 1895 v W; 1896 v W; 1897 v W.

KEIR, L. (Dumbarton) (5): 1885 v W; 1886 v Ni; 1887 v E, W; 1888 v E.

KELLY, H. T. (Blackpool) (1): 1952 v USA.

KELLY, J. (Renton, Celtic) (8): 1888 v E; 1889 v E; 1890 v E; 1892 v E; 1893 v E; 1894 v W; 1896 v Ni.

KELLY, J. C. (Barnsley) (2): 1949 v W, Ni.

KELSO, R. (Renton, Dundee) (8): 1885 v W, Ni; 1886 v W; 1887 v E, W; 1888 v E, Ni; 1898 v Ni.

KELSO, T. (Dundee) (1): 1914 v W.

KENNAWAY, J. (Celtic) (1): 1909 v A.

KENNEDY, A. (Eastern, Third Lanark) (6): 1875 v E; 1876 v E, W; 1878 v E; 1882 v W; 1884 v W.

KENNEDY, J. (Celtic) (6): 1964 v W, Fr, WG; 1965 v W, Ni, Fin.

KENNEDY, J. (Celtic) (1): 2004 v R.

KENNEDY, J. (Hibernian) (1): 1897 v W.

KENNEDY, S. (Aberdeen) (8): 1978 v Bul, W, E, Pe, Holl; 1979 v A, Por; 1982 v Por.

KENNEDY, S, (Partick Th.) (1): 1905 v W.

KENNEDY, S. (Rangers) (5): 1975 v Se, Por, W, Ni, E.

KER, G. (Queen's Park) (5): 1880 v E; 1881 v E, W; 1882 v W, E.

KER, W. (Granville, Queen's Park) (2): 1872 v E; 1873 v E.

KERR, A. (Partick Th.) (2): 1955 v A, H.

KERR, B. (Newcastle Utd, Coventry) (3): 2003 v Nz; 2004 v Est; 2004: v Trin.

KERR, P. (Hibernian) (1): 1924 v Ni.

KEY, G. (Hearts) (1): 1902 v Ni.

KEY, W. (Queen's Park) (1): 1907 v Ni.

KING, A. (Hearts, Celtic) (6): 1896 v E, W; 1897 v Ni; 1898 v Ni; 1899 v Ni, W.

KING, J. (Hamilton Accies) (2): 1933 v Ni; 1934 v Ni.

KING, W. S. (Queen's Park) (1): 1929 v W.

KINLOCH, J. D. (Partick Th.) (1): 1922 v Ni.

KINNAIRD, A. F. (Wanderers) (1): 1873 v E.

KINNEAR, D. (Rangers) (1): 1938 v Cz.

KYLE, K. (Sunderland) (9): 2002 v Skor, SA, HK; 2003 v D, Fi, Can, Por, Nz; 2004 v D.

LAMBERT, P. (Motherwell, Borussia Dortmund, Celtic) (40): 1995 v, Ec; 1997 v La, Se (2), A, Blr; 1998 v Blr, La, Fin, Co, US, Br, N, M. 1999 v Lth, CzR (2), G, Fi; 2000 v Bos, Lth, Holl, Ei; 2001 v Bel, Sm; 2002 v Cro, Bel, Fr, Nig; 2003 v D, Fi, Ice (2), Por, Ei, Lth, G; 2004 v N, G.

LAMBIE, J. A. (Queen's Park) (3): 1886 v Ni; 1887 v Ni; 1888 v E.

LAMBIE, W. A. (Queen's Park) (9): 1892 v Ni; 1893 v W; 1894 v E; 1895 v E, Ni; 1896 v E, Ni; 1897 v E, Ni.

LAMONT, D. (Pilgrims): 1885 v Ni.

LANG, A. (Dumbarton) (1): 1880 v W.

LANG, J. J. (Clydesdale, Third Lanark) (2): 1876 v W; 1878 v W.

LATTA, A. (Dumbarton) (2): 1888 v W; 1889 v E.

LAW, D. (Huddersfield Town, Manchester Utd, Torino, Manchester City) (55): 1959 v W, Ni, Holl, Por; 1960 v Ni, W; 1960 v E, Pol, A; 1961 v Ni; 1962 v Cz (2), E; 1963 v W, Ni, E, A, N, Ei, Sp; 1964 v W, E, N, WG; 1965 v W, Ni, E, Fin (2), Pol, Sp; 1966 v Ni, E, Pol; 1967 v W, E, USSR; 1968 v Ni; 1969 v Ni, A, WG; 1972 v Pe, Ni, W, E, Y, Cz, Br; 1974 v Cz (2), WG (2), Ni, Z.

LAW, G. (Rangers) (3): 1910 v E, Ni, W.

LAW, T. (Chelsea) (2): 1928 v E, 1930 v E.

LAWRENCE, J. (Newcastle Utd.) (1): 1911 v E.

LAWRENCE, T. (Liverpool) (3): 1963 v Ei; 1969 v W, WG.

LAWSON, D. (St Mirren) (1): 1923 v E.

LECKIE, R. (Queen's Park) (1): 1872 v E.

LEGGAT, G. (Aberdeen, Fulham) (18): 1956 v E; 1957 v W; 1958 v Ni, H, Pol, Y, Par; 1959 v E, W, Ni, WG, Holl; 1960 v E, Ni, W, Pol, A, H.

LEIGHTON, J. (Aberdeen, Manchester Utd, Hibernian, Aberdeen) (91): 1983 v EG, Sw (2), Bel, W, E, Ca (2); 1984 v U, Bel, W, E, Fr; 1985 v Y, Ice, Sp (2), W, E, Ice; 1986 v W, EG, Aus (2), Is, D, WG, U; 1987 v Bul, Ei (2), L, Bel, E; 1988 v H, Bel, Bul, L, S.Ar, Ma, Sp, Co, E; 1989 v N, Cy (2), Fr, E, Ch; 1990 v Y, Fr, N, Arg, Ma, Cr, Se, Br; 1994 v Ma, A, Holl; 1995 v Gr, Ru, Sm, J, Ec, Fi. 1996 v Gr, Fin, Se, Sm, Aus, D, US;1997 v Se (2), Est, A, W, Ma, Blr.1998 v Blr, La, D, Fin, US, Br, N, M. 1999 v Lth, Est.

LENNIE, W. (Aberdeen) (2): 1908 v W, Ni.

LENNOX, R. (Celtic) (10): 1967 v Ni, E, USSR; 1968 v W, L; 1969 v D, A. WG, Cy; 1970 v W.

LESLIE, L. G. (Airdrie) (5): 1961 v W, Ni, Ei (2), Cz.

LEVEIN, C. (Hearts) (16): 1990 v Arg, EG, Eg, Pol, Ma, Se; 1991 R, Sm; 1993 v Por (2), G; 1994 v Sw, Holl; 1995 v Fin, Fi, Ru.

LIDDELL, W. (Liverpool) (28): 1947 v W, Ni; 1948 v E, W, Ni; 1950 v E, W, Por, Fr; 1951 v W, Ni, E, A; 1952 v W, Ni, E, USA, D, Se; 1953 v W, Ni, E; 1954 v W; 1955 v Por, Y, A, H; 1956 v Ni.

LIDDLE, D. (East Fife) (3): 1931 v A, I, Sw.

LINDSAY, D. (St Mirren) (1): 1903 v Ni.

LINDSAY, J. (Dumbarton) (8): 1880 v W; 1881 v W, E; 1884 v W, E; 1885 v W, E; 1886 v E.

LINDSAY, J. (Renton) (3): 1888 v E; 1893 v E, Ni.

LINWOOD, A. B. (Clyde) (1): 1950 v W.

LITTLE, R. J. (Rangers) (1): 1953 v Se.

LIVINGSTONE, G. T. (Man City, Rangers) (2): 1906 v E; 1907 v W.

LOCHHEAD, A. (Third Lanark) (1): 1889 v W.

LOGAN, J. (Ayr Utd) (1): 1891 v W.

LOGAN, T. (Falkirk) (1): 1913 v Ni.

LOGIE, J. T. (Arsenal) (1): 1953 v Ni.

LONEY, W. (Celtic) (2): 1910 v W, Ni.

LONG, H. (Clyde) (1): 1947 v Ni.

LONGAIR, W. (Dundee) (1): 1894 v Ni.

LORIMER, P. (Leeds Utd) (21): 1970 v A; 1971 v W, Ni; 1972 v Ni, W, E; 1973 v D (2), E (2); 1974 v WG, E, Bel, N, Z, Br, Y; 1975 v Sp; 1976 v D (2), R.

LOVE, A. (Aberdeen) (3): 1931 v A, I, Sw.

_OW, A. (Falkirk) (1): 1934 v Ni.
_OW, T. P. (Rangers) (1): 1897 v Ni.
_OW, W. L. (Newcastle U) (5): 1911 v E, W; 1912 v Ni; 1920 v E, Ni.
_OWE, J. (Cambuslang) (1): 1891 v Ni.
_OWE, J. (St Bernard's) (1): 1887 v Ni.
_UNDIE, J. (Hibernian) (1): 1886 v W.
_YALL, J. (Sheffield W.) (1): 1905 v E.

McADAM, J. (Third Lanark) (1): 1880 v W.
McALLISTER, B. (Wimbledon) (3): 1997 v W, Ma, Blr.
McALLISTER, G. (Leicester City, Leeds Utd, Coventry) (57): 1990 v EG, Pol, Ma; 1991 v R, Sw (2), Bul, USSR, Sm, (2); 1992 v Ni, Fin, US, Ca, N, Holl, G, CIS; 1993 v Sw, Por, I, Ma; 1994 v Sw, I, Ma, Holl (2), A; 1995 v Fin, Ru (2), Gr, Sm. 1996 v Gr, Fin, Se, Sm, Aus, _, US, U, Holl, E, Sw; 1997 v A (2), La, Est (2), Se, W, Ma, Blr; 1998 v Blr, La, Fr; 1999 v CzR.
McALLISTER, J. (Livingston) (1): 2004 v Trin.
McARTHUR, D. (Celtic) (3): 1895 v E, Ni; 1899 v W.
McATEE, A. (Celtic) (1): 1913 v W.
McAULAY, J. (Dumbarton, Arthurlie) (2): 1882 v W; 1884 v Ni.
McAULAY, J. (Dumbarton) (8): 1883 v E, W; 1884 v E; 1885 v E, W; 1886 v E; 1887 v E, W.
McAULEY, R. (Rangers) (2): 1932 v Ni, W.
McAVENNIE, F. (West Ham Utd., Celtic) (5): 1986 v Aus (2), D, WG; _988 v S.Ar.
McBAIN, E. (St Mirren) (1): 1894 v W.
McBAIN, N. (Manchester Utd., Everton) (3): 1922 v E; 1923 v Ni; _924 v W.
McBRIDE, J. (Celtic) (2): 1967 v Ni.
McBRIDE, P. (Preston NE) (6): 1904 v E; 1906 v E; 1907 v E, W; 1908 _ E; 1909 v W.
McCALL, J. (Renton) (5): 1886 v W; 1887 v E, W; 1888 v E; 1890 v _.
McCALL, S. M. (Everton, Rangers) (40) 1990 v Arg, EG, Eg, Pol, Ma, _r, Se, Br; 1991 v Sw, USSR, Sm (2); 1992 v Sw, R, US, Ca, N, Holl, _, CIS; 1993 v Sw, Por (2); 1994 v I, Holl (2), A; 1995 v Fin, Ru, Gr; _996 v Gr, D, US, U, Holl, E, Sw; 1997 v A, La;. 1998 v D.
McCALLIOG, J. (Sheffield W., Wolverhampton W.) (5): 1967 v E, _SSR; 1968 v Ni; 1969 v D; 1971 v Por.
McCALLUM, N. (Renton) (1): 1888 v Ni.
McCANN, R. J. (Motherwell) (5): 1959 v WG; 1960 v E, Ni, W; 1961 _ E.
McCANN, N. (Hearts, Rangers, Southampton) (21): 1999 v Lth, _zR. 2000 v Bos; Est, E, Fr, Holl, Ei; 2001 v La, Sm, Aus; 2002 v _ro, Fr, Nig; 2003 v Ei; 2004 v Fi, G, Holl (2), R, D.
McCARTNEY, W. (Hibernian) (1): 1902 v Ni.
McCLAIR, B. (Celtic, Manchester Utd) (30): 1987 v L, Ei, E, Br; 1988

v Bul, Ma, Sp; 1989 v N, Y, I, Cy, Fr; 1990 v N, Arg; 1991 v Bul (2), Sm; 1992 v Sw, R, Ni, US, Ca, N, Holl, G, CIS; 1993 v Sw, Por, Est (2)

McCLORY, A. (Motherwell) (3): 1927 v W; 1928 v Ni; 1935 v W.

McCLOY, P. (Ayr Utd) (2): 1924 v E; 1925 v E.

McCLOY, P. (Rangers) (4): 1973 v W, Ni, Sw, Br.

McCOIST, A. (Rangers, Kilmarnock) (61): 1986 v Holl; 1987 v L, Ei Bel, E, Br; 1988 v H, Bel, Ma, Sp, Co, E; 1989 v Y, Fr, Cy, E; 1990 v Y, Fr, N, EG, Eg, Pol, Ma, Cr, Se, Br; 1991 v R, Sw, Bul (2), USSR 1992 v Sw, Sm, Ni, Fin, US, Ca, N, Holl, G, CIS; 1993 v Sw, Por (2) I, Ma. 1996 v Gr, Fin, Sm, Aus, D, U, E, Sw; 1997 v A (2), Se, Est 1998 v Blr. 1999 v Lth, Est.

McCOLL, A. (Renton) (1): 1888 v Ni.

McCOLL, I. M. (Rangers) (14): 1950 v E, Fr; 1951 v W, Ni, Bel; 1957 v E, Ni, W, Y, Sp, Sw, WG; 1958 v Ni, E.

McCOLL, R. S. (Queen's Park, Newcastle Utd.) (13): 1896 v W, Ni 1897 v Ni; 1898 v Ni; 1899 v Ni; E, W; 1900 v E, W; 1901 v E, W 1902 v E; 1908 v Ni.

McCOLL, W. (Renton) (1): 1895 v W.

McCOMBIE, A. (Sunderland, Newcastle Utd.) (4): 1903 v E, W; 1905 v E, W.

McCORKINDALE, J. (Partick Th.) (1): 1891 v W.

McCORMICK, R. (Abercorn) (1): 1886 v W.

McCRAE, D. (St Mirren) (2): 1929 v N, G.

McCREADIE, A. (Rangers) (2): 1893 v W; 1894 v E.

McCREADIE, E. G. (Chelsea) (23): 1965 v E, Sp, Fin, Pol; 1966 v Por, Ni, W, Pol, I; 1967 v E, USSR; 1968 v Ni, W, E, Holl; 1969 v W Ni, E, D, A, W, Cy (2).

McCULLOCH, D. (Hearts, Brentford, Derby Co.) (7): 1935 v W; 1936 v E; 1937 v W, Ni; 1938 v Cz; 1939 v H, W.

MacDONALD, A. (Rangers) (1): 1976 v Sw.

McDONALD, J. (Edinburgh University) (1): 1886 v E.

McDONALD, J. (Sunderland) (2): 1956 v W, Ni.

MacDOUGALL, E. J. (Norwich City) (7): 1975 v Se, Por, W, Ni, E 1976 v D, R.

McDOUGALL, J. (Liverpool) (2): 1931 v I, A.

McDOUGALL, J. (Airdrie) (1): 1926 v Ni.

McDOUGALL, J. (Vale of Leven) (5): 1877 v E, W; 1878 v E; 1879 v E, W.

McFADDEN, J. (Motherwell, Everton) (14): 2002 v SA; 2003 v Can A, Nz; 2004 v Fi, G, Lth, Holl (2), W, R, D, Est, Trin.

McFADYEN, W. (Motherwell) (2): 1934 v A, W.

MACFARLANE, A. (Dundee) (5): 1904 v W; 1906 v W; 1908 v W 1909 v Ni; 1911 v W.

McFARLANE, R. (Morton) (1): 1896 v W.

MACFARLANE, W. (Hearts) (1): 1947 v L.

McGARR, E. (Aberdeen) (2): 1970 v Ei, A.

McGARVEY, F. (Liverpool, Celtic) (7): 1979 v Ni, Arg; 1984 v U, Bel, EG, Ni, W.

McGEOCH, A. (Dumbreck) (4): 1876 v E, W; 1877 v E, W.

McGHEE, J. (Hibernian) (1): 1886 v N.

McGHEE, M. (Aberdeen) (4): 1983 v Ca (2); 1984 v Ni, E.

McGINLAY, J. (Bolton W.) (13): 1994 v A, Holl; 1995 v Fi (2), Ru (2), Gr, Sm; 1996 v Se; 1997 v Se, Est (2), A.

McGONAGLE, W. (Celtic) (6): 1933 v E; 1934 v A, E, Ni; 1935 v Ni, W.

McGRAIN, D. (Celtic) (62): 1973 v W, Ni, E, Sw, Br; 1974 v Cz (2), WG, W, E, Bel, N, Z, Br, Y; 1975 v Sp, Se, Por, W, Ni, E, R; 1976 v D (2), Sw, Ni, W, E; 1977 v Fin, Cz, W (2), Se, Ni, E, Ch, Arg, Br; 1978 v EG, Cz; 1980 v Bel, Por, Ni, W, E, Pol, H; 1981 v Se, Por, Is, (2), Ni (2), W, E; 1982 v Se, Sp, Holl, Ni, E, Nz, USSR.

McGREGOR, J. C. (Vale of Leven) (4): 1877 v E, W; 1878 v E; 1880 v E.

McGRORY, J. E. (Kilmarnock) (3): 1965 v Ni, Fin; 1966 v Por.

McGRORY, J. (Celtic) (7): 1928 v Ni; 1931 v E; 1932 v Ni, W; 1933 v E, Ni; 1934 v Ni.

McGUIRE, W. (Beith) (2): 1881 v E, W.

McGURK, F. (Birmingham City) (1): 1934 v W.

McHARDY, H. (Rangers) (1): 1885 v N.

McINALLY, A. (Aston Villa, Bayern Munich) (8): 1989 v Cy, Ch; 1990 v Y, Fr, Arg, Pol, Ma, Cr.

McINALLY, J. (Dundee Utd) (10): 1987 v Bel, Br; 1988 v Ma; 1991 v Bul (2); 1992 v US, N, CIS; 1993 v G, Por.

McINALLY, T. B. (Celtic) (2): 1926 v Ni; 1927 v W.

McINNES, D. (WBA) (2): 2003 v D, Por.

McINNES, T. (Cowlairs) (1): 1889 v Ni.

McINTOSH, W. (Third Lanark) (1): 1905 v Ni.

McINTYRE, A. (Vale of Leven) (2): 1878 v E; 1882 v E.

McINTYRE, H. (Rangers) (1): 1880 v W.

McINTYRE, J. (Rangers) (1): 1884 v W.

McKAY, D. (Celtic) (14): 1959 v E, WG, Holl, Por; 1960 v E, Pol, A, H, T; 1961 v W, Ni; 1962 v Ni, Cz, U.

McKAY, J. (Blackburn R.) (1): 1924 v W.

McKAY, R. (Newcastle Utd.) (1): 1928 v W.

McKEAN, R. (Rangers) (1): 1976 v Sw.

McKENZIE, D. (Brentford) (1): 1938 v Ni.

MACKENZIE, J. A. (Partick Th.) (9): 1954 v W, E, N, Fin, A, U; 1955 v E, H; 1956 v A.

McKEOWN, M. (Celtic) (2): 1889 v Ni; 1890 v E.

McKIE, J. (East Stirling) (1): 1898 v W.

McKILLOP, T. R. (Rangers) (1): 1938 v Holl.

McKIMMIE, S. (Aberdeen) (40): 1989 v E, Ch; 1990 v Arg, Eg, Cr, Br; 1991 v R (2), Sw, Bul, Sm; 1992 v Sw, Ni, Fin, US, Ca, N, Holl, G, CIS. 1993 v Por, Est; 1994 v Sw, I, Holl (2), A; 1995 v Fin, Fi (2), Ru (2), Gr. 1996 v Gr, Fin, Se, D, U, Holl, E.

McKINLAY, D. (Liverpool) (2): 1922 v W, Ni.

McKINLAY, T. (Celtic) (22): 1996 v Gr, Fin, D, U, E, Sw; 1997 v A (2), La, Se (2), Est (2), W, Ma, Blr; 1998 v Blr, La, Fr, US, Br, M.

McKINLAY, W. (Dundee Utd, Blackburn R.) (29): 1994 v Ma, Holl (2), A; 1995 v Fi (2), Ru (2), Gr, Sm, J, Ec; 1996 v Fin, Se, Sm, Aus, D, Holl; 1997 v Se, Est; 1998 v La, Fr, D, Fin, Co, US, Br. 1999 v Est, Fi.

McKINNON, A. (Queen's Park) (1): 1874 v E.

McKINNON, R. (Rangers) (28): 1966 v W, E, I (2), Holl, Br; 1967 v W, Ni, E; 1968 v Ni, W, E, Holl; 1969 v D, A, WG, Cy; 1970 v Ni, W, E, Ei, WG, A; 1971 v D, Bel, Por, USSR, D.

McKINNON, R. (Motherwell) (3): 1994 v Ma; 1995 v J, Fi.

MACKINNON, W. (Dumbarton) (4): 1883 v E, W; 1884 v E, W.

McKINNON, W. W. (Queen's Park) (9): 1872 v E; 1873 v E; 1874 v E; 1875 v E; 1876 v E, W; 1877 v E; 1878 v E; 1879 v E.

McLAREN, A. (St Johnstone) (5): 1929 v N, G, Holl; 1933 v W, Ni.

McLAREN, A. (Preston NE) (4): 1947 v E, Bel, L; 1948 v W.

McLAREN, A. (Hearts, Rangers) (24): 1992 v US, Ca, N; 1993 v I, Ma, G, Est (2); 1994 v I, Ma, Holl, A; 1995 v Fin, Fi (2), Ru (2), Gr, Sm, J, Ec; 1996 v Fin, Se, Sm.

McLAREN, A. (Kilmarnock) (1): 2001 v Pol.

McLAREN, J. (Hibernian, Celtic) (3): 1888 v W; 1889 v E; 1890 v E.

McLEAN, A. (Celtic) (4): 1926 v W, Ni; 1927 v W, E.

McLEAN, D. (St Bernard's) (2): 1896 v W; 1897 v Ni.

McLEAN, D. (Sheffield W.) (1): 1912 v E.

McLEAN, G. (Dundee) (1): 1968 v Holl.

McLEAN, T. (Kilmarnock) (6): 1969 v D, Cy, W; 1970 v Ni, W; 1971 v D.

McLEISH, A. (Aberdeen) (77): 1980 v Por, Ni, W, E, Pol, H; 1981 v Se, Is (2), Ni (2), E; 1982 v Se, Sp, Ni, Br; 1983 v Bel, Sw, W, E, Ca (3); 1984 v U, Bel, EG, Ni, W, E, Fr; 1985 v Y, Ice, (2), Sp (2), W, E; 1986 v W, EG, Aus (2), E, Holl, D; 1987 v Bel, E, Br; 1988 v Bel, Bul, L, S.Ar, Ma, Sp, Co, E; 1989 v N, Y, I, Cy (2), Fr, E, Ch; 1990 v Y, Fr, N, Arg, EG, Eg, Cr, Se, Br; 1991 v R, Sw, USSR, Bul; 1993 v Ma.

McLEOD, D. (Celtic) (4): 1905 v Ni; 1906 v E, W, Ni.

McLEOD, J. (Dumbarton) (5): 1888 v Ni; 1889 v W; 1890 v Ni; 1892 v E; 1893 v W.

MacLEOD, J. M. (Hibernian) (4): 1961 v E, Ei (2), Cz.

MACLEOD, M. (Celtic, Borussia Dort., Hibernian) (20): 1985 v E; 1987 v Ei, L, E, Br; 1988 v Co, E; 1989 v I, Ch; 1990 v Y, Fr, N, Arg, EG, Pol, Se, Br; 1991 v R, Sw, USSR.

McLEOD, W. (Cowlairs) (1): 1886 v Ni.

McLINTOCK, A. (Vale of Leven) (3): 1875 v E; 1876 v E; 1880 v E.

McLINTOCK, F. (Leicester City, Arsenal) (9): 1963 v N, Ei, Sp; 1965 v Ni; 1967 v USSR; 1970 v Ni; 1971 v W, Ni, E.

McLUCKIE, J. S. (Manchester City) (1): 1934 v W.

McMAHON, A. (Celtic) (6): 1892 v E; 1893 v E, Ni; 1894 v E; 1901 v Ni. 1902 v W.

McMENEMY, J. (Celtic) (12): 1905 v Ni; 1909 v Ni; 1910 v E, W; 1911 v Ni, W, E; 1912 v W; 1914 v W, Ni, E; 1920 v Ni.

McMENEMY, J. (Motherwell) (1): 1934 v W.

McMILLAN, J. (St Bernard's) (1): 1897 v W.

McMILLAN, I. L. (Airdrie, Rangers) (6): 1952 v E, USA, D; 1955 v E; 1956 v E; 1961 v Cz.

McMILLAN, T. (Dumbarton) (1): 1887 v Ni.

McMULLAN, J. (Partick Th., Manchester City) (16): 1920 v W; 1921 v W, Ni, E; 1924 v E, Ni; 1925 v E; 1926 v W, E; 1927 v E, W; 1928 v E, W; 1929 v W, E, Ni.

McNAB, A. (Morton) (2): 1921 v E, Ni.

McNAB, A. (Sunderland, WBA) (2): 1937 v A; 1939 v E.

McNAB, C. D. (Dundee) (6): 1931 v E, W, A, I, Sw; 1932 v E.

McNAB, J. S. (Liverpool) (1): 1923 v W.

McNAIR, A. (Celtic) (15): 1906 v W; 1907 v Ni; 1908 v E, W; 1909 v E; 1910 v W; 1912 v E, W, Ni; 1913 v E; 1914 v E, Ni; 1920 v E, W, Ni.

McNAMARA J. (Celtic) (25): 1997 v La, Se, Est, W; 1998 v D, Co, US, N, M; 2000 v Holl; 2001 v Sm; 2002 v Bel, Fr; 2003 v Ice (2), Lth, Nz, G; 2004 v Fi, G, Lth, Holl (2), W, Trin.

McNAMEE, D. (Livingston) (2): 2004 v Est, Trin.

J. McNAUGHT, W. (Raith R.) (5): 1951 v A, W, Ni; 1952 v E; 1955 v Ni.

McNAUGHTON, K. (Aberdeen) (2): 2002 v Nig; 2003 v D.

McNEIL, H. (Queen's Park) (10): 1874 v E; 1875 v E; 1876 v E, W; 1877 v W; 1878 v E; 1879 v E, W; 1881 v E, W.

McNEIL, M. (Rangers) (2): 1876 v W; 1880 v E.

McNEILL, W. (Celtic) (29): 1961 v E, Ei (2), Cz; 1962 v Ni, E, Cz, U; 1963 v Ei, Sp; 1964 v W, E, WG;`1965 v E, Fin, Pol, Sp; 1966 v Ni, Pol; 1967 v USSR; 1968 v E; 1969 v Cy (2), W, E; 1970 v WG; 1972 v Ni, W, E.

McPHAIL, J. (Celtic) (5): 1950 v W; 1951 v W, Ni, A; 1954 v Ni.

McPHAIL, R. (Airdrie, Rangers) (17): 1927 v E; 1929 v W; 1931 v E, Ni; 1932 v W, Ni, Fr; 1933 v E, Ni; 1934 v A, Ni; 1935 v E; 1937 v G, E, Cz; 1938 v W, Ni.

McPHERSON, D. (Kilmarnock) (1): 1892 v Ni.

McPHERSON, D. (Hearts, Rangers) (27): 1989 v Cy, E; 1990 v N, Ma, Cr, Se, Br; 1991 v Sw, Bul (2), USSR, Sm (2); 1992 v Sw, R, Ni, Fin, US, Ca, N, Holl, G, CIS; 1993 v Sw, I, Ma, Por.

McPHERSON, J. (Clydesdale) (1): 1875 v W.

McPHERSON, J. (Vale of Leven) (8): 1879 v E, W; 1880 v E; 1881 v W; 1883 v E, W; 1884 v E; 1885 v Ni.

McPHERSON, J. (Kilmarnock, Cowlairs, Rangers) (9): 1888 v W; 1889 v E; 1890 v W; 1892 v W; 1894 v E; 1895 v E, Ni; 1897 Ni.

McPHERSON, J. (Hearts) (1): 1891 v E.

McPHERSON, R. (Arthurlie) (1): 1882 v E.

McQUEEN, G. (Leeds Utd., Manchester Utd.) (30): 1974 v Bel; 1975 v Sp (2), Por, W, Ni, E, R; 1976 v D; 1977 v Cz, W (2), Ni, E; 1978 v

EG, Cz, W, Bul, Ni, W; 1979 v A, N, Por, Ni, E, N; 1980 v Pe, A, Bel; 1981 v W.

McQUEEN, M. (Leith Ath.) (2): 1890 v W; 1891 v W.

McRORIE, D. M. (Morton) (1): 1931 v W.

McSPADYEN, A. (Partick Th.) (2): 1939 v E, H.

McSTAY, P. (Celtic) (76): 1984 v U, Bel, EG, Ni, W, E; 1985 v Ice, Sp (2), W; 1986 v EG, Aus, Is, U, Y; 1987 v Bul, Ei (2), L, Bel, E, Br; 1988 v H, Bel, Bul, L, S.Ar, Sp, Co, E; 1989 v N, Y, I, Cy (2), Fr, E, Ch; 1990 v Y, Fr, N, Arg, EG, Eg, Pol, Ma, Cr, Se, Br; 1991 v R, USSR, Bul; 1992 v Sm, Fin, US, Ca, N, Holl, G, CIS; 1993 v Sw, Por (2), I, Ma, Est (2); 1994 v I, Holl; 1995 v Fin, Fi, Ru; 1996 v Aus, 1997 v Est (2), A.

McSTAY, W. (Celtic) (13): 1921 v W, Ni; 1925 v E, Ni, W; 1926 v E, Ni, W; 1927 v E, Ni, W; 1928 v W, Ni.

McSWEGAN, G. (Hearts) (2): 2000 v Bos, Lth.

McTAVISH, J. (Falkirk) (1): 1910 v Ni.

McWHATTIE, G. C. (Queen's Park) (2): 1901 v W, Ni.

McWILLIAM, P. (Newcastle Utd.) (8): 1905 v E; 1906 v E; 1907 v E, W; 1909 v E, W; 1910 v E; 1911 v W.

MACARI, L. (Celtic, Manchester Utd.) (24): 1972 v W, E, Y, Cz, Br; 1973 v D, E (2), W, Ni; 1975 v Se, Por, W, E, R; 1977 v Ni, E, Ch, Arg; 1978 v EG, W, Bul, Pe, Ir.

MACAULEY, A. R. (Brentford, Arsenal) (7): 1947 v E; 1948 v E, W, Ni, Bel, Sw, Fr.

MACKAY, D. C. (Hearts, Tottenham H.) (22): 1957 v Sp; 1958 v Fr; 1959 v W, Ni, WG, E; 1960 v W, Ni, A, Pol, H, T; 1961 v W, Ni, E; 1963 v E, A, N; 1964 v Ni, W, N; 1966 v Ni.

MACKAY, G. (Hearts) (4): 1988 v Bul, L, S.Ar, Ma.

MACKAY, M. (Norwich) (3): 2004 v D, Est, Trin.

MADDEN, J. (Celtic) (2): 1893 v W; 1895 v W.

MAIN, F. R. (Rangers) (1): 1938 v W.

MAIN, J. (Hibernian) (1): 1909 v Ni.

MALEY, W. (Celtic) (2): 1893 v E, Ni.

MALPAS, M. (Dundee Utd.) (55): 1984 v Fr; 1985 v E, Ice; 1986 v W, Aus (2), Is, R, E, Holl, D, WG; 1987 v Bul, Ei, Bel; 1988 v Bel, Bul, L, S.Ar, Ma; 1989 v N, Y, I, Cy (2), Fr, E, Ch; 1990 v Y, Fr, N, Eg, Pol, Ma, Cr, Se, Br; 1991 v R (2), Bul (2), USSR, Sm (2); 1992 v Sw, Ni, Fin, US, Ca, N, Holl, G; 1993 v Sw, Por, I.

MARSHALL, H. (Celtic) (2): 1899 v W; 1900 v Ni.

MARSHALL, G. (Celtic) (1): 1992 v US.

MARSHALL, J. (Middlesbrough, Llanelly) (7): 1921 v E, W, Ni; 1922 v E, W, Ni; 1924 v W.

MARSHALL, J. (Third Lanark) (4): 1885 v Ni; 1886 v W; 1887 v E, W.

MARSHALL, J. (Rangers) (3): 1932 v E; 1933 v E; 1934 v E.

MARSHALL, R. W. (Rangers) (2): 1892 v Ni; 1894 v Ni.

MARTIN, B. (Motherwell) (2): 1995 v. J, Ec.

MARTIN, F. (Aberdeen) (6): 1954 v N (2), A, U; 1955 v E, H.

MARTIN, N. (Hibernian, Sunderland) (3): 1965 v Fin, Pol; 1966 v I.

MARTIS, J. (Motherwell) (1): 1961 v W.

MASON, J. (Third Lanark) (7): 1949 v E, W, Ni; 1950 v Ni; 1951 v Ni, Bel, A.

MASSIE, A. (Hearts, Aston Villa) (18): 1932 v Ni, W, Fr; 1933 v Ni; 1934 v E, Ni; 1935 v E, Ni, W; 1936 v W, Ni, E; 1937 v G, E, W, Ni, A; 1938 v W.

MASSON, D. S. (QPR, Derby Co.) (17): 1976 v Ni, W, E; 1977 v Fin, Cz, W, Ni, E, Ch, Arg, Br; 1978 v EG, Cz, W, Ni, E, Pe.

MATHERS, D. (Partick Th.) (1): 1954 v Fin.

MATTEO, D. (Leeds Utd) (6): 2001 v Aus, Sm, Bel; 2002 v Cro, Bel, Fr.

MAXWELL, W. S. (Stoke City) (1): 1898 v S.

MAY, J. (Rangers) (5): 1906 v W, Ni; 1908 v E, Ni; 1909 v W.

MEECHAN, P. (Celtic) (1): 1896 v W.

MEIKLEJOHN, D. D. (Rangers) (15): 1922 v W; 1924 v W; 1925 v W, Ni, E; 1928 v W, Ni; 1929 v E, Ni; 1930 v E, Ni; 1931 v E; 1932 v W, Ni; 1934 v A.

MENZIES, A. (Hearts) (1): 1906 v E.

MERCER, R. (Hearts) (2): 1912 v W; 1913 v Ni.

MIDDLETON, R. (Cowdenbeath) (1): 1930 v Ni.

MILLAR, A. (Hearts) (1): 1939 v W.

MILLAR, J. (Rangers) (3): 1897 v E; 1898 v E, W.

MILLAR, J. (Rangers) (2): 1963 v A, Ei.

MILLER, C. (Dundee United) (1): 2001 v Pol.

MILLER, K. (Rangers, Wolves) (12): 2001 v Pol; 2003 v A, Ice, Lth, G; 2004 v Lth, Holl (2), W, R, Est, Trin.

MILLER, J. (St Mirren) (5): 1931 v E, I, Sw; 1932 v Fr; 1934 v E.

MILLER, P. (Dumbarton) (3): 1882 v E; 1883 v E, W.

MILLER, T. (Liverpool, Manchester Utd.) (3): 1920 v E; 1921 v E, Ni.

MILLER, W. (Third Lanark) (1): 1876 v W.

MILLER, W. (Celtic) (6): 1947 v E, W, Bel, L; 1948 v W, Ni.

MILLER, W. (Aberdeen) (65): 1975 v R; 1978 v Bul; 1980 v Bel, W, E, Pol, H; 1981 v Se, Por, Is, Ni (2), W, E; 1982 v Ni, Por, Holl, Br, USSR; 1983 v EG, Sw (2), W, E, Ca (3); 1984 v U, Bel, EG, W, E, Fr; 1985 v Y, Ice, Sp (2), W, E, Ice; 1986 v W, EG, Aus (2), Is, R, E, Holl, D, WG, U; 1987 v Bul, E, Br; 1988 v H, L, S.Ar, Ma, Sp, Co, E; 1989 v N, Y; 1990 v Y.

MILLS, W. (Aberdeen) (3): 1936 v W, Ni; 1937 v W.

MILNE, J. V. (Middlesbrough) (2): 1938 v E; 1939 v E.

MITCHELL, D. (Rangers) (5): 1890 v Ni; 1892 v E; 1893 v E, Ni; 1894 v E.

MITCHELL, J. (Kilmarnock) (3): 1908 v Ni; 1910 v Ni, W.

MITCHELL, R. C. (Newcastle Utd.) (2): 1951 v D, Fr.

MOCHAN, N. (Celtic) (3): 1954 v N, A, U.

MOIR, W. (Bolton) (1): 1950 v E.

MONCUR, R. (Newcastle Utd.) (16): 1968 v Holl; 1970 v Ni, W, E, Ei; 1971 v D, Bel, W, Por, Ni, E, D; 1972 v Pe, Ni, W, E.

MORGAN, H. (St Mirren, Liverpool) (2): 1898 v W; 1899 v E.

MORGAN, W. (Burnley, Manchester Utd.) (21): 1968 v Ni; 1972 v Pe, Y, Cz, Br; 1973 v D (2), E (2), W, Ni, Sw, Br; 1974 v Cz (2), WG (2), Ni, Bel, Br, Y.

MORRIS, D. (Raith R.) (6): 1923 v Ni; 1924 v E, Ni; 1925 v E, W, Ni.

MORRIS, H. (East Fife) (1): 1950 v Ni.

MORRISON, T. (St Mirren) (1): 1927 v E.

MORTON, A. L. (Queen's Park, Rangers) (31): 1920 v W, Ni; 1921 v E; 1922 v E, W; 1923 v E, W, Ni; 1924 v E, W, Ni; 1925 v E, W, Ni; 1927 v E, Ni; 1928 v E, W, Ni; 1929 v E, W, Ni; 1930 v E, W, Ni; 1931 v E, W, Ni; 1932 v E, W, Fr.

MORTON, H. A. (Kilmarnock) (2): 1929 v G, Holl.

MUDIE, J. K. (Blackpool) (17): 1957 v W, Ni, E, Y, Sw, Sp (2), WG; 1958 v Ni, E, W, Sw, H, Pol, Y, Par, Fr.

MUIR, W. (Dundee) (1): 1907 v Ni.

MUIRHEAD, T. A. (Rangers) (8): 1922 v Ni; 1923 v E; 1924 v W; 1927 v Ni; 1928 v Ni; 1929 v W, Ni; 1930 v W.

MULHALL, G. (Aberdeen, Sunderland) (3): 1960 v Ni; 1963 v Ni; 1964 v Ni.

MUNRO, A. D. (Hearts, Blackpool) (3): 1937 v W, Ni; 1938 v Holl.

MUNRO, F. M. (Wolverhampton W.) (9): 1971 v Ni, E, D, USSR; 1975 v Se, W, Ni, E, R.

MUNRO, I. (St Mirren) (7): 1979 v Arg, N; 1980 v Pe, A, Bel, W, E.

MUNRO, N. (Abercorn) (2): 1888 v W; 1889 v E.

MURDOCH, J. (Motherwell) (1): 1931 v Ni.

MURDOCH, R. (Celtic) (12): 1966 v W, E, I (2); 1967 v Ni; 1968 v Ni; 1969 v W, Ni, E, WG, Cy; 1970 v A.

MURPHY, F. (Celtic) (1): 1938 v Holl.

MURRAY, I. (Hibernian) (1): 2003 v Can.

MURRAY, J. (Renton) (1): 1895 v W.

MURRAY, J. (Hearts) (5): 1958 v E, H, Pol, Y, Fr.

MURRAY, J. W. (Vale of Leven) (1): 1890 v W.

MURRAY, P. (Hibernian) (2): 1896 v W; 1897 v W.

MURRAY, S. (Aberdeen) (1): 1972 v Bel.

MURTY, G. (Reading) (1): 2004 v W.

MUTCH, G. (Preston NE) (1): 1938 v E.

NAPIER, C. E. (Celtic, Derby County) (5): 1932 v E; 1935 v E, W; 1937 v Ni, A.

NAREY, D. (Dundee Utd.) (35): 1977 v Se; 1979 v Psor, Ni, Arg; 1980 v Por, Ni, Pol, H; 1981 v W, E; 1982 v Holl, W, E, Nz, Br, USSR; 1983 v EG, Sw, Bel, Ni, W, E, Ca (3); 1986 v Is, R, Holl, WG, U; 1987 v Bul, E, Bel; 1989 v I, Cy.

NAYSMITH, G. (Hearts, Everton) (22): 2000 v Ei; 2001 v La, Sm, Cro; 2002 v Cro, Bel; 2003 v D, Ice (2), Por, Ei, A, Lth, Nz, G; 2004 v N, Fi, G, Lth, Holl (2), W.

NEIL, R. G. (Hibernian, Rangers) (2): 1896 v W; 1900 v W.

NEILL, R. W. (Queen's Park) (5): 1876 v W; 1877 v E, W; 1878 v W; 1880 v E.
NELLIES, P. (Hearts) (2): 1914 v W, Ni.
NELSON, J. (Cardiff C.) (4): 1925 v W, Ni; 1928 v E; 1930 v Fr.
NEVIN, P. (Chelsea, Everton, Tranmere) (28): 1986 v R, E; 1987 v L, Ei, Bel; 1988 v L; 1989 v Cy, E; 1991 v R, Bul, Sm; 1992 v US, G, CIS; 1993 v Ma, Por, Est; 1994 v Sw, Ma, Holl (2), A. 1995 v Fi, Ru, Sm; 1996 v Se, Sm, Aus.
NIBLO, T. (Aston Villa) (1): 1904 v E.
NIBLOE, J. (Kilmarnock) (11): 1929 v E, N, Holl; 1930 v W; 1931 v E, Ni, A, I, Sw; 1932 v E, Fr.
NICHOLAS, C. (Celtic, Arsenal, Aberdeen) (20): 1983 v Sw, Ni, E, Ca (3); 1984 v Bel, Fr; 1985 v Y, Ice, Sp, W; 1986 v Is, R, E, D, U; 1987 v Bul, E; 1989 v Cy.
NICOL, S. (Liverpool) (27): 1985 v Y, Ice, Sp, W; 1986 v W, EG, Aus, E, D, WG, U; 1988 v H, Bul, S.Ar, Sp, Co, E; 1989 v N, Y, Cy, Fr; 1990 v Y, Fr; 1991 v Sw, USSR, Sm; 1992 Sw.
NICOLSON, B. (Dunfermline) (2): 2001 v Pol; 2002 v La.
NISBET, J. (Ayr Utd.) (3): 1929 v N, G, Holl.
NIVEN, J. B. (Moffat) (1): 1885 v Ni.

O'CONNOR, G. (Hibernian) (3): 2002 v Nig, Skor, HK.
O'DONNELL, F. (Preston NE, Blackpool) (6): 1937 v E, A, Cz; 1938 v E, W, Holl.
O'DONNELL, P. (Motherwell) (1): 1994 v Sw.
OGILVIE, D. H. (Motherwell) (1): 1934 v A.
O'HARE, J. (Derby County) (13): 1970 v W, Ni, E; 1971 v D, Bel, W, Ni; 1972 v Por, Bel, Holl, Pe, Ni, W.
O'NEIL, J. (Hibs) (1): 2001 v Pol.
O'NEIL, B. (Celtic, Wolfsburg) (6): 1996 v Aus; 1999 v G; 2000 v Lth, Holl, Ei; 2001 v Aus.
ORMOND, W. E. (Hibernian) (6): 1954 v E, N, Fin, A, U; 1959 v E.
O'ROURKE, F. (Airdrie) (1): 1907 v Ni.
ORR, J. (Kilmarnock) (1): 1892 v W.
ORR, R. (Newcastle Utd.) (2): 1902 v E; 1904 v E.
ORR, T. (Morton) (2): 1952 v Ni, W.
ORR, W. (Celtic) (3): 1900 v Ni; 1903 v Ni; 1904 v W.
ORROCK, R. (Falkirk) (1): 1913 v W.
OSWALD, J. (Third Lanark, St Bernard's, Rangers) (3): 1889 v E; 1895 v E; 1897 v W.

PARKER, A. H. (Falkirk, Everton) (15): 1955 v Por, Y, A; 1956 v E, Ni, W, A; 1957 v Ni, W, Y; 1958 v Ni, W, E, Sw, Par.
PARLANE, D. (Rangers) (12): 1973 v W, Sw, Br; 1975 v Sp, Se, Por, W, Ni, E, R; 1976 v D; 1977 v W.
PARLANE, R. (Vale of Leven) (3): 1878 v W; 1879 v E, W.
PATERSON, G. D. (Celtic) (1): 1939 v Ni.
PATERSON, J. (Leicester City) (1): 1920 v E.

PATERSON, J. (Cowdenbeath) (3): 1931 v A, I, Sw.

PATON, A. (Motherwell) (2): 1952 v D, Se.

PATON, D. (St Bernard's) (1): 1896 v W.

PATON, M. (Dumbarton) (5): 1883 E; 1884 v W; 1885 v W, E; 1886 v E.

PATON, R. (Vale of Leven) (2): 1879 v E, W.

PATRICK, J. (St Mirren) (2): 1897 E, W.

PAUL, J. McD. (Queen's Park) (3): 1909 v E, W, Ni.

PAUL, W. (Partick Th.) (3): 1888 v W; 1889 v W; 1890 v W.

PAUL, W. (Dykebar) (1): 1891 v Ni.

PEARSON, S. (Motherwell, Celtic) (2): 2004: v Holl, W.

PEARSON, T. (Newcastle Utd.) (2): 1947 v E, Bel.

PENMAN, A. (Dundee) (1): 1966 v Holl.

PETTIGREW, W. (Motherwell) (5): 1976 v Sw, Ni, W; 1977 v W, Se.

PHILLIPS, J. (Queen's Park) (3): 1877 v E, W; 1878 v W.

PLENDERLEITH, J. B. (Manchester City) (1): 1961 v Ni.

PORTEOUS, W. (Hearts) (1): 1903 v Ni.

PRESSLEY, S. (Hearts) (17): 2000 v E, Fr, Ei; 2003 v Ice (2), Can, Por, A, Lth, Nz, G; 2004 v N, G, Lth, Holl (2), R, D, Est, Trin.

PRINGLE, C. (St Mirren) (1): 1921 v W.

PROVAN, D. (Rangers) (5): 1964 v Ni, N; 1966 v I (2), Holl.

PROVAN, D. (Celtic) (10): 1980 v Bel (2), Por, Ni; 1981 v Is, W, E; 1982 v Se, Por, Ni.

PURSELL, P. (Queen's Park) (1): 1914 v W.

QUASHIE, N. (Portsmouth) (2): 2004 v Est, Trin.

QUINN, J. (Celtic) (11): 1905 v Ni; 1906 v Ni, W; 1908 v Ni, E; 1909 v E; 1910 v E, Ni, W; 1912 v E, W.

QUINN, P. (Motherwell) (4): 1961 v E, Ei (2); 1962 v U.

RAE, G. (Dundee, Rangers) (8): 2001 v Pol; 2002 v La, G; 2004 v N, Fi, G, Lth, Holl, R.

RAE, J. (Third Lanark) (2): 1889 v W; 1890 v Ni.

RAESIDE, J. S. (Third Lanark) (1): 1906 v W.

RAISBECK, A. G. (Liverpool) (8): 1900 v E; 1901 v E; 1902 v E; 1903 v E, W; 1904 v E; 1906 v E; 1907 v E.

RANKIN, G. (Vale of Leven) (2): 1890 v Ni; 1891 v E.

RANKIN, R. (St Mirren) (3): 1929 v N, G, Holl.

REDPATH, W. (Motherwell) (9): 1949 v W, Ni; 1951 v E, D, Fr, Bel, A; 1952 v Ni, E.

REID, J, G. (Airdrie) (3): 1914 v W; 1920 v W; 1924 v W.

REID, R. (Brentford) (2): 1938 v E, Ni.

REID, W. (Rangers) (9): 1911 v E, W, Ni; 1912 v Ni; 1913 v E, W, Ni; 1914 v E, Ni.

REILLY, L. (Hibernian) (38): 1949 v E, W, Fr; 1950 v W, Ni, Sw, Fr; 1951 v W, E, D, Fr, Bel, A; 1952 v Ni, W, E, USA, D, Se; 1953 v Ni, W, E, Se; 1954 v W; 1955 v H (2), Por, Y, A, E; 1956 v E, W, Ni, A; 1957 v E, Ni, W, Y.

RENNIE, H. G. (Hearts, Hibs) (13): 1900 v E, Ni; 1901 v E; 1902 v E, Ni, W; 1903 v Ni, W; 1904 v Ni; 1905 v W; 1906 v Ni; 1908 v Ni, W.

RENNY-TAILYOUR, H. W. (Royal Engineers) (1): 1873 v E.

RHIND, A. (Queen's Park) (1): 1872 v E.

RICHMOND, A. (Queen's Park) (1): 1906 v W.

RICHMOND, J. T. (Clydesdale, Queen's Park) (3): 1877 v E; 1878 v E; 1882 v W.

RING, T. (Clyde) (12): 1953 v Se; 1955 v W, Ni, E, H; 1957 v E, Sp (2), Sw, WG; 1958 v Ni, Sw.

RIOCH, B. D. (Derby County, Everton) (24): 1975 v Por, W, Ni, E, R; 1976 v D (2), R, Ni, W, E; 1977 v Fin, Cz, W (2), Ni, E, Ch, Br; 1978 v Cz, Ni, E, Pe, Holl.

RITCHIE, A. (East Stirling) (1): 1891 v W.

RITCHIE, H. (Hibernian) (2): 1923 v W; 1928 v Ni.

RITCHIE, J. (Queen's Park) (1): 1897 v W.

RITCHIE, P. (Hearts, Bolton, Walsall) (7): 1999 v G, Czr, E; 2000 v Lth, Fr, Holl; 2004 v W.

RITCHIE, W. (Rangers) (1): 1962 v U.

ROBB, D. T. (Aberdeen) (5): 1971 v W, E, Por, D, USSR.

ROBB, W. (Rangers, Hibernian) (2): 1926 v W; 1928 v W.

ROBERTSON, A. (Clyde) (5): 1955 v Por, A, H; 1958 v Sw, Par.

ROBERTSON, D. (Rangers) (3): 1991 v Ni; 1994 v Sw, Holl.

ROBERTSON, G. (Motherwell, Sheffield W.) (4): 1910 v W; 1912 v W; 1913 v E, Ni.

ROBERTSON, G. (Kilmarnock) (1): 1938 v Cz.

ROBERTSON, H. (Dundee) (1): 1962 v Cz.

ROBERTSON, J. (Dundee) (2): 1931 v A, I.

ROBERTSON, J. (Hearts) (16): 1991 v R, Sw, Bul, Sm (2); 1992 v Ni, Fin; 1993 v I, Ma, G, Est; 1995 v J, Ec, Fi. 1996 v Gr, Se.

ROBERTSON, J. N. (Nottingham F., Derby County) (28): 1978 v Ni, W, Ir; 1979 v Por, N; 1980 v Pe, A, Bel (2), Por; 1981 v Se, Por, Is, Ni (2), E; 1982 v Se, Ni (2), E, Nz, Br, USSR; 1983 v EG, Sw; 1984 v U, Bel.

ROBERTSON, J. G. (Tottenham H.) (1): 1965 v W.

ROBERTSON, J. T. (Everton, Southampton, Rangers) (16): 1898 v E; 1899 v E; 1900 v E, W; 1901 v W, Ni, E; 1902 v W, Ni, E; 1903 v E, W; 1904 v E, W, Ni; 1905 v W.

ROBERTSON, P. (Dundee) (1): 1903 v Ni.

ROBERTSON, T. (Queen's Park) (4): 1889 v Ni; 1890 v E; 1891 v W; 1892 v Ni.

ROBERTSON, T. (Hearts) (1): 1898 v Ni.

ROBERTSON, W. (Dumbarton) (1): 1887 v E, W.

ROBINSON, R. (Dundee) (4): 1974 v WG; 1975 v Se, Ni, R.

ROSS, M. (Rangers) (13): 2002 v Skor, SA, HK; 2003 v D, Fi, Ice, Can, Por, Nz, G; 2004 v N, G, Holl.

ROUGH, A. (Partick Th, Hibernian) (53): 1976 v Sw, Ni, W, E; 1977 v Fin, Cz, W (2), Se, Ni, E, Ch, Arg, Br; 1978 v Cz, W, Ni, E, Pe, Ir, Holl; 1979 v A, Por, W, Arg, N; 1980 v Pe, A, Bel (2), Por, W, E, Pol, H; 1981 v Se, Por, Is (2), Ni, W, E; 1982 v Se, Ni, Sp, Holl, W, E, Nz, Br, USSR; 1986 v W, E.

ROUGVIE, D. (Aberdeen) (1): 1984 v Ni.

ROWAN, A. (Caledonian, Queen's Park) (2): 1880 v E; 1882 v W.

RUSSELL, D. (Hearts, Celtic) (6): 1895 v E, Ni; 1897 v W; 1898 v Ni; 1901 v W, Ni.

RUSSELL, J. (Cambuslang) (1): 1890 v Ni.

RUSSELL W. F. (Airdrie) (2): 1924 v W; 1925 v E.

RUTHERFORD, E. (Rangers) (1): 1948 v F.

ST JOHN, I. (Motherwell, Liverpool) (21): 1959 v WG; 1960 v E, Ni, W, Pol, A; 1961 v E; 1962 v Ni, W, E, Cz (2), U; 1963 v W, Ni, E, N, Ei, Sp; 1964 v Ni; 1965 v E.

SAWERS, W. (Dundee) (1): 1895 v W.

SCARFF, P. (Celtic) (1): 1931 v W.

SCHAEDLER, E. (Hibernian) (1): 1974 v WG.

SCOTT, A. S. (Rangers, Everton) (16): 1957 v Ni, Y, WG; 1958 v W, Sw; 1959 v Por; 1962 v Ni, W, E, Cz, U; 1964 v W, N; 1965 v Fin; 1966 v Por, Br.

SCOTT, J. (Hibernian) (1): 1966 v Holl.

SCOTT, J. (Dundee) (2): 1971 v D, USSR.

SCOTT, M. (Airdrie) (1): 1898 v W.

SCOTT, R. (Airdrie) (1): 1894 v Ni.

SCOULAR, J. (Portsmouth) (9): 1951 v D, Fr, A; 1952 v E, USA, D, Se; 1953 v W, Ni.

SELLAR, W. (Battlefield, Queen's Park) (9): 1885 v E; 1886 v E; 1887 v E, W; 1888 v E; 1891 v E; 1892 v E; 1893 v E, Ni.

SEMPLE, J. (Cambuslang) (1): 1886 v W.

SEVERIN, S. (Hearts) (8): 2002 v La, Skor, SA, HK; 2003 v D, Ice, Can, Por.

SHANKLY, W. (Preston NE) (5): 1938 v E; 1939 v E, W, Ni, H.

SHARP, G. M. (Everton) (12): 1985 v Ice; 1986 v W, Aus (2), Is, R, U; 1987 v Ei; 1988 v Bel, Bul, L, Ma.

SHARP, J. (Dundee, Woolwich Arsenal, Fulham) (5): 1904 v W; 1907 v W, E; 1908 v E; 1909 v W.

SHAW, D. (Hibernian) (8): 1947 v W, Ni; 1948 v E, Bel, Sw, Fr; 1949 v W, Ni.

SHAW, F. W. (Pollokshields Ath.) (2): 1884 v E, W.

SHAW, J. (Rangers) (4): 1947 v E, Bel, L; 1948 v Ni.

SHEARER, D. (Aberdeen) (7) 1994 v A, Holl; 1995 v Fin, Ru, Sm, Fi. 1996 v Gr.

SHEARER, R. (Rangers) (4): 1961 v E, Ei (2), Cz.

SILLARS, D. C. (Queen's Park) (5): 1891 v Ni; 1892 v E; 1893 v W; 1894 v E; 1895 v W.

SIMPSON, J. (Third Lanark) (3): 1895 v E, W, Ni.

SIMPSON, J. (Rangers) (14): 1935 v E, W, Ni; 1936 v E, W, Ni; 1937 v G, E, W, Ni, A, Cz; 1938 v W, Ni.

SIMPSON, N. (Aberdeen) (4): 1983 v Ni; 1984 v Fr; 1987 v E; 1988 v E.

SIMPSON, R. C. (Celtic) (5): 1967 v E, USSR; 1968 v Ni, E; 1969 v A.

SINCLAIR, G. L. (Hearts) (3): 1910 v Ni; 1912 v W, Ni.

SINCLAIR, J. W. E. (Leicester City) (1): 1966 v Por.

SKENE, L. H. (Queen's Park) (1): 1904 v W.

SLOAN, T. (Third Lanark) (1): 1904 v W.

SMELLIE, R. (Queen's Park) (6): 1887 v Ni; 1888 v W; 1889 v E; 1891 v E; 1893 v E, Ni.

SMITH, A. (Rangers) (20): 1898 v E; 1900 v E, Ni, W; 1901 v E, Ni, W; 1902 v E, Ni, W; 1903 v E, Ni, W; 1904 v Ni; 1905 v W; 1906 v E, Ni; 1907 v W; 1911 v E, Ni.

SMITH, D. (Aberdeen, Rangers) (2): 1966 v Holl; 1968 v Holl.

SMITH, G. (Hibernian) (18): 1947 v E, Ni; 1948 v W, Bel, Sw, Fr; 1952 v E, USA; 1955 v Por, Y, A, H; 1956 v E, Ni, W; 1957 v Sp (2), Sw.

SMITH, H. G. (Hearts) (3): 1988 v S.Ar; 1991 v Ni; 1992 v Ca.

SMITH, J. (Rangers) (2): 1935 v Ni; 1938 v Ni.

SMITH, J. (Ayr United) (1): 1924 v E.

SMITH, J. (Aberdeen, Newcastle Utd.) (4): 1968 v Holl; 1974 v WG, Ni, W.

SMITH, J. (Celtic) (2): 2003 v Ei, A.

SMITH, J. E. (Celtic) (2): 1959 v H, Por.

SMITH, Jas (Queen's Park) (1): 1872 v E.

SMITH, J. (Mauchline, Edinburgh University, Queen's Park) (10): 1877 v E, W; 1879 v E, W; 1880 v E; 1881 v W, E; 1883 v E, W; 1884 v E.

SMITH, N. (Rangers) (12): 1897 v E; 1898 v W; 1899 v E, W, Ni; 1900 v E, W, Ni; 1901 v Ni, W; 1902 v E, Ni.

SMITH, R, (Queen's Park) (2): 1872 v E; 1873 v E.

SMITH, T. M. (Kilmarnock, Preston NE) (2): 1934 v E; 1938 v E.

SOMERS, P. (Celtic) (4): 1905 v E, Ni; 1907 v Ni; 1909 v W.

SOMERS, W. S. (Third Lanark, Queen's Park) (3): 1879 v E, W; 1880 v W.

SOMERVILLE, G. (Queen's Park) (1): 1886 v E.

SOUNESS, G. J. (Middlesbrough, Liverpool, Sampdoria) (54): 1975 v EG, Sp, Se; 1978 v Bul, W, E, Holl; 1979 v A, N, W, Ni, E; 1980 v Pe, A, Bel, Por, Ni; 1981 v Por, Is (2); 1982 v Ni, Por, Sp, W, E, Nz, Br, USSR; 1983 v EG, Sw (2), Bel, W, E, Ca (3); 1984 v U, Ni, W; 1985 v Y, Ice (2), Sp (2), W, E; 1986 v EG, Aus (2), R, E, D, WG.

SPEEDIE, D. R. (Chelsea, Coventry City) (10): 1985 v E; 1986 v W, EG, Aus, E; 1989 v Y, I, Cy (2), Ch.

SPEEDIE, F. (Rangers) (3): 1903 v E, W, Ni.

SPENCER, J. (Chelsea) (14): 1995 v Ru, Gr, Sm, J; 1996 v Fin, Aus, D, US, U, Holl, E, Sw; 1997 v La, W.

SPIERS, J. H. (Rangers) (1): 1908 v W.

STANTON, P. (Hibernian) (16): 1966 v Holl; 1969 v Ni; 1970 v Ei, A; 1971 v D, Bel, Por, USSR, D; 1972 v Por, Bel, Holl, W; 1973 v W, Ni; 1974 v WG.

STARK, J. (Rangers) (2): 1909 v E, Ni.

STEEL, W. (Morton, Derby County, Dundee) (30): 1947 v E, Bel, L; 1948 v Fr, E, W, Ni; 1949 v E, W, Ni, Fr; 1950 v E, W, Ni, Sw, Por, Fr; 1951 v W, Ni, E, A (2), D, Fr, Bel; 1952 v W; 1953 v W, E, Ni, Se.

STEELE, D. M. (Huddersfield) (3): 1923 v E, W, Ni.

STEIN, C. (Rangers, Coventry City) (21): 1969 v W, Ni, D, E, Cy (2); 1970 v A, Ni, W, E, Ei, WG; 1971 v D. USSR, Bel, D; 1972 v Cz; 1973 v E (2), W, Ni.

STEPHEN, J. F. (Bradford) (2): 1947 v W; 1948 v W.

STEVENSON, G. (Motherwell) (12): 1928 v W, Ni; 1930 v Ni, E, Fr; 1931 v E, W; 1932 v W, Ni; 1933 v Ni; 1934 v E; 1935 v Ni.

STEWART, A. (Queen's Park) (2): 1888 v Ni; 1889 v W.

STEWART, A. (Third Lanark) (1): 1894 v W.

STEWART, D. (Dumbarton) (1): 1888 v Ni.

STEWART, D. (Queen's Park) (3): 1893 v W; 1894 v Ni; 1897 v Ni.

STEWART, D. S. (Leeds Utd.) (1): 1978 v EG.

STEWART, G. (Hibernian, Man City) (4): 1906 v W, E; 1907 v E, W.

STEWART, J. (Kilmarnock, Middlesbrough) (2): 1977 v Ch; 1979 v N.

STEWART, M. (Manchester Utd) (3): 2002 v Nig, Skor, SA.

STEWART, R. (West Ham Utd.) (10): 1981 v W, Ni, E; 1982 v Ni, Por, W; 1984 v Y; 1987 v Ei (2), L.

STEWART, W. E. (Queen's Park) (2): 1898 v Ni; 1900 v Ni.

STOCKDALE, R. (Middlesbrough) (5): 2002 v Nig, Skor, SA, HK; 2003 v D.

STORRIER, D. (Celtic) (3): 1899 v E, W, Ni.

STRACHAN, G. (Aberdeen, Manchester Utd., Leeds Utd.) (50): 1980 v Ni, W, E, Pol, H; 1981 v Sw, Por; 1982 v Ni, Por, Sp, Holl, Nz, Br, USSR; 1983 v EG, Sw (2), Bel, Ni, W, E, Ca (3); 1984 v EG, Ni, E, Fr; 1985 v Sp, E, Ice; 1986 v W, Aus, R, D, WG, U; 1987 v Bul, Ei (2); 1988 v H; 1989 v Fr; 1990 v Fr; 1991 v USSR, Bul, Sm; 1992 v Sw, R, Ni, Fin.

STURROCK, P. (Dundee Utd.) (20): 1981 v W, Ni, E; 1982 v Por, Ni, W, E; 1983 v EG, Sw, Bel, Ca (3); 1984 v W; 1985 v Y; 1986 v Is, Holl, D, U; 1987 v Bel.

SULLIVAN, N. (Wimbledon, Spurs) (28): 1997 v W; 1998 Fr, Co. 1999 v Fi (2), CzR (2); G. 2000 v Bos (2), Est, E (2) Fr, Holl, Ei; 2001 v La, Sm (2), Cro, Bel, Pol; 2002 v Cro, Bel, La, Fr, Skor; 2003 v Ei.

SUMMERS, W. (St Mirren) (1): 1926 v E.

SYMON, J. S. (Rangers) (1): 1939 v H.

TAIT, T. S. (Sunderland) (1): 1911 v W.

TAYLOR, J. (Queen's Park) (6): 1872 v E; 1873 v E; 1874 v E; 1875 v E; 1876 v E, W.

TAYLOR, J. D. (Dumbarton, St Mirren) (4): 1892 v W; 1893 v W; 1894 v Ni; 1895 v Ni.

TAYLOR, W. (Hearts) (1): 1892 v E.

TELFER, P. (Coventry) (1): 2000 v Fr.

TELFER, W. (Motherwell) (2): 1933 v Ni; 1934 v Ni.

TELFER, W. D. (St Mirren) (1): 1954 v W.

TEMPLETON, R. (Aston Villa, Newcastle Utd., Woolwich Arsenal, Kilmarnock) (11): 1902 v E; 1903 v E, W; 1904 v E; 1905 v W; 1908 v Ni; 1910 v E, Ni; 1912 v E, Ni; 1913 v W.

THOMPSON, S. (Dundee United, Rangers) (13): 2002 v Fr, Nig, HK; 2003 v D, Fi, Ice, Can, Ei, A, G; 2004 v Fi, G, R

THOMSON, A. (Arthurlie) (1): 1886 v Ni.

THOMSON, A. (Third Lanark) (1): 1889 v W.

THOMSON, A. (Airdrie) (1): 1909 v W.

THOMSON, A. (Celtic) (3): 1926 v E; 1932 v Fr; 1933 v W.

THOMSON, C. (Hearts, Sunderland) (21): 1904 v Ni; 1905 v E, Ni, W; 1906 v W, Ni; 1907 v E, W, Ni; 1908 v E, W, Ni; 1909 v W; 1910 v E; 1911 v Ni; 1912 v E, W; 1913 v E, W; 1914 v E, Ni.

THOMSON, C. (Sunderland) (1): 1937 v Cz.

THOMSON, D. (Dundee) (1): 1920 v W.

THOMSON, J. (Celtic) (4): 1930 v Fr; 1931 v E, W, Ni.

THOMSON, J. J. (Queen's Park) (3): 1872 v E; 1873 v E; 1874 v E.

THOMSON, J. R. (Everton) (1): 1933 v W.

THOMSON, R. (Celtic) (1): 1932 v W.

THOMSON, R. W. (Falkirk) (1): 1927 v E.

THOMSON, S. (Rangers) (2): 1884 v W, Ni.

THOMSON, W. (Dumbarton) (4): 1892 v W; 1893 v W; 1898 v Ni, W.

THOMSON, W. (Dundee) (1): 1896 v W.

THOMSON, W. (St Mirren) (7): 1980 v Ni; 1981 v Ni (2); 1982 v Por; 1983 v Ni, Ca; 1984 v EG.

THORNTON, W. (Rangers) (7): 1947 v W, Ni; 1948 v E, Ni; 1949 v Fr; 1952 v D, Se.

TONER, W. (Kilmarnock) (2): 1959 v W, Ni.

TOWNSLEY, T. (Falkirk) (1926 v W.

TROUP, A. (Dundee, Everton) (5): 1920 v E; 1921 v W, Ni; 1922 v Ni; 1926 v E.

TURNBULL, E. F. (Hibernian) (8): 1948 v Bel, Sw; 1951 v A; 1958 v H, Pol, Y, Par, Fr.

TURNER, T. (Arthurlie) (1): 1884 v W.

TURNER, W. (Pollokshields Ath.) (2): 1885 v Ni; 1886 v Ni.

URE, J. F. (Dundee, Arsenal) (11): 1962 v W, Cz; 1963 v W, Ni, E, A, N, Sp; 1964 v Ni, N; 1968 v Ni.

URQUHART, D. (Hibernian) (1): 1934 v W.

VALLANCE, T. (Rangers) (7): 1877 v E, W; 1878 v E; 1879 v E, W; 1881 v E, W.

VENTERS, A. (Cowdenbeath, Rangers) (3): 1934 v Ni; 1936 v E; 1939 v E.

WADDELL, T. S. (Queen's Park) (6): 1891 v Ni; 1892 v E; 1893 v E, Ni; 1895 v E, Ni.

WADDELL, W. (Rangers) (17): 1947 v W; 1949 v E, W, Ni, Fr; 1950 v E, Ni; 1951 v E, D, Fr, Bel, A; 1952 v Ni, W; 1954 v Ni; 1955 v W, Ni.

WALES, H. M. (Motherwell) (1): 1933 v W.

WALKER, A. (Celtic) (3): 1988 v Co; 1995 v Fin, Fi.

WALKER, F. (Third Lanark) (1): 1922 v W.

WALKER, G. (St Mirren) (4): 1930 v Fr; 1931 v Ni, A, Sw.

WALKER, J. (Hearts, Rangers) (5): 1895 v Ni; 1897 v W; 1898 v Ni; 1904 v W, Ni.

WALKER, J. (Swindon T.) (9): 1911 v E, W, Ni; 1912 v E, W, Ni; 1913 v E, W, Ni.

WALKER, N. (Hearts) (2): 1993 v G, 1996 US.

WALKER, R. (Hearts) (29): 1900 v E, Ni; 1901 v E, W; 1902 v E, W, Ni; 1903 v E, W, Ni; 1904 v E, W; 1905 v E, W, Ni; 1906 v Ni; 1907 v Ni; 1908 v E, W, Ni; 1909 v E, W; 1912 v E, W, Ni; 1913 v E, W.

WALKER, T. (Hearts) (20): 1935 v E, W; 1936 v E, W, Ni; 1937 v G, E, W, Ni, A, Cz; 1938 v E, W, Ni, Cz, Holl; 1939 v E, W, Ni, H.

WALKER, W. (Clyde) (2): 1909 v Ni; 1910 v Ni.

WALLACE, I. A. (Coventry City) (3): 1978 v Bul; 1979 v Por, W.

WALLACE, W. S. B. (Hearts, Celtic) (7): 1965 v Ni; 1966 v E, Holl; 1967 v E, USSR; 1968 v Ni; 1969 v E.

WARDHAUGH, J. (Hearts) (2): 1955 v H; 1957 v Ni.

WARK, J. (Ipswich Town, Liverpool) (29): 1979 v W, Ni, E, Arg, N; 1980 v Pe, A, Bel (2); 1981 v Is, Ni; 1982 v Se, Sp, Holl, Ni, Nz, Br, USSR; 1983 v EG, Sw (2), Ni, E; 1984 v U, Bel, EG, E, Fr; 1985 v Y.

WATSON, A. (Queen's Park) (3): 1881 v E, W; 1882 v E.

WATSON, J. (Sunderland, Middlesbrough) (6): 1903 v E, W; 1904 v E; 1905 v E; 1909 v E, Ni.

WATSON, J. (Motherwell, Huddersfield) (2): 1948 v Ni; 1954 v Ni.

WATSON, J. A. K. (Rangers) (1): 1878 v W.

WATSON, P. R. (Blackpool) (1): 1934 v A.

WATSON, R. (Motherwell) (1): 1971 v USSR.

WATSON, W. (Falkirk) (1): 1898 v W.

WATT, F. (Kilbirnie) (4): 1889 v W, Ni; 1890 v W; 1891 v E.

WATT, W. W. (Queen's Park) (1): 1887 v Ni.

WAUGH, A. (Hearts) (1): 1938 v Cz.

WEBSTER, A. (Hearts) (8): 2003 v A, Nz, G; 2004 v N, Fi, W, Est, Trin.

WEIR, A. (Motherwell) (6): 1959 v WG; 1960 v E, Por, A, H, T.

WEIR, D. (Hearts, Everton) (37): 1997 v W, Ma; 1998 Fr, D, Fin, N, M; 1999 v Est, Fi, CzR (2), G, Fi; 2000 v Bos (2), Est, Lth, E (2), Holl;

2001 v La, Sm (2), Cro, Aus, Bel, Pol; 2002 v Cro, Bel, La, Fr, Nig, Skor, SA, HK; 2003 v D, Fi.

WEIR, J. (Third Lanark) (1): 1887 v Ni.

WEIR, J. B. (Queen's Park) (4): 1872 v E; 1874 v E; 1875 v E; 1878 v W.

WEIR, P. (St Mirren, Aberdeen) (6): 1980 v N, W, Pol, H; 1983 v Sw; 1984 v Ni.

WHITE, J. (Albion Rovers, Hearts) (2): 1922 v W; 1923 v Ni.

WHITE, J. A. (Falkirk, Tottenham H.) (22): 1959 v WG, Holl, Por; 1960 v Ni, W, Pol, A, T; 1961 v W; 1962 v Ni, W, E, Cz (2); 1963 v W, Ni, E; 1964 v Ni, W, E, N, WG.

WHITE, W. (Bolton W.) (2): 1907 v E; 1908 v E.

WHITELAW, A. (Vale of Leven) (2): 1887 v Ni; 1890 v W.

WHYTE, D. (Celtic, Middlesbrough, Aberdeen) (12): 1988 v Bel, L; 1989 v Ch; 1992 v US; 1993 v Por, I; 1995 v J, Ec, US; 1997 v La; 1998 v Fin; 1999 v G.

WILKIE, L. (Dundee) (11): 2002 v SA, HK; 2003 v Ice (2), Can, Por, A, Lth; 2004 v Fi, Holl (2).

WILLIAMS, G. (Nottingham Forest) (5): 2002 v Nig, Skor, SA, HK, Por.

WILSON, A. (Sheffield W.) (6): 1907 v E; 1908 v E; 1912 v I; 1913 v E, W; 1914 v Ni.

WILSON, A. (Portsmouth) (1): 1954 v Fin.

WILSON, A. N. (Dunfermline, Middlesbrough) (12): 1920 v E, W, Ni; 1921 v E, W, Ni; 1922 v E, W, Ni; 1923 v E, W, Ni.

WILSON, D. (Queen's Park) (1): 1900 v W.

WILSON, D. (Oldham) (1): 1913 v E.

WILSON, D. (Rangers) (22): 1961 v E, W, Ni, Ei (2), Cz; 1962 v Ni, W, E, Cz, U; 1963 v W, E, A, N, Ei, Sp; 1964 v E, WG; 1965 v Ni, E, Fin.

WILSON, G. W. (Hearts, Everton, Newcastle Utd.) (6): 1904 v W; 1905 v E, Ni; 1906 v W; 1907 v E; 1909 v E.

WILSON, H. (Newmilns, Sunderland, Third Lanark) (4): 1890 v W; 1897 v E; 1902 v W; 1904 v Ni.

WILSON, I. A. (Leicester, Everton) (5): 1987 v E, Br; 1988 v Bel, Bul, L.

WILSON, J. (Vale of Leven) (4): 1888 v W; 1889 v E; 1890 v E; 1891 v E.

WILSON, P. (Celtic) (4): 1926 v Ni; 1930 v Fr; 1931 v Ni; 1933 v E.

WILSON, P. (Celtic) (1): 1975 v Sp.

WILSON, R. P. (Arsenal) (2): 1972 v Por, Holl.

WINTERS, R. (Aberdeen) (1): 1999 v G.

WISEMAN, W. (Queen's Park) (2): 1927 v W; 1930 v Ni.

WOOD, G. (Everton, Arsenal) (4): 1979 v Ni, E, Arg; 1982 v Ni.

WOODBURN, W. A. (Rangers) (24): 1947 v E, Bel, L; 1948 v W, Ni; 1949 v E, Fr; 1950 v E, W, Ni, Por, Fr; 1951 v E, W, Ni, A (2), D, Fr, Bel; 1952 v E, W, Ni, USA.

WOTHERSPOON, D. N. (Queen's Park) (2): 1872 v E; 1873 v E.
WRIGHT, K. (Hibs) (1): 1992 v Ni.
WRIGHT, S. (Aberdeen) (2): 1993 v G, Est.
WRIGHT, T. (Sunderland) (3): 1953 v W, Ni, E.
WYLIE, T. G. (Rangers) (1): 1890 v Ni.

YEATS, R. (Liverpool) (2): 1965 v W; 1966 v I.
YORSTON, B. C. (Aberdeen) (1): 1931 v Ni.
YORSTON, H. (Aberdeen) (1): 1955 v W.
YOUNG, A. (Hearts, Everton) (8): 1960 v E, A, H, T; 1961 v W, Ni, Ei; 1966 v Por.
YOUNG, A. (Everton) (2): 1905 v E; 1907 v W.
YOUNG, G. A. (Rangers) (53): 1947 v E, Ni, Bel, L; 1948 v E, Ni, Bel, Sw, Fr; 1949 v E, W, Ni, Fr; 1950 v E, W, Ni, Sw, Por, Fr; 1951 v E, W, Ni, A (2), D, Fr, Bel; 1952 v E, W, Ni, USA, D, Se; 1953 v W, E, Ni, Se; 1954 v Ni, W; 1955 v W, Ni, Por, Y; 1956 v Ni, W, E, A; 1957 v E, Ni, W, Y, Sp, Sw.
YOUNG, J. (Celtic) (1): 1906 v Ni.
YOUNGER, T. (Hibernian, Liverpool) (24): 1955 v Por, Y, A, H; 1956 v E, Ni, W, A; A: 1957 v E, Ni, W, Y, Sp (2), Sw, WG; 1958 v Ni, W, E, Sw, H, Pol, Y, Par.

WORLD CUP WINNERS

Year	Winners		Runners-up		Venue
1930	URUGUAY	4	Argentina	2	Uruguay
1934	ITALY	2	Czechosl'kia	1	Italy
			(after extra time)		
1938	ITALY	4	Hungary	2	France
1950	URUGUAY	2	Brazil	1	Brazil
1954	W GERMANY	3	Hungary	2	Switzerland
1958	BRAZIL	5	Sweden	2	Sweden
1962	BRAZIL	3	Czechosl'kia	1	Chile
1966	ENGLAND	4	W Germany	2	Wembley
			(after extra time)		
1970	BRAZIL	4	Italy	1	Mexico
1974	W GERMANY	2	Holland	1	W Germany
1978	ARGENTINA	3	Holland	1	Argentina
			(after extra time)		
1982	ITALY	3	W Germany	1	Spain
1986	ARGENTINA	3	W Germany	2	Mexico
1990	W GERMANY	1	Argentina	0	Italy
1994	BRAZIL	0	Italy	0	America
		(after extra time, Brazil won 3-2 on penalties)			
1998	FRANCE	3	Brazil	0	France
2002	BRAZIL	2	Germany	0	Japan

EUROPEAN CHAMPIONSHIP WINNERS

Year	Winners	Runners-up	Venue
1960	RUSSIA.................2	Yugoslavia........1	France
1964	SPAIN..................2	Russia 1	Spain
1968	ITALY 2	Yugoslavia........0	Italy
	(aet in replay after 1-1 draw)		
1972	W GERMANY.......3	Russia 0	Belgium
1976	CZECHOSLOVAKIA...2	W Germany...........2	Yugoslavia
	(Czechoslovakia won 5-3 on penalties)		
1980	W GERMANY.......2	Belgium 1	Italy
1984	FRANCE................2	Spain 0	France
1988	HOLLAND 2	Russia 0	West Germany
1992	DENMARK 2	Germany 0	Sweden
1996	GERMANY 2	Czech Rep 1	Wembley
	(1-1 full time. Germany scored Golden Goal in extra time)		
2000	FRANCE...............2	Italy 1	Holland
	(1-1 full time. France scored Golden Goal in extra time)		

SCOTLAND'S Darren Fletcher celebrates scoring the only goal of Euro 2004 qualifier against Lithuania at Hampden

EUROPEAN SUPER CUP

(Champions Cup v Cup-Winners' Cup winners)

Year	Team 1	Score	Team 2	Score
1972	AJAX	3	Rangers	2
	Rangers	1	AJAX	3
1973	AC Milan	0	AJAX	1
	AJAX	6	AC Milan	0
	1974 – Not contested			
1975	Bayern Munich	0	DYNAMO KIEV	1
	DYNAMO KIEV	2	Bayern Munich	0
1976	Bayern Munich	2	ANDERLECHT	1
	ANDERLECHT	4	Bayern Munich	1
1977	Hamburg	1	LIVERPOOL	1
	LIVERPOOL	6	Hamburg	0
1978	ANDERLECHT	3	Liverpool	1
	Liverpool	2	ANDERLECHT	1
1979	NOTTS FOREST	1	Barcelona	0
	Barcelona	1	NOTTS FOREST	1
1980	Nottingham Forest	2	VALENCIA	1
	VALENCIA	1	Nottingham Forest	0
	1981 – Not contested			
1982	Barcelona	1	ASTON VILLA	0
	ASTON VILLA	3	Barcelona	0
1983	Hamburg	0	ABERDEEN	0
	ABERDEEN	2	Hamburg	0
1984	JUVENTUS	2	Liverpool	0
	1985 Juventus v Everton not played due to			
	Uefa ban on English clubs			
1986	ST BUCHAREST	1	Dynamo Kiev	0
1987	Ajax	0	FC PORTO	1
	FC PORTO	1	Ajax	0
1988	MECHELEN	3	PSV Eindhoven	0
	PSV Eindhoven	1	MECHELEN	0
1989	Barcelona	1	AC MILAN	1
	AC MILAN	1	Barcelona	0
1990	Sampdoria	1	AC MILAN	1
	AC MILAN	2	Sampdoria	0
1991	MANCHESTER UTD.	1	Red Star Belgrade	0
1992	Werder Bremen	1	BARCELONA	1
	BARCELONA	2	Werder Bremen	1
1993	PARMA	0	AC Milan	1
	AC Milan	0	PARMA	2
	(aet, 90 min. 0-1, agg.1-2 for Parma)			
1994	Arsenal	0	AC MILAN	0
	AC MILAN	2	Arsenal	0
1995	Real Zaragoza	1	AJAX	1
	AJAX	4	Real Zaragoza	0
1996	Paris St Germain	0	JUVENTUS	1
	JUVENTUS	6	Paris St Germain	1
1997	BARCELONA	0	Borussia Dortmund	1
	Borussia Dortmund	1	BARCELONA	2
1998	Real Madrid	0	CHELSEA	1
1999	LAZIO	1	Manchester United	0
2000	GALATASARAY	2	Real Madrid	1
	(1-1 full time. Galatasaray scored golden goal in extra time)			
2001	LIVERPOOL	3	Bayern Munich	2
2002	REAL MADRID	3	Feyenoord	1
2003	AC MILAN	1	FC Porto	0

EUROPEAN CUP FINALS

Year	Winners		Runners-up	
1956	REAL MADRID	4	Rheims	3
	(Paris, 38,000)			
1957	REAL MADRID	2	Fiorentina	0
	(Madrid, 124,000)			
1958	REAL MADRID	3	AC Milan	2
	After extra time (Brussels, 67,000)			
1959	REAL MADRID	2	Rheims	0
	(Stuttgart, 80,000)			
1960	REAL MADRID	7	Eintracht	3
	(Glasgow, 127,261)			
1961	BENFICA	3	Barcelona	2
	(Berne, 28,000)			
1962	BENFICA	5	Real Madrid	3
	(Amsterdam, 65,000)			
1963	AC MILAN	2	Benfica	1
	(Wembley, 45,000)			
1964	INTER MILAN	3	Real Madrid	1
	(Vienna, 74,000)			
1965	INTER MILAN	1	Benfica	0
	(Milan, 80,000)			
1966	REAL MADRID	2	Partisan Belgrade	1
	(Brussels, 55,000)			
1967	CELTIC	2	Inter Milan	1
	(Lisbon, 56,000)			
1968	MAN UNITED	4	Benfica	1
	(Wembley, 100,000)			
1969	AC MILAN	4	Ajax	1
	(Madrid, 50,000)			
1970	FEYENOORD	2	Celtic	1
	(Milan, 50,000)			
1971	AJAX	2	Panathinaikos	0
	(Wembey, 90,000)			
1972	AJAX	2	Inter Milan	0
	(Rotterdam, 67,000)			
1973	AJAX	1	Juventus	0
	(Belgrade, 93,500)			
1974	BAYERN MUNICH	4	Atletico Madrid	0
	(Brussels, 65,000) (after 1-1 draw)			
1975	BAYERN MUNICH	2	Leeds	0
	(Paris, 50,000)			
1976	BAYERN MUNICH	1	St Etienne	0
	(Glasgow, 54,864)			

EUROPEAN CUP FINALS (continued)

7	LIVERPOOL...............3	Borussia MG..................1	
	(Rome, 57,000)		
8	LIVERPOOL...............1	Bruges 0	
	(Wembley, 92,000)		
9	NOTTS FOREST 1	Malmo 0	
	(Munich, 57,500)		
0	NOTTS FOREST 1	Hamburg 0	
	(Madrid, 50,000)		
1	LIVERPOOL...............1	Real Madrid 0	
	(Paris, 48,360)		
2	ASTON VILLA............1	Bayern Munich...............0	
	(Rotterdam, 46,000)		
3	HAMBURG..................1	Juventus 0	
	(Athens, 75,000)		
4	LIVERPOOL...............1	Roma 1	
	(Rome, 69,693)		

Liverpool won 4-2 on penalties

5	JUVENTUS.................1	Liverpool 0	
	(Brussels, 58,000)		
6	S BUCHAREST 0	Barcelona.......................0	

Steaua Bucharest won 2-0 on penalties (Seville, 70,000)

7	PORTO......................2	Bayern Munich...............1	
	(Vienna, 59,000)		
8	PSV 0	Benfica...........................0	
	(Stuttgart, 70,000)		

PSV Eindhoven won 6-5 on penalties

9	AC MILAN 4	Steau Bucharest 0	
	(Barcelona, 97,000)		
0	AC MILAN 1	Benfica...........................0	
	(Vienna, 57,500)		
1	R.S. BELGRADE 0	Marseille.........................0	
	(Bari, 56,000)		

Red Star won 5-3 on penalties

2	BARCELONA 1	Sampdoria 0	
	After extra time		
	(Wembley, 70,000)		
3	MARSEILLE................1	AC Milan 0	
	(Munich, 65,000)		
4	AC MILAN 4	Barcelona.......................0	
	(Athens, 75,000)		
5	AJAX 1	AC Milan 0	
	(Vienna, 49,000)		

1996   JUVENTUS..................1   Ajax ....
        (Rome, 67,000)
        (1-1 full time. Juventus won 4-2 on penalties)
1997   B DORTMUND 3   Juventus ....
        (Munich, 55,500)
1998   REAL MADRID 1   Juventus ....
        (Amsterdam, 45,000)
1999   MANCHESTER UTD ..2   Bayern Munich.............
        (Barcelona, 90,000)
2000   REAL MADRID 3   Valencia........................
        (Paris, 73,000)
2001   BAYERN MUNICH......1   Valencia........................
        (Milan, 80,000)
        (1-1 full-time. Bayern won 5-4 on penalties)
2002   REAL MADRID 2   Bayer Leverkusen ....
        (Glasgow, 52,000)
2003   AC MILAN 0   Juventus ....
        (0-0 after extra time. AC Milan won 3-2 on penalties)
        (Manchester, 63,000)
2004   PORTO 3   Monaco.........................
        (Gelsenkirchen, 52,000)

**PORTO players savour their 3-0 Champions League Fi
victory over French side Monaco at Gelsenkirchen's
AufSchalke Arena in Schalke**

UROPEAN CUP-WINNERS' CUP FINALS

1	Rangers......................0	FIORENTINA 2
	(Ibrox, 80,000)	
	FIORENTINA 2	Rangers.............................1
	(Florence, 50,000)	
	Aggregate 4-1	
2	ATLETICO MADRID ..1	Fiorentina 1
	(Glasgow, 27,389)	
	ATLETICO MADRID ..3	Fiorentina 0
	(Stuttgart, 45,000)	
3	SPURS 5	Atletico Madrid 1
	(Rotterdam, 25,000)	
4	SPORTING LISBON ..1	MTK Budapest..................0
	(Antwerp, 18,000)	
	After 3-3 draw in Brussels	
5	WEST HAM.................2	Munich 1860 0
	(Wembley, 100,000)	
6	BOR. DORTMUND 2	Liverpool 1
	(Hampden, 41,657)	
7	BAYERN MUNICH 1	Rangers.............................0
	(Nuremberg, 69,480 aet)	
8	AC MILAN..................2	S.V. Hamburg....................0
	(Rotterdam, 60,000)	
9	S BRATISLAVIA..........3	Barcelona 2
	(Basle, 40,000)	
0	MANCHESTER CITY 2	Gornik 1
	(Vienna, 10,000)	
1	CHELSEA 2	Real Madrid 1
	(Athens, 24,000, after 1-1 draw)	
2	RANGERS 3	Moscow Dynamo...............2
	(Barcelona, 35,000)	
3	AC MILAN 1	Leeds United.....................0
	(Salonika, 45,000)	
4	AC MAGDEBURG......2	AC Milan 0
	(Rotterdam, 5,000)	
5	DYNAMO KIEV 3	Ferencvaros 0
	(Basle, 13,000)	
6	ANDERLECHT............4	West Ham 2
	(Brussels, 58,000)	
7	SV HAMBURG 2	Anderlecht.........................0
	(Amsterdam, 65,000)	
8	ANDERLECHT............4	Austria Wein 0
	(Amsterdam, 48,679)	

1979	BARCELONA.............4	Fortuna Dusseldorf ....
	(Basel, 58,000)	
1980	VALENCIA 0	Arsenal ....
	(Brussels, 40,000, Valencia won 5-4 on penalties)	
1981	DYNAMO TBILISI 2	Carl Zeiss Jena ....
	(Dusseldorf, 9,000)	
1982	BARCELONA.............2	Standard Liege...............
	(Barcelona, 100,000)	
1983	ABERDEEN 2	Real Madrid.....................
	(Gothenburg, 17,804)	
1984	JUVENTUS 2	FC Porto.........................
	(Basle, 60,000)	
1985	EVERTON 3	Vienna Rapide................
	(Rotterdam, 30,000)	
1986	DYNAMO KIEV 3	Atletico Madrid................
	(Lyon, 39,300)	
1987	AJAX 1	Lokomotiv Leipzig............
	(Athens, 35,000)	
1988	MICHELEN 1	Ajax ....
	(Strasbourg, 39,446)	
1989	BARCELONA.............2	Sampdoria ....
	(Berne, 45,000)	
1990	SAMPDORIA 2	Anderlecht......................
	(Gothenburg, 20,103)	
1991	MANCHESTER UTD ..2	Barcelona........................
	(Rotterdam, 50,000)	
1992	WERDER BREMEN 2	Monaco...........................
	(Lisbon, 50,000)	
1993	Antwerp.....................1	PARMA............................
	(Wembley, 50,000)	
1994	Parma 0	ARSENAL.........................
	(Copenhagen, 33,765)	
1995	Arsenal 1	REAL ZARAGOZA............
	(aet, 90 minutes 1-1) (Paris, 42,000)	
1996	PARIS ST GERMAIN ..1	Rapid Vienna...................
	(Brussels, 50,000)	
1997	BARCELONA.............1	Paris St Germain..............
	(Rotterdam, 40,000)	
1998	CHELSEA 1	VfB Stuttgart ....
	(Stockholm)	
1999	LAZIO 2	Real Mallorca ....
	(Villa Park, 30,000)	

UEFA CUP FINALS

(FORMERLY FAIRS CITIES CUP)

58	London 2	BARCELONA 2	
	BARCELONA 6	London 0	
		(agg: 8-2)	
60	Birmingham................0	BARCELONA 0	
	BARCELONA 4	Birmingham......................1	
		(agg: 4-1)	
61	Birmingham................2	ROMA 2	
	ROMA 2	Birmingham......................0	
		(agg: 4-2)	
62	VALENCIA 6	Barcelona.........................2	
	Barcelona 1	VALENCIA 1	
		(agg 7-3)	
63	Dynamo Zagreb 1	VALENCIA 2	
	VALENCIA 2	Dynamo Zagreb 0	
		(agg: 4-1)	
64	REAL ZARAGOZA......2	Valencia............................1	
		(Barcelona)	
65	FERENCVAROS 1	Juventus 0	
		(Turin)	
66	BARCELONA 0	Real Zaragoza...................1	
	Real Zaragoza............2	BARCELONA 4	
		(agg: 4-3)	
67	DINAMO ZAGREB 2	Leeds United.....................0	
	Leeds United..............0	DINAMO ZAGREB 0	
		(agg: 2-0)	
68	LEEDS UNITED 1	Ferencvaros 0	
	Ferencvaros 0	LEEDS UNITED..................0	
		(agg: 1-0)	
69	NEWCASTLE UTD 3	Ujpest Dozsa....................0	
	Ujpest Dozsa..............2	NEWCASTLE UTD 3	
		(agg: 6-2)	
70	Anderlecht.................3	ARSENAL...........................1	
	ARSENAL 3	Anderlecht........................0	
		(agg: 4-3)	
71	Juventus 2	LEEDS UNITED..................2	
	LEEDS UNITED 1	Juventus 1	
		(agg: 3-3)	
		Leeds won on away goals	
72	Wolves.......................1	TOTTENHAM 2	
	TOTTENHAM 1	Wolves 1	
		(agg: 3-2)	

1973	LIVERPOOL..............3	Borussia M....................
	Borussia M 2	LIVERPOOL ....
	(agg: 3-2)	
1974	Tottenham Hostpur 2	FEYENOORD ....
	FEYENOORD 2	Tottenham Hotspur .....
	(agg: 4-2)	
1975	BORUSSIA M 0	Twente ....
	Twente........................1	BORUSSIA M ....
	(agg: 5-1)	
1976	LIVERPOOL..............3	FC Bruges ....
	Bruges.......................1	LIVERPOOL ....
	(agg 4-3)	
1977	JUVENTUS 1	Athletic Bilbao.............
	Athletic Bilbao............2	JUVENTUS ....
	(agg: 2-2. Juventus won on away goals)	
1978	Bastia 0	PSV EINDHOVEN ....
	PSV EINDHOVEN 3	Bastia ....
	(agg: 3-0)	
1979	Red Star Belgrade 1	BORUSSIA M ....
	BORUSSIA M 1	Red Star Belgrade...........
	(agg: 2-1)	
1980	Borussia M 3	EINTRACHT.................
	EINTRACHT 1	Borussia M ....
	(agg: 3-3. Eintracht won on away goals)	
1981	IPSWICH 3	AZ 67 ....
	AZ 67.........................4	IPSWICH ....
	(agg: 5-4)	
1982	GOTHENBURG 1	Hamburg ....
	Hamburg 0	GOTHENBURG ....
	(agg: 4-0)	
1983	ANDERLECHT............1	Benfica ....
	Benfica 1	ANDERLECHT..............
	(agg: 2-1)	
1984	Anderlecht.................1	TOTTENHAM...............
	TOTTENHAM 1	Anderlecht ....
	(agg: 2-2. Tottenham won 4-3 on penalties)	
1985	Videoton 0	REAL MADRID ....
	REAL MADRID 0	Videoton ....
	(agg: 3-1)	
1986	REAL MADRID 5	Cologne ....
	Cologne......................2	REAL MADRID ....
	(agg: 5-3)	

7 GOTHENBURG 1   Dundee United 0
   Dundee United 1   GOTHENBURG................1
                      (agg: 2-1)

8 Espanyol 3   BAYER LEVERKUSEN 0
   BAYER LEVERKUSEN ..3   Espanyol 0
      (agg: 3-3. Leverkusen won 3-2 on penalties)

9 NÁPOLI 2   Stuttgart 1
   Stuttgart 3   NÁPOLI 3
                      (agg: 5-4)

0 JUVENTUS 3   Fiorentina 1
   Fiorentina 0   JUVENTUS 0
                      (agg: 3-1)

1 INTER MILAN 2   Roma 0
   Roma..........................0   INTER MILAN 0
                      (agg: 2-1)

2 Torino 2   AJAX..............................2
   AJAX 0   Torino 0
      (agg: 2-2. Ajax win on away goals rule)

3 Borussia Dortmund 1   JUVENTUS 3
   JUVENTUS 3   Borussia Dortmund..........0
                      (agg: 6-1)

4 Salzburg 0   INTER MILAN 1
   INTER MILAN 1   Salzburg 0
                      (agg: 2-0)

5 PARMA 1   Juventus 0
   Juventus 1   PARMA 1
                      (agg: 2-1)

6 BAYERN MUNICH......2   Bordeaux 0
   Bordeaux....................1   BAYERN MUNICH 3
                      (agg: 5-1)

7 Schalke 1   INTER MILAN 0
   INTER MILAN 1   Schalke............................0
      (agg: 1-1. Schalke win 4-1 on penalties)

8 INTER MILAN 3   Lazio 0
                       (Paris)

9 PARMA 3   Marseille 0
                      (Moscow)

0 GALATASARAY 0   Arsenal 0
      (Galatasaray won 4-1 on penalties)
                    (Copenhagen)

1 LIVERPOOL 5   Alaves..............................4
      (4-4 full-time. Liverpool win with golden goal)
                     (Dortmund)

2 Borussia Dortmund ..2   FEYENOORD 3
                    (Rotterdam)

3 Celtic 2   PORTO 3
                 (2-2 after 90 mins.)
                      (Seville)

4 VALENCIA 2   Marseille 0
                    (Gothenburg)

GAMES TO REMEMBER

1967   CELTIC..............2   Inter Milan ....
(European Cup Final, Lisbon, May 25. Attendance 56,000)
CELTIC: Simpson, Craig, Gemmell, Murdoch, McNeill, Cla
Johnstone, Wallace, Chalmers, Auld, Lennox. Scorers: Gemm
(63), Chalmers (85).
INTER MILAN: Sarti, Burgnich, Facchetti, Bedin, Guarneri, Picc
Domenghini, Cappellini, Mazzola, Bicicli, Corso. Scorer: Mazzola
pen)

1967   England 2   SCOTLAND ....
(Home Internationals, Wembley, April 15. Att: 100,000)
SCOTLAND: Simpson, Gemmell, McCreadie, Greig, McKinno
Baxter, Wallace, Bremner, McCalliog, Law, Lennox. Scorers: La
Lennox, McCalliog.
ENGLAND: Banks, Cohen, Wilson, Stiles, J Charlton, Moore, B
Greaves, R Charlton, Hurst, Peters. Scorers: J. Charlton, Hurst.

1972   RANGERS 3   Moscow Dynamo ....
(Cup-Winners' Cup Final, Barcelona, May 24. Att: 35,000)
RANGERS: McCloy, Jardine, Mathieson, Greig, D Johnstone, Smi
McLean, Conn, Stein, MacDonald, W Johnston. Scorers: Stein (2
Johnston (40, 49).
MOSCOW DYNAMO: Pilgui, Basalev, Dolmatov, Zyko
Dobbonosov, (Gerschkovitch), Zhukov, Baidatchini, Jakub
(Eschtrekov), Sabo, Makovikov, Evryuzhikbin. Scorers: Eschtrek
(55) Makovikov (87).

1983   ABERDEEN 2   Real Madrid ....
(Cup-Winners' Cup Final, Gothenburg, May 11. Att: 17,804)
ABERDEEN: Leighton, Rougvie, McMaster, Cooper, McLeish, Mil
Strachan, Simpson, McGhie, Black (Hewitt), Weir. Subs: Kenne
Gunn, Watson, Hewitt, Angus. Scorers: Black (7), Hewitt (112).
REAL MADRID: Agustin, Jan jose, Camacho, Metgod, Bon
Gallego, Jaunito, Angel, Santillana, Stielike, Isidro. Scorer: Juan
(14 pen).

2003   SCOTLAND 1   Holland ....
(Euro 2004 play-off 1st leg, Glasgow, November 15. Att: 50,67
SCOTLAND: Douglas, McNamara, Pressley, Wilkie, Naysmi
Fletcher, Dailly, Ferguson, McCann (Pearson), Dickov (Mille
McFadden (Hutchison). Scorer McFadden (22).
HOLLAND: Van der Sar, Ooijer, Stam, Frank de Boer, v
Bronckhorst (Seedorf), Van der Meyde, Cocu, Davids (Van d
Vaart), Overmars, Kluivert (Makaay), van Nistelrooy.

2004   CELTIC.................1   Barcelona ....
(Uefa Cup 4th rd 1st leg, Glasgow, March 11. Att: 59,539)
CELTIC: Douglas, Varga, Balde, McNamara, Agathe, Lenno
Petrov, Pearson, Thompson (Sylla), Larsson, Beattie (Marsha
Scorer: Thompson (59).
BARCELONA: Victor Valdes, Reiziger (Gerard Lopez), Puy
Oleguer, Gabri, Cocu, Xavi, Motta, Ronaldinho, Luis Garc
(Quaresma), Saviola.

SCOTTISH CLUBS IN EUROPE
A COMPLETE HISTORY
Abbreviations EC (European Champions Cup), ECWC
European Cup-Winners' Cup), FC (Fairs Cities Cup) UEFA
efa Cup) w (won) l (lost) p (preliminary) q (qualifying round)

ABERDEEN

ponents	Venue	Res	Scorers	Rnd
1967-68 ECWC				
Reykjavic	H	W10-1	Munro 3, Storrie 2	1
land)			Smith 2, McMillan,	
			Petersen,Taylor	
	A	W4-1	Storrie 2 Buchan, Munro	
ndard Liege	A	L0-3		2
lgium)	H	W2-0	Munro, Melrose	
1968-69 FC				
via Sofia	A	D0-0		1
lgaria)	H	W2-0	Robb, Taylor	
al Zaragossa	H	W2-1	Forrest, Smith	2
ain)	A	L0-3		
1970-71 ECWC				
nved	H	W3-1	Graham, Harper, S Murray	1
ngary)	A	L1-3	S Murray	
1971-72 UEFA				
lta Vigo	A	W2-0	Harper, o.g.	1
ain)	H	W1-0	Harper	
ventus	A	L0-2		2
ly)	H	D1-1	Harper	
1972-73 UEFA				
russia Moench.	H	L2-3	Harper, Jarvie	1
est Germany)	A	L3-6	Harper 2, Jarvie	
1973-74 UEFA				
n Harps	H	W4-1	R Miller, Jarvie 2,	1
ep of Ireland)			Graham	
	A	W3-1	Robb, Graham, R Miller	
ttenham H	H	D1-1	Hermiston pen	2
ngland)	A	L1-4	Jarvie	
1977-78 UEFA				
WD Molenbeek	A	D0-0		1
elgium)	H	L1-2	Jarvie	
1978-79 ECWC				
rek Stanke	A	L2-3	Jarvie, Harper	1
lgaria)	H	W3-0	Strachan, Jarvie, Harper	
rtuna Dusseldorf	A	L0-3		2
est Germany)	H	W2-0	McLelland, Jarvie	
1979-80 UEFA				
ntracht Frankfurt	H	D1-1	Harper	1
est Germany)	A	L0-1		
1980-81 EC				
stria Vienna	H	W1-0	McGhee	1
ustria)	A	D0-0		

Opponents	Venue	Res	Scorers	R
Liverpool	H	L0-1		
(England)	A	L0-4		
1981-82 UEFA				
Ipswich Town	A	D1-1	Hewitt	
(England)	H	W3-1	Strachan, pen, Weir 2	
Arges Pitesti	H	W3-0	Strachan, Weir, Hewitt	
Romania	A	D2-2	Strachan, pen,Hewitt	
SV Hamburg	H	W3-2	Black, Watson, Hewitt	
(West Germany)	A	L1-3	McGhee	
1982-83 ECWC				
Sion	H	W7-0	Black 2, Strachan,	
(Switzerland)			Hewitt, Simpson,	
			McGhee, Kennedy	
	A	W4-1	Hewitt, Miller, McGhee 2	
Dinamo Tirana	H	W1-0	Hewitt	
(Albania)	A	D0-0		
Lech Poznan	H	W2-0	McGhee, Weir	
(Poland)	A	W1-0	Bell	
Bayern Munich	H	D0-0		Q
(West Germany)	H	W3-2	Simpson, McLeish, Hewitt	
Waterschei	H	W5-1	Black, Simpson	S
(Belgium)			McGhee 2, Weir	
	A	L0-1		
Real Madrid	N	W2-1	Black, Hewitt	
(Spain)				
1983-84 (European Super Cup)				
Hamburg	A	D0-0		
(West Germany)	H	W2-0	Simpson, McGhee	
1983-84 ECWC				
Akranes	A	W2-1	McGhee 2	
(Iceland)	H	D1-1	Strachan, pen	
Beveren	A	D0-0		
(Belgium)	H	W4-1	Strachan 2, 1 pen,	
			Simpson, Weir	
Ujpest Dozsa	A	L0-2		Q
(Hungary)	H	W3-0	McGhee 3	
Porto	A	L0-1		S
(Portugal)	H	L0-1		
1984-85 EC				
Dynamo Berlin	H	W2-1	Black 2	
(East Germany)	A	L1-2	Angus	
1985-86 EC				
Akranes	A	W3-1	Black, Hewitt, Stark	
(Iceland)	H	W4-1	Simpson, Hewitt	
			Gray, Falconer	
Servette	A	D0-0		
(Switzerland)	H	W1-0	McDougall	
IFK Gothenburg	H	D2-2	J Miller, Hewitt	Q
(Sweden)	A	D0-0		
1986-87 ECWC				
Sion	H	W2-1	Bett (pen), Wright	
(Switzerland)	A	L0-3		

ponents	Venue	Res	Scorers	Rnd
		1987-88 UEFA		
hemians	A	D0-0		1
p of Ireland)	H	W1-0	Bett pen	
venoord	H	W2-1	Falconer, J Miller	2
olland)	A	L0-1		
		1988-89 UEFA		
namo Dresden	H	D0-0		1
st Germany)	A	L0-2		
		1989-90 UEFA		
pid Vienna	H	W2-1	C Robertson, Grant	1
ustria)	A	L0-1		
		1990-91 ECWC		
lamis	A	W2-0	Mason, Gillhaus	1
yprus)	H	W3-0	C Robertson, Gillhaus, Jess	
gia Warsaw	H	D0-0		2
oland)	A	L0-1		
		1991-92 UEFA		
Copenhagen	H	L0-1		1
enmark)	A	L0-2		
		1993-94 ECWC		
ur	A	W3-0	Shearer, Jess 2	1
eland)	H	W4-0	Jess 2, Miller, Irvine	
rino	A	L2-3	Paatelainen, Jess	
aly)	H	L1-3	Richardson	
		1994-95 UEFA		
onto Riga	A	D0-0		P
atvia)	H	D1-1	Kane	
		1996-97 UEFA		
nius	A	W4-1	Dodds 2, Glass, Shearer	Q
thuania)	H	L1-3	Irvine	
rry Town	H	W3-1	Windass, Glass, Young	1
ales)	A	D3-3	Dodds 2, Rowson	
ondby	H	L0-2		2
enmark)	A	D0-0		
		2000-01 UEFA		
hemians	H	L1-2	Winters	Q
ep of Ireland)	A	W1-0	Morrison og	
		2002-2003 UEFA		
stru Otaci	H	W1-0	Mackie	Q
oldova)	A	D0-0		
rtha Berlin	H	D0-0		1
ermany)	A	L1-0		

AIRDRIE

1992-93 ECWC

ponents	Venue	Res	Scorers	Rnd
arta Prague	H	L0-1		1
zechoslovakia)	A	L1-2	Black	

CELTIC

Opponents	Venue	Res	Scorers	R
		1962-63 FC		
Valencia	A	L2-4	Carrol 2	
(Spain)	H	D2-2	Crerand, o.g.	
		1963-64 ECWC		
Basle	A	W5-1	Divers, Hughes 3, Lennox	
(Switzerland)	H	W5-0	Johnstone, Divers 2	
			Murdoch, Chalmers	
Dynamo Zagreb	H	W3-0	Chalmers 2, Hughes	
(Yugoslavia)	A	L1-2	Murdoch	
Slovan Bratislava	H	W1-0	Murdoch pen	(
(Czechoslovakia)	A	W1-0	Hughes	
MTK Budapest	H	W3-0	Johnstone, Chalmers 2	!
(Hungary)	A	L0-4		
		1964-65 FC		
Leixoes	A	D1-1	Murdoch	
(Portugal)	H	W3-0	Murdoch, pen, Chalmers	
Barcelona	A	L1-3	Hughes	
(Spain)	H	D0-0		
		1965-66 ECWC		
Go Ahead	A	W6-0	Gallacher 2, Hughes	
(Holland)			Johnstone 2 Lennox	
	H	W1-0	McBride	
Aarhus	A	W1-0	McBride	
(Denmark)	H	W2-0	McNeill, Johnstone	
Dynamo Kiev	H	W3-0	Gemmell, Murdoch 2	(
(USSR)	A	D1-1	Gemmell	
Liverpool	H	W1-0	Lennox	!
(England)	A	L0-2		
		1966-67 EC		
Zurich	H	W2-0	Gemmell, McBride	
(Switzerland)	A	W3-0	Gemmell 2, 1 pen, McBride	
Nantes	A	W3-1	McBride, Lennox,	
(France)			Chalmers	
	H	W3-1	Johnstone, Lennox, Chalmers	
Vojvodina	A	L0-1		(
(Yugoslavia)	H	W2-0	Chalmers, McNeill	
Dukla Prague	H	W3-1	Johnstone, Wallace, 2	!
(Czechoslovakia)	A	D0-0		
Inter Milan	N	W2-1	Gemmell, Chalmers	
(Italy)				
		1967-68 EC		
Dymano Kiev	H	L1-2	Lennox	
(USSR)	A	D1-1	Lennox	

ponents	Venue	Res	Scorers	Rnd
		1968-69 EC		
Etienne (ance)	A	L0-2		1
H	W4-0	Gemmell pen, Craig Chalmers, McBride	
d Star Belgrade (goslavia)	H	W5-1	Murdoch, Johnstone 2, Lennox, Wallace	2
	A	D1-1	Wallace	
Milan ly)	A	D0-0		QF
	H	L0-1		
		1969-70 EC		
sle (vitzerland)	A	D0-0		1
	H	W2-0	Hood, Gemmell	
nfica (rtugal)	H	W3-0	Gemmell, Wallace, Hood	2
	A	L0-3		
rentina ly)	H	W3-0	Auld, Wallace, o.g.	QF
	A	L0-1		
eds United gland)	H	W1-0	Connelly	SF
	H	W2-1	Hughes, Murdoch	
yenoord olland)	N	L1-2	Gemmell	F
		1970-71 EC		
V Kokkola nland)	H	W9-0	Hood 3, Wilson 2, Hughes McNeill, Johnstone, Davidson	1
	A	W5-0	Wallace 2, Callaghan Davidson, Lennox	
terford ep of Ireland)	A	W7-0	Wallace 3, Murdoch 2 Macari 2	2
	H	W3-2	Hughes, Johnstone 2	
ıx olland)	A	L0-3		QF
	H	W1-0	Johnstone	
		1971-72 EC		
; 1903 penhagen enmark)	A	L1-2	Macari	1
	H	W3-0	Wallace 2, Callaghan	
ema W alta)	H	W5-0	Gemmell, Macari 2 Hood, Brogan	2
	A	W2-1	Hood, Lennox	
best Dozsa ungary)	A	W2-1	Macari, o.g.	QF
	H	D1-1	Macari	
er Milan ıly)	A	D0-0		SF
	H	D0-0	lost on penalties	
		1972-73 EC		
senborg orway)	H	W2-1	Macari, Deans	1
	A	W3-1	Macari, Hood, Dalglish	
best Dozsa ungary)	H	W2-1	Dalglish 2	2
	A	L0-3		

Opponents	Venue	Res	Scorers	R
		1973-74 EC		
Turku	A	W6-1	Callaghan 2, Hood, Johnstone, Deans, Connelly, pen	
(Finland)	H	W3-0	Deans, Johnstone 2	
Vejle	H	D0-0		
(Denmark)	A	W1-0	Lennox	
Basle	A	L2-3	Wilson, Dalglish	C
(Switzerland)	H	W4-2	Dalglish, Deans, Callaghan, Murray	
Atletico Madrid	H	D0-0		S
(Spain)	A	L0-2		
		1974-75 EC		
Olympiakos	H	D1-1	Wilson	
(Greece)	A	L0-2		
		1975-76 ECWC		
Valur	A	W2-0	Wilson McDonald	
(Iceland)	H	W7-0	Edvaldsson, Dalglish McCluskey, pen, Deans Hood 2, Callaghan	
Boavista	A	D0-0		
(Portugal)	H	W3-1	Dalglish, Edvaldsson, Deans	
Zwickau	H	D1-1	Dalglish	C
(East Germany)	A	L0-1		
		1976-77 UEFA		
Wisla Krakow	H	D2-2	McDonald, Dalglish	
(Poland)	A	L0-2		
		1977-78 EC		
Jeunesse D'Esch	H	W5-0	McDonald, Wilson, Craig 2, McLaughlin	
(Luxembourg)	A	W6-1	Lennox 2, Glavin, Edvaldsson 2, Craig	
SW Innsbruck	H	W2-1	Craig, Burns	
(Austria)	A	L0-3		
		1979-80 EC		
Partizan Tirana	A	L0-1		
(Albania)	H	W4-1	McDonald, Aitken 2 Davidson	
Dundalk	H	W3-2	McDonald, Burns McCluskey	
(Rep of Ireland)	A	D0-0		
Real Madrid	H	W2-0	McCluskey, Doyle	Q
(Spain)	A	L0-3		

ponents	Venue	Res	Scorers	Rnd
		1980-81 ECWC		
osgyor (ungary)	H	W6-0	McGarvey 2, Sullivan McCluskey 2, o.g.	P
	A	L1-2	Nicholas	
nisorara (omania)	H	W2-1	Nicholas 2	1
	A	L0-1	lost on away goals	
		1981-82 EC		
ventus (aly)	H	W1-0	MacLeod	1
	A	L0-2		
		1982-83 EC		
ax (olland)	H	D2-2	Nicholas, McGarvey	1
	A	W2-1	Nicholas, McCluskey	
al Sociedad (pain)	A	L0-2		2
	H	W2-1	MacLeod 2	
		1983-84 UEFA		
arhus (enmark)	H	1-0	Aitken	1
	A	W4-1	MacLeod, McGarvey, Aitken, Provan	
orting Lisbon (ortugal)	A	L0-2		2
	H	W5-0	Burns, McAdam, McClair MacLeod, McGarvey	
otts Forest (ngland)	A	D0-0		3
	H	L1-2	MacLeod	
		1984-85 ECWC		
ent (elgium)	A	L0-1		1
	H	W3-0	McGarvey 2, McStay	
apid Vienna (ustria)	A	L1-3	McClair	2
	H	W3-0	McClair, MacLeod, Burns	
(UEFA ordered match to be replayed)				
	N	L0-1		
		1985-86 ECWC		
tletico Madrid (pain)	A	D1-1	Johnston	1
	H	L1-2	Aitken	
		1986-87 EC		
hamrock Rov (ep of Ireland)	A	W1-0	MacLeod	1
	H	W2-0	Johnston 2	
ymano Kiev (SSR)	H	D1-1	Johnston	2
	A	L1-3	McGhee	
		1987-88 UEFA		
or Dortmund (Vest Germany)	H	W2-1	Walker, Whyte	1
	A	L0-2		
		1988-89 EC		
onved (ungary)	A	L0-1		1
	H	W4-0	Stark, Walker, McAvennie, McGhee	
Verder Bremen (Vest Germany)	H	L0-2		2
	A	D0-0		

Opponents	Venue	Res	Scorers	R
		1989-90 ECWC		
Part Belgrade	A	L1-2	Galloway	
(Yugoslavia)	H	W5-4	Dziekanowski 4 Walker	
		1991-92 UEFA		
Ekeren	H	W2-0	Nicholas 2, 1 pen	
(Belgium)	A	D1-1	Galloway	
Neuchatel Xamax	A	L1-5	O'Neill	
(Switzerland)	H	W1-0	Miller	
		1992-93 UEFA		
Cologne	A	L0-2		
(Germany)	H	W3-0	McStay, Creaney, Collins	
Bor Dortmund	A	L0-1		
(Germany)	H	L1-2	Creaney	
		1993-94 UEFA		
Young Boys	A	D0-0		
(Switzerland)	H	W1-0	og	
Sporting Lisbon	H	W1-0	Creaney	
(Portugal)	A	L0-2		
		1995-96 ECWC		
Dinamo Batumi	A	W3-2	Thom 2, Donnelly	
(Georgia)	H	W4-0	Thom 2, Donnelly, Walker	
Paris St Germain	A	L0-1		
(France)	H	L0-3		
		1996-97 UEFA		
Kosice	A	D0-0		
(Poland)	H	W1-0	Cadete	
Hamburg	H	L0-2		
(Germany)	A	L0-2		
		1997-98 UEFA		
Inter Cable-Tel	A	W3-0	Thom pen,	
(Wales)			Johnson pen, Wieghorst	
	H	W5-0	Thom pen, Jackson,	
			Johnson, Hannah, Hay	
Tirol Innsbruck	A	L1-2	Stubbs	
(Austria)	H	W6-3	Donnelly 2, 1 pen, Thom	
			Burley 2, Wieghorst	
Liverpool	H	D2-2	McNamara, Donnelly	
(England)	A	D0-0		
		1998-99 EC		
St Patrick's	H	D0-0		
(Rep of Ireland)	A	W2-0	Brattbakk, Larsson	
Croatia Zagreb	H	W1-0	Jackson	
(Croatia)	A	L0-3		
		UEFA		
Vitoria Guimareas	A	W2-1	Larsson, Donnelly	
(Portugal)	H	W2-1	Stubbs, Larsson	
FC Zurich	H	D1-1	Brattbakk	
(Switzerland)	A	L4-2	O'Donnell, Larsson	

Opponents	Venue	Res	Scorers	Rnd
		1999-2000 UEFA		
Cwmbran Town (Wales)	A	W6-0	Berkovic, Larsson 2, Tebily, Viduka, Brattbakk	Q
	H	W4-0	Brattbakk, Smith, Mjallby, Johnson	
Hapoel Tel Aviv (Israel)	H	W2-0	Larsson 2	1
	A	W1-0	Larsson	
Lyon (France)	A	L0-1		2
	H	L0-1		
		2000-2001 UEFA		
Jeunesse Esch (Luxembourg)	A	W4-0	Moravcik 2, Larsson, Petta	Q
	H	W7-0	Burchill 3, Berkovic 2, Riseth, Petrov	
HJK Helsinki (Finland)	H	W2-0	Larsson 2	1
	A	L1-2	Sutton	
Bordeaux (France)	A	D1-1	Larsson pen	2
	H	L1-2 (aet)	Moravcik	
		2001-2002 EC		
Ajax (Holland)	A	W3-1	Petta, Agathe, Sutton	Q3
	H	L0-1		
		FIRST GROUP STAGE		
Juventus (Italy)	A	L2-3	Petrov, Larsson	
Porto (Portugal)	H	W1-0	Larsson	
Rosenborg (Norway)	H	W1-0	Thompson	
Porto	A	L0-3		
Rosenborg	A	L0-2		
Juventus	H	W4-3	Valgaeren, Sutton 2, Larsson	
		UEFA		
Valencia (Spain)	A	L0-1		3
	H	W1-0	Larsson	
	(aet, Valencia won 5-4 on penalties)			
		2002-2003 EC		
FC Basel (Switzerland)	H	W3-1	Larsson pen, Sutton, Sylla	Q3
	A	L2-0		
		UEFA		
FK Suduva (Lithuania)	H	W8-1	Larsson 3, Petrov, Sutton, Lambert, Hartson, Valgaeren	1
	A	W2-0	Fernandez, Thompson	
Blackburn (England)	H	W1-0	Larsson	2
	A	W2-0	Larsson, Sutton	
Celta Vigo (Spain)	H	W1-0	Larsson	3
	A	L2-1	Hartson	
VfB Stuttgart (Germany)	H	W3-1	Lambert, Maloney, Petrov	4
	A	L3-2	Thompson, Sutton	
Liverpool (England)	H	D1-1	Larsson	QF
	A	W2-0	Thompson, Hartson	
Boavista (Portugal)	H	D1-1	Larsson	SF
	A	W1-0	Larsson	
Porto	N	L 2-3 (aet)	Larsson 2	F

2003-2004 EC

FBK Kaunas (Lithuania)	A	W4-0	Larsson, Sutton, Maloney, Miller	Q2
	H	W1-0	Gvildys (og)	
MTK Hungaria (Hungary)	A	W4-0	Larsson, Agathe, Petrov, Sutton	Q3
	H	W1-0	Sutton	

GROUP STAGE

Bayern Munich (Germany)	A	L1-2	Thompson	
	H	D0-0		
Lyon (France)	H	W2-0	Miller, Sutton	
	A	L2-3	Hartson, Sutton	
Anderlecht (Belgium)	A	L0-1		
	H	W3-1	Larsson, Miller, Sutton	

UEFA

Teplice (Czech Republic)	H	W3-0	Larsson 2, Sutton	3
	A	L0-1		
Barcelona (Spain)	H	W1-0	Thompson	4
	A	D0-0		
Villarreal (Spain)	H	D1-1	Larsson	QF
	A	L0-2		

DUNDEE

Opponents	Venue	Res	Scorers	Rnd
1962-63 EC				
FC Cologne (West Germany)	H	W8-1	Gilzean 3, Wishart, Smith Robertson, Penman, og	P
	A	L0-4		
Sporting Lisbon (Portugal)	A	L0-1		1
	H	W4-1	Gilzean 3, Cousin	
Anderlecht (Belgium)	A	W4-1	Gilzean 2, Cousin, Smith	QF
	H	W2-1	Cousin, Smith	
AC Milan (Italy)	A	L1-5	Cousin	SF
	H	W1-0	Gilzean	
1964-65 ECWC				
Bye				1
Real Zaragossa (Spain)	H	D2-2	Murray, Houston	2
	A	L1-2	Robertson	
1967-68 FC				
DWS Amsterdam (Holland)	A	L1-2	McLean	1
	H	W3-0	Wilson, McLean 2, 1 pen	
FC Liege (Belgium)	H	W3-1	Stuart 2, Wilson	2
	A	W4-1	McLean 4	
Bye in Round 3				
Zurich (Switzerland)	H	W1-0	Easton	QF
	A	W1-0	Wilson	
Leeds United (England)	H	D1-1	Wilson	SF
	A	L0-2		

1971-72 UEFA

Akademisk	H	W4-2	Bryce 2, Wallace, Lambie	1
(Denmark)	A	W1-0	Duncan	
Cologne	A	L1-2	Kinninmonth	2
(West Germany)	H	W4-2	Duncan 3, Wilson	
AC Milan	A	L0-3		3
(Italy)	H	W2-0	Wallace, Duncan	

1973-74 UEFA

Twente Ensch.	H	L1-3	Stewart	1
(Holland)	A	L2-4	Johnston, Scott	

1974-75 UEFA

RWD Molenbeek	A	L0-1		1
(Belgium)	H	L2-4	Duncan, Scott	
Vllaznia Shkoder	A	W2-0	Lovell, Novo	Q
(Albania)	H	W4-0	Novo 2, Sara, Rae	
Perugia	H	L1-2	Novo	1
(Italy)	A	L0-1		

DUNDEE UNITED

Opponents	Venue	Res	Scorers	Rnd
			1966-67 FC	
Bye				1
Barcelona	A	W2-1	Hainey, Seeman	2
(Spain)	H	W2-0	Mitchell, Hainey	
Juventus	A	L0-3		3
(Italy)	H	W1-0	Dossing	
			1969-70 FC	
Newcastle Utd	H	L1-2	Scott	1
(England)	A	L0-1		
			1970-71 FC	
Grasshoppers	H	W3-2	Reid I, Markland, Reid A	1
(Switzerland)	A	D0-0		
Sparta Prague	A	L1-3	Traynor	2
(Czechoslovakia)	H	W1-0	Gordon	
			1974-75 ECWC	
Jiul Petrosani	H	W3-0	Narey, Copland, Gardner	1
(Romania)	A	L0-2		
Bursaspor	A	D0-0		2
(Turkey)	A	L0-1		
			1975-76 UEFA	
Keflavik	A	W2-0	Narey 2	1
(Iceland)	H	W4-0	Hall 2, Hegarty, pen, Sturrock	
Porto	H	L1-2	Rennie	2
(Portugal)	A	D1-1	Hegarty	

Opponents	Venue	Res	Scorers	Rnd
1977-78 UEFA				
KB Copenhagen	H	W1-0	Sturrock	1
(Denmark)	A	L0-3		
1978-79 UEFA				
Standard Liege	A	L0-1		1
(Belgium)	H	D0-0		
1979-80 UEFA				
Anderlecht	H	D0-0		1
(Belgium)	A	D1-1	Kopel	
(Diosgyor)	H	L0-1		2
Hungary	A	L1-3	Kopel	
1980-81 UEFA				
Slask Wroclaw	A	D0-0		1
(Poland)	H	W7-2	Dodds 2, Pettigrew 3, Stark, Payne pen	
Lokeren	H	D1-1	Pettigrew	
(Belgium)	A	D0-0		
1981-82 UEFA				
Monaco	A	W5-2	Bannon 2, 1 pen, Dodds 2, Kirkwood	1
(France)	H	L1-2	Milne	
Borussia M.	A	L0-2		2
(West Germany)	H	W5-0	Milne, Kirkwood, Hegarty, Sturrock, Bannon	
Winterslag	A	D0-0		3
(Belgium)	H	W5-0	Bannon, Narey, Hegarty Milne 2	
Rankicki Nis	H	W2-0	Narey, Dodds	QF
(Yugoslavia)	A	L0-3		
1982-83 UEFA				
PSV Eindhoven	H	D1-1	Dodds	1
(Holland)	A	W2-0	Kirkwood, Hegarty	
Viking Stavanger	A	W3-1	Milne 2, Sturrock	2
(Norway)	H	D0-0		
Werder Bremen	H	W2-1	Milne, Narey	3
(West Germany)	A	D1-1	Hegarty	
Bohemians	A	L0-1		QF
(Czechoslovakia)	H	D0-0		
1983-84 EC				
Hamrun Spartans	A	W3-0	Reilly, Bannon, Stark	1
(Malta)	H	W3-0	Milne, Kirkwood 2	
Standard Liege	A	D0-0		2
(Belgium)	H	W4-0	Milne 2, Hegarty, Dodds	
Rapid Vienna	A	L1-2	Stark	QF
(Austria)	H	W1-0	Dodds	
AS Roma	H	W2-0	Dodds, Stark	SF
(Italy)	A	L0-3		

Opponents	Venue	Res	Scorers	Rnd
		1984-85 UEFA		
AIK Stockholm	A	L0-1		1
(Sweden)	H	W3-0	Sturrock, Milne 2	
ASK Linz	A	W2-1	Kirkwood, Bannon pen 2	
(Austria)	H	W5-1	Hegarty, Coyne 2,	
			Gough Beaumont	
Manchester Utd	A	D2-2	Hegarty, Sturrock	3
(England)	H	L2-3	Dodds, Hegarty	
		1985-86 UEFA		
Bohemians	A	W5-2	Sturrock 3, Bannon 2	1
(Rep of Ireland)	H	D2-2	Milne, Redford	
Vardar Skopje	A	W2-0	Redford, Gough	2
(Yugoslavia)	H	D1-1	Hegarty	
Neuchatel Xamax	W2-1	Dodds, Redford	3
(Switzerland)	A	L1-3	Redford	
		1986-87 UEFA		
Lens	A	L0-1		1
(France)	H	W2-0	Milne, Coyne	
Uni. Craiova	H	W3-0	Redford 2, Clark	2
(Romania)	A	L0-1		
Hadjuk Split	H	W2-0	McInally, Clark	3
(Yugoslavia)	A	D0-0		
Barcelona	H	W1-0	Gallacher	QF
(Spain)	A	W2-1	Clark, Ferguson	
Borussia Moench.	H	D0-0		SF
(West Germany)	A	W2-0	Ferguson, Redford	
IFK Gothenburg	A	L0-1		F
(Sweden)	H	D1-1	Clark	
		1987-88 UEFA		
Coleraine	A	W1-0	Sturrock	1
(Northern Ireland)	H	W3-1	Gallacher, Sturrock, Clark	
Vitkovice	H	L1-2	Ferguson	2
(Czechoslovakia)	A	D1-1	og	
		1988-89 ECWC		
Floriana	A	D0-0		1
(Malta)	H	W1-0	Meade	
Din. Bucharest	H	L0-1		2
(Romania)	A	D1-1	Beaumont	
		1989-90 UEFA		
Glentoran	A	W3-1	Cleland, McInally, Hinds	1
(Northern Ireland)	H	W2-0	Clark, Gallacher	
Antwerp	A	L0-4		2
(Belgium)	H	W3-2	Paatelainen, O'Neill, Clark	

Opponents	Venue	Res	Scorers	Rnd
		1990-91 UEFA		
Harnfjardar (Iceland)	A	W3-1	Jackson, Cleland, og	1
Arnhem (Holland)	H	D2-2	Connolly, og	
	A	L1-0		2
	H	L0-4		
		1993-94 UEFA		
Brondby (Denmark)	A	L0-2		1
	H	W3-1	McKinlay, Crabbe, Clark	
		1994-95 ECWC		
Tatran Presov (Slovakia)	H	W3-2	Petric, Nixon, Hannah	1
	A	L3-1	Nixon	
		1997-98 UEFA		
C E Principat (Andorra)	A	W8-0	Zetterlund, Winters 4, McSwegan 3	Q
	H	W9-0	Olofsson, Zetterlund, Winters 2, McLaren, McSwegan 3 Thomson	
Trabzonspor (Turkey)	A	L0-1		Q
	H	D1-1	McLaren	

DUNFERMLINE

Opponents	Venue	Res	Scorers	Rnd
		1961-62 ECWC		
St Patrick's Ath. (Rep of Ireland)	H	W4-1	Melrose, Peebles, Dickson, Macdonald	1
	A	W4-0	Peebles 2, Dickson 2	
Vardar Skopje (Yugoslavia)	H	W5-0	Smith, Dickson 2, Melrose, Peebles	2
	A	L0-2		
Ujpest Dozsa (Hungary)	A	L3-4	Smith, Macdonald 2	QF
	H	L0-1		
		1962-63 FC		
Everton (England)	A	L0-1		1
	H	W2-0	Miller, Melrose	
Valencia (Spain)	A	L0-4		2
	H	W6-2	Melrose, Sinclair 2 McLean, Peebles, Smith	
	N	L0-1		
		1964-65 FC		
Oergryte (Sweden)	H	W4-2	McLaughlin 2, Sinclair 2	1
	A	D0-0		
Stuttgart (West Germany)	H	W1-0	Callaghan	2
	A	D0-0		
Athletico Bilbao (Spain)	A	L0-1		3
	H	W1-0	Smith	
	A	L1-2	Smith	

Opponents	Venue	Res	Scorers	Rnd
		1965-66 FC		
Bye				1
KB Copenhagen (Denmark)	H	W5-0	Fleming, Paton 2, Robertson, Callaghan	2
	A	W4-2	Edwards, Paton, Fleming, Ferguson	
Spartak Brno (Czechoslovakia)	H	W2-0	Paton, Ferguson, pen	3
	A	D0-0		
Real Zaragossa (Spain)	H	W1-0	Paton	QF
	A	L2-4	Ferguson 2	
		1966-67 FC		
Frigg Oslo (Norway)	A	W3-1	Fleming 2, Callaghan	1
	H	W3-1	Delaney 2 Callaghan	
Dynamo Zagreb (Yugoslavia)	H	W4-2	Delaney, Edwards, Ferguson 2	2
	A	L0-2		
		1968-69 ECWC		
Apoel (Cyprus)	H	W10-1	Robertson 2, Renton 2 Barry, Callaghan W 2, Gardner Edwards, Callaghan T	1
	A	W2-0	Gardner, Callaghan W	
Olymp. Piraeus (Greece)	H	W4-0	Edwards 2, Fraser, Mitchell	2
	A	L0-3		
West Bromwich (England)	H	D0-0		QF
	A	W1-0	Gardner	
Slovan Bratislava (Czechoslovakia)	H	D1-1	Fraser	SF
	A	L0-1		
		1969-70 FC		
Bordeaux (France)	H	W4-0	Paton 2, Mitchell, Gardner	1
	A	L0-2		
Gwardia Warsaw (Poland)	H	W2-1	McLean, Gardner	2
	A	W1-0	Renton	
Anderlecht (Belgium)	A	L0-1		3
	H	W3-2	McLean 2, Mitchell	

**BERT PATON
played in
Europe for
Dunfermline
before going
on to manage
the Pars**

HEARTS

Opponents	Venue	Res	Scorers	Rnd
		1958-59 EC		
Standard Liege	A	L1-5	Crawford	P
(Belgium)	H	W2-1	Bauld	
		1960-61 EC		
Benfica	H	L1-2	Young	P
(Portugal)	A	L0-3		
		1961-62 FC		
Union St Gilloise	A	W3-1	Blackwood, Davidson 2	1
(Belgium)	H	W2-0	Wallace, Stenhouse	
Inter Milan	H	L0-1		2
(Italy)	A	L0-4		
		1963-64 FC		
Lausanne	A	D2-2	Traynor, Ferguson	1
(Switzerland)	H	D2-2	Cumming, Hamilton J	
	A	L2-3	Wallace, Ferguson	
		1965-66 FC		
Bye				1
Valerengen	H	W1-0	Wallace	2
(Norway)	A	W3-1	Kerrigan 2, Traynor	
Real Zaragossa	H	D3-3	Anderson, Wallace, Kerrigan	3
(Spain)	A	D2-2	Anderson, Wallace	
	A	L0-1		
		1976-77 ECWC		
Lokomotiv Leipzig	A	L0-2		1
(East Germany)	H	W5-1	Kay, Gibson 2, Brown, Busby	
SV Hamburg	A	L2-4	Park, Busby	2
(West Germany)	H	L1-4	Gibson	
		1984-85 UEFA		
Paris St Germain	A	L0-4		1
(France)	H	D2-2	Robertson 2	
		1986-87 UEFA		
Dukla Prague	H	W3-2	Foster, Clark, Robertson	1
(Czechoslovakia)	A	L0-1		
		1988-89 UEFA		
St Patrick's Ath	A	W2-0	Foster pen, Galloway	1
(Rep of Ireland)	H	W2-0	Black, Galloway	
FK Austria	H	D0-0		2
(Austria)	A	W1-0	Galloway	
Velez Mostar	H	W3-0	Bannon, Galloway, Colquhoun	3
(Yugoslavia)	A	L1-2	Galloway	
Bayern Munich	H	W1-0	Ferguson	QF
(West Germany)	A	L0-2		

Opponents	Venue	Res	Scorers	Rnd
		1990-91 UEFA		
Dnepr	A	D1-1	Robertson	1
(USSR)	H	W3-1	McPherson, Robertson 2	
Bologna	H	W3-1	Foster 2, Ferguson	2
(Italy)	A	L0-3		
		1992-93 UEFA		
Slavia Prague	A	L0-1		1
(Czech Rep)	H	W4-2	Mackay, Baird, Levein, Snodin	
Standard Liege	H	L0-1		2
(Belgium)	A	L0-1		
		1993-94 UEFA		
Atletico Madrid	H	W2-1	Robertson, Colquhoun	1
(Spain)	A	L0-3		
		1996-97 ECWC		
Red Star Belgrade	A	D0-0		1
(Yugoslavia)	H	D1-1	McPherson	
		1998-99 ECWC		
Lantana	A	W1-0	Makel	Q
(Estonia)	H	W5-0	Hamilton, Fulton, McCann, Flogel, Holmes	
Real Mallorca	H	L0-1		1
(Spain)	A	D1-1	Hamilton	
		2000-2001 UEFA		
IBV	A	W2-0	Severin, Jackson	Q
(Iceland)	H	W3-0	McSwegan, Tomaschek, O'Neil	
Stuttgart	A	L0-1		
(Germany)	H	W3-2	Pressley, Petric, Cameron pen	1
		2003-2004 UEFA		
Zeljeznicar	H	W2-0	de Vries, Webster	1
(Bosnia)	A	D0-0		
Bordeaux	A	W1-0	de Vries	2
(France)	H	L0-2		

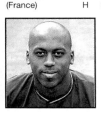

**MARK DE VRIES was
on target for Hearts
twice in the Uefa Cup
last season**

HIBERNIAN

Opponents	Venue	Res	Scorers	Rnd
			1955-56 EC	
Rot-Weiss Essen	A	W4-0	Turnbull 2, Reilly, Ormond	1
(West Germany)	H	D1-1	Buchanan J	
Djurgaarden	H	W3-1	Combe, Mulkerrin, og	QF
(Sweden)	A	W1-0	Turnbull pen	
Reims	A	L0-2		SF
(France)	H	L0-1		
			1960-61 FC	
Barcelona	A	D4-4	McLeod, Preston Baker 2	QF
(Spain)	H	W3-2	Kinloch 2, 1 pen, Baker	
AS Roma	H	D2-2	Baker, McLeod	SF
(Italy)	A	D3-3	Baker 2, Kinloch	
	A	L0-6		
			1961-62 FC	
Belenenses	H	D3-3	Fraser 2, Baird pen	1
(Portugal)	A	W3-1	Baxter 2, Stevenson	
Red Star Belgrade	A	L0-4		2
(Yugoslavia)	H	L0-1		
			1962-63 FC	
Stavenet	H	W4-0	Byrne 2, Baker, og	1
(Denmark)	A	W3-2	Stevenson 2, Byrne	
DOS Utrecht	A	W1-0	Falconer	2
(Holland)	H	W2-1	Baker, Stevenson	
Valencia	A	L0-5		QF
(Spain)	H	W2-1	Preston, Baker	
			1965-66 FC	
Valencia	H	W2-0	Scott, McNamee	1
(Spain)	A	L0-2		
	A	L0-3		
			1967-68 FC	
Porto	H	W3-0	Cormack 2, Stevenson	1
(Portugal)	A	L1-3	Stanton pen	
Napoli	A	L1-4	Stein	2
(Italy)	H	W5-0	Duncan, Quinn, Cormack Stanton, Stein	
Leeds United	A	L0-1		3
(England)	H	D1-1	Stein	
			1968-69 FC	
Ljubljana	A	W3-0	Stevenson, Stein, Marinello	1
(Yugoslavia)	H	W2-1	Davis 2	
Lokomotiv Leipzig	H	W3-1	McBride 3	2
(East Germany)	A	W1-0	Grant	
SV Hamburg	A	L0-1		3
(West Germany)	H	W2-1	McBride 2	

Opponents	Venue	Res	Scorers	Rnd
			1970-71 FC	
Malmo FF	H	W6-0	McBride 3 Duncan 2, Blair	1
(Sweden)	A	W3-2	Duncan, McEwan, Stanton	
Vitoria Giumaraes	H	W2-0	Duncan, Stanton	2
(Portugal)	A	L1-2	Graham	
Liverpool	H	L0-1		3
(England)	A	L0-2		
			1972-73 ECWC	
Sporting Lisbon	A	L1-2	Duncan	1
(Portugal)	H	W6-1	Gordon 2, O'Rourke 3, og	
Besa	H	W7-1	Cropley, O'Rourke 3,	2
(Albania)			Duncan 2, Brownlie	
	A	D1-1	Gordon	
Hadjuk Split	H	W4-2	Gordon 3, Duncan	QF
(Yugoslavia)	A	L0-3		
			1973-74 UEFA	
Keflavik	H	W2-0	Black, Higgins	1
(Iceland)	A	D1-1	Stanton	
Leeds United	A	D0-0		2
(England)	H	D0-0		
			1974-75 UEFA	
Rosenborg	A	W3-2	Stanton, Gordon, Cropley	1
(Norway)	H	W9-1	Harper 2, Munro 2, Stanton 2,	
			Cropley 2 pens, Gordon	
Juventus	H	L2-4	Stanton, Cropley	2
(Italy)	A	L0-4		
			1975-76 UEFA	
Liverpool	H	W1-0	Harper	1
(England)	A	L1-3	Edwards	
			1976-77 UEFA	
Sochaux	H	W1-0	Brownlie	1
(France)	A	D0-0		
Osters Vaxjo	H	W2-0	Blackley, Brownlie pen	2
(Sweden)	A	L1-4	Smith	
			1978-79 UEFA	
Norrkoping	H	W3-2	Higgins 2, Temperley	1
(Sweden)	A	D0-0		
Strasbourg	A	L0-2		2
(France)	H	W1-0	McLeod pen	
			1989-90 UEFA	
Videoton	H	W1-0	Mitchell	1
(Hungary)	A	W3-0	Houchen, Evans, Collins	
FC Liege	H	D0-0		
(Belgium)	A	L0-1		

Opponents	Venue	Res	Scorers	Rnd
		1992-93 UEFA		
Anderlecht	H	D2-2	Beaumont, McGinlay	1
(Belgium)	A	D1-1	Jackson	
		2001-02 UEFA		
AEK Athens	A	L0-2		1
(Greece)	H	W3-2 (aet)	Luna 2, Zitelli	

KILMARNOCK

Opponents	Venue	Res	Scorers	Rnd
		1964-65 FC		
Eintracht Frankfurt	A	L0-3		1
(West Germany)	H	W5-1	Hamilton, McIlroy, Sneddon McFadzean, McInally	
Everton	H	L0-2		2
(England)	A	L1-4	McIlroy	
		1965-66 EC		
Nendori Tirana	A	D0-0		P
(Albania)	H	W1-0	Black	
Real Madrid	H	D2-2	McLean pen, McInally	1
(Spain)	A	L1-5	McIlroy	
		1966-67 FC		
Bye				1
Antwerp	A	W1-0	McInally	2
(Belgium)	H	W7-2	McInally 2, Queen 2 McLean 2, Watson	
La Gantoise	H	W1-0	Murray	3
(Belgium)	A	W2-1	McInally, McLean	
Lokomotiv Leipzig	A	L0-1		QF
(East Gemany)	H	W2-0	McFadzean, McIlroy	
Leeds United	A	L2-4	McIlroy 2	SF
(England)	H	D0-0		
		1969-70 FC		
Zurich	A	L2-3	McLean J, Mathie	1
(Switzerland)	H	W3-1	McGrory, Morrison, McLean T	
Slavia Sofia	H	W4-1	Mathie 2, Cook, Gilmour	2
(Bulgaria)	A	L0-2		
Dynamo Bacau	H	D1-1	Mathie	3
(Romania)	A	L0-2		
		1970-71 FC		
Coleraine	A	D1-1	Mathie	1
(Northern Ireland)	H	L2-3	McLean T, Morrison	
		1997-98 ECWC		
Shelbourne	H	W2-1	Wright 2	Q
(Rep of Ireland)	A	D1-1	McIntyre	
Nice	A	L1-3	Wright	1
(France)	H	D1-1	Reilly	

Opponents	Venue	Res	Scorers	Rnd
		1998-99 UEFA		
Zeljeznicar	A	D1-1	McGowne	P
(Bosnia)	H	W1-0	Mahood	
Sigma Olomouc	A	L0-2		P
(Czech Rep)	H	L0-2		
		1999-2000 UEFA		
KR Reyjkavic	A	L0-1		Q
(Iceland)	H	W2-0	Wright, Bagan	
Kaislerslautern	A	L0-3		1
(Germany)	H	L0-2		
		2001-2002 UEFA		
Glenavon	A	W1-0	Innes	Q
(Northern Ireland)	H	W1-0	Mitchell	
Viking Stavanger	H	D1-1	Dargo	1
(Norway)	A	L0-2		

LIVINGSTON

Opponents	Venue	Res	Scorers	Rnd
		2002-2003 UEFA		
Vaduz	A	D1-1	Rubio	Q
(Liechtenstein)	H	D0-0		
Sturm Graz	A	L2-5	Zarate, Lovell	1
(Austria)	H	W4-3	Wilson 2 (1 pen), Xausa, Andrews	

BARRY WILSON
hit a double
against Austrian
side Sturm Graz in
the Uefa Cup

MORTON

Opponents	Venue	Res	Scorers	Rnd
		1968-69 FC		
Chelsea	A	L0-5		1
(England)	H	L3-4	Thorop, Mason, Taylor	

MOTHERWELL

Opponents	Venue	Res	Scorers	Rnd
		1991-92 FC		
Katowice	A	L0-2		1
(Poland)	H	W3-1	Kirk 2, Cusack	
		1994-95 UEFA		
Hanvar	H	W3-0	Coyne, McGrillen, Kirk	P
(Faroe Islands)	A	W4-1	Kirk 2, Davies, Burns	
Bor Dortmund	A	L0-1		1
(Germany)	H	L0-2		
		1995-96 UEFA		
My-Pa 47	H	L1-3	McSkimming	P
(Finland)	A	W2-0	Burns, Arnott	

PARTICK THISTLE

Opponents	Venue	Res	Scorers	Rnd
		1963-64 FC		
Glentoran	A	W4-1	Hainey, Yard 2, Wright	1
(Northern Ireland)	H	W3-0	Smith 2, Harvey, pen,	
Spartak Brno	H	W3-2	Yard, Harvey, pen,	2
(Czechoslovakia)			Ferguson	
	A	L0-4		
		1972-73 UEFA CUP		
Honved	A	L0-1		1
(Hungary)	H	L0-3		

RAITH ROVERS

Opponents	Venue	Res	Scorers	Rnd
		1995-96 UEFA		
Gotu	H	W4-0	Dair, Rougier, Cameron	P
(Faroe Islands)			McAnespie	
	A	D2-2	Lennon, Crawford	
Akranes	H	W3-1	Lennon 2, Wilson	1
(Iceland	A	L0-1		
Bayern Munich	H	L0-2		2
(Germany)	A	L1-2	Lennon	

RANGERS

Opponents	Venue	Res	Scorers	Rnd
		1956-57 EC		
Bye				P
Nice	H	W2-1	Murray, Simpson	1
(France)	A	L1-2	Hubbard pen	
	N	L1-3	og	
		1957-58 EC		
St Etienne	H	W3-1	Kichenbrand, Scott,	P
(France)			Simpson	
	A	L1-2	Wilson	
AC Milan	H	L1-4	Murray	1
(Italy)	A	L0-2		
		1959-60 EC		
Anderlecht	H	W5-2	Millar, Scott, Matthew,	P
(Belgium)			Baird 2	
	A	W2-0	Matthew, McMillan	
Red Star	H	W4-3	McMillan, Scott, Wilson	1
Bratislava			Millar	
(Czechoslovakia)	A	D1-1	Scott	
Sparta Rotterdam	A	W3-2	Wilson, Baird, Murray	QF
(Holland)	H	L0-1		
	N	3-2	Baird 2, og	
Eintracht Frankfurt	A	L1-6	Caldow pen	SF
(West Germany)	H	L3-6	McMillan 2, Wilson	
		1960-61 ECWC		
Ferencvaros	H	W4-2	Davis, Millar 2, Brand	P
(Hungary)	A	L1-2	Wilson	
Borussia Moench	A	W3-0	Millar, Scott, McMillan	QF
(West Germany)	H	W8-0	Baxter, Brand 3, Millar 2	
			Davis, og	
Wolves	A	W2-0	Scott, Brand	SF
(England)	H	D1-1	Scott	
Fiorentina	H	L0-2		F
(Italy)	A	L1-2	Scott	
		1961-62 EC		
Monaco	A	W3-2	Baxter, Scott 2	P
(France)	H	W3-2	Christie 2, Scott	
Vorwaerts	A	W2-1	Caldow pen, Brand	1
(East Germany)	H	W4-1	McMillan 2 Henderson, og	
Standard Liege	A	L1-4	Wilson	
(Belgium)	H	W2-0	Brand, Caldow	
		1962-63 ECWC		
Seville	H	W4-0	Millar 3, Brand	1
(Spain)	A	L0-2		
Tottenham	A	L2-5	Brand, Millar	2
(England)	H	L2-3	Brand, Wilson	
		1963-64 EC		
Real Madrid	H	L0-1		P
(Spain)	A	L0-6		

Opponents	Venue	Res	Scorers	Rnd
		1964-65 EC		
Red Star Belgrade	H	W3-1	Brand 2, Forrest	P
(Yugoslavia)	A	L2-4	Greig, McKinnon	
	N	W3-1	Forrest 2, Brand	
Rapid Vienna	H	W1-0	Wilson	1
(Austria)	A	W2-0	Forrest, Wilson	
Inter Milan	A	L1-3	Forrest	QF
(Italy)	H	W1-0	Forrest	
		1966-67 ECWC		
Glentoran	A	D1-1	McLean	1
(Northern Ireland)	H	W4-0	Johnston, Smith D, Setterington, McLean	
Bor Dortmund	H	W2-1	Johansen, Smith A	2
(West Germany)	A	D0-0		
Real Zaragoza	H	W2-0	Smith, Willoughby	QF
(Spain)	A	L0-2		
Slavia Sofia	A	W1-0	Wilson	SF
(Bulgaria)	H	W1-0	Henderson	
Bayern Munich	N	L0-1		F
(West Germany)				
		1967-68 FC		
Dynamo Dresden	A	D1-1	Ferguson	1
(East Germany)	H	W2-1	Penman, Greig	
FC Cologne	H	W3-0	Ferguson 2, Henderson	2
(West Germany)	A	L1-3	Henderson	
		Bye		3
Leeds United	H	D0-0		QF
(England)	A	L0-2		
		1968-69 FC		
Vojvodina	H	W2-0	Greig pen, Jardine	1
(Yugoslavia)	A	L0-1		
Dundalk	H	W6-1	Henderson 2, Greig Ferguson 2, og	2
(Rep of Ireland)	A	W3-0	Mathieson, Stein 2	
DWS Amsterdam	A	W2-0	Johnstone, Henderson	3
(Holland)	H	W2-1	Smith, Stein	
Athletic Bilbao	H	W4-1	Ferguson, Penman, Persson, Stein	QF
(Spain)	A	L0-2		
Newcastle Utd	H	D0-0		SF
(England)	A	L0-2		
		1969-70 ECWC		
Steaua Bucharest	H	W2-0	Johnston 2	1
(Romania)	A	D0-0		
Gornik Zabrze	A	L1-3	Persson	2
(Poland)	H	L1-3	Baxter	
		1970-71 FC		
Bayern Munich	A	L0-1		1
(West Germany)	H	D1-1	Stein	

Opponents	Venue	Res	Scorers	Rnd
		1971-72 ECWC		
Rennes	A	D1-1	Johnston	1
(France)	H	W1-0	MacDonald	
Sporting Lisbon	H	W3-2	Stein 2, Henderson	2
(Portugal)	A	L3-4	Stein 2, Henderson	
Torino	A	D1-1	Johnston	QF
(Italy)	H	W1-0	MacDonald	
Bayern Munich	A	D1-1	og	SF
(West Germany)	H	W2-0	Jardine, Parlane	
Dynamo Moscow	N	W3-2	Johnston 2, Stein	F
(USSR)				
		1972-73 European Super Cup		
Ajax	H	L1-3	MacDonald	
(Holland)	A	L2-3	MacDonald, Young	
		1973-74 ECWC		
Ankaragucu	A	W2-0	Conn, McLean	1
(Turkey)	H	W4-0	Greig 2, O'Hara, Johnstone	
Borussia Moench.	A	L0-3		2
(West Germany)	H	W3-2	Conn, Jackson, MacDonald	
		1975-76 EC		
Bohemians	H	W4-1	Fyfe, Johnstone, O'Hara	1
(Rep of Ireland)			og	
	A	D1-1	Johnston	
St Etienne	A	L0-2		2
(France)	H	L1-2	MacDonald	
		1976-77 EC		
Zurich	H	D1-1	Parlane	1
(Switzerland)	A	L0-1		
		1977-78 ECWC		
Young Boys	H	W1-0	Greig	P
(Switzerland)	A	D2-2	Johnstone, Smith	
Twente Enschede	H	D0-0		1
(Holland)	A	L0-3		
		1978-79 EC		
Juventus	A	L0-1		1
(Italy)	H	W2-0	MacDonald, Smith	
PSV Eindhoven	H	D0-0		2
(Holland)	A	W3-2	MacDonald, Johnstone	
			Russell	
FC Cologne	A	L0-1		QF
(West Germany)	H	D1-1	McLean	
		1979-80 ECWC		
Lillestrom	H	W1-0	Smith	P
(Norway)	A	W2-0	MacDonald A, Johnstone	
Fortuna Dusseldorf	H	W2-1	MacDonald A, McLean	1
(West Germany)	A	D0-0		
Valencia	A	D1-1	McLean	2
(Spain)	H	L1-3	Johnstone	

Opponents	Venue	Res	Scorers	Rnc
		1981-82 ECWC		
Dukla Prague	A	L0-3		
(Czechoslovakia)	H	W2-1	Bett, MacDonald J	
		1982-83 UEFA		
Borussia Dortmund	A	D0-0		
(West Germany)	H	W2-0	Cooper, Johnstone	
FC Cologne	H	W2-1	Johnstone, McClelland	2
(West Germany)	A	L0-5		
		1983-84 ECWC		
Valetta	A	W8-0	Paterson, McPherson 4	1
(Malta)			MacDonald, Prytz 2	
	H	W10-0	Mitchell 2, MacDonald 3	
			Dawson, MacKay, Davis 2,	
			Redford	
Porto	H	W2-1	Clark, Mitchell	2
(Portugal)	A	L0-1		
		1984-85 UEFA		
Bohemians	A	L2-3	McCoist, McPherson	1
(Rep of Ireland)	H	W2-0	Paterson, Redford	
Inter Milan	A	L0-3		2
(Italy)	H	W3-1	Mitchell, Ferguson 2	
		1985-86 UEFA		
Osasuna	H	W1-0	Paterson	1
(Spain)	A	L0-2		
		1986-87 UEFA		
Ilves	H	W4-0	Fleck 3, McCoist	1
(Finland	A	L0-2		
Boavista	H	W2-1	McPherson, McCoist	2
(Portugal)	A	W1-0	Ferguson	
Borussia Moench.	H	D1-1	Durrant	3
(West Germany)	A	D0-0		
		1987-88 EC		
Dynamo Kiev	A	L0-1		1
(USSR)	H	W2-0	Falco, McCoist	
Gornik Zabrze	H	W3-1	McCoist, Durrant, Falco	2
(Poland)	A	D1-1	McCoist pen	
Steaua Bucharest	A	L0-2		QF
(Romania)	H	W2-1	Gough, McCoist pen	
		1988-89 UEFA		
Katowice	H	W1-0	Walters	1
(Poland)	A	W4-2	Butcher 2, Durrant	
			Ferguson	
FC Cologne	A	L0-2		2
(West Germany)	H	D1-1	Drinkell	

Opponents	Venue	Res	Scorers	Rnd
		1989-90 EC		
Bayern Munich	H	L1-3	Walters, pen	1
(West Germany)	A	D0-0		
		1990-91 EC		
Valetta	A	W4-0	McCoist, Hateley, Johnston 2	1
(Malta)	H	W6-0	Dodds, Spencer, Johnston 3, McCoist	
Red Star Belgrade	A	L0-3		2
(Yugoslavia)	H	D1-1	McCoist	
		1991-92 EC		
Sparta Prague	A	L0-1		1
(Czechoslovakia)	H	W2-1	McCall 2	
		1992-93 EC		
Lyngby	H	W2-0	Hateley, Huistra	1
(Denmark)	A	W1-0	Durrant	
Leeds United	H	W2-1	og, McCoist	
(England)	A	W2-1	Hateley, McCoist	
		GROUP STAGES		
Marseille	H	D2-2	McSwegan, Hateley	
(France)				
CSKA Moscow	A	W1-0	Ferguson	
(Russia)				
FC Bruges	A	D1-1	Huistra	
(Belgium)				
FC Bruges	H	W2-1	Durrant, Nisbet	
Marseille	A	D1-1	Durrant	
CSKA Moscow	H	D0-0		
		1993-94 EC		
Levski Sofia	H	W3-2	McPherson, Hateley 2	1
(Bulgaria)	A	L1-2	Durrant	
		1994-95 EC		
AEK Athens	A	L2-0		1
(Greece)	H	L0-1		
Anorthosis	H	W1-0	Durie	P
(Cyprus)	A	D0-0		
		1995-96 EC		
		GROUP STAGES		
Steau Bucharest	A	L0-1		
(Romania)				
Borussia Dort	H	D2-2	Gough, Ferguson	
(Germany)				
Juventus	A	L1-4	Gough	
(Italy)				
Juventus	H	L0-4		
Steau Bucharest	H	D1-1	Gascoigne	
Borussia Dort	A	D2-2	Laudrup, Durie	

Opponents	Venue	Res	Scorers	Rne
		1996-97 EC		
Vladikavkaz	H	W3-1	McInnes, McCoist, Petric	C
(Russia)	A	W7-2	McCoist 3, van Vossen	
			Laudrup 2, Miller	
		GROUP STAGES		
Grasshoppers	A	L0-3		
(Switzerland)				
Auxerre	H	L1-2	Gascoigne	
(France)				
Ajax	L	4-1	Durrant	
(Holland)				
Ajax	H	L0-1		
Grasshoppers	H	W2-1	McCoist 2, 1 pen	
Auxerre	A	L1-2	Gough	
		1997-98 EC		
Gotu	A	W5-0	Negri, Durie 2, McCoist 2	C
(Faroe Islands)	H	W6-0	Durie, Negri 2, McCoist	
			Albertz, Ferguson	
Gothenburg	A	L0-3		C
(Sweden)	H	D1-1	Miller	
		UEFA		
Strasbourg	A	L1-2	Albertz	1
(France)	A	L1-2	Gattuso	
		1998-99 UEFA		
Shelbourne	A	W5-3	Albertz 2, 1 pen,	C
(Rep of Ireland)			Amato 2, van Bronckhorst	
	H	W2-0	Johansson 2	
PAOK Salonika	H	W2-0	Kanchelskis, Wallace	C
(Greece)	A	D0-0		
Beitar	A	D1-1	Albertz	4
(Israel)	H	W4-2	Gattuso, Porrini,	
			Johansson, Wallace	
Bayer Leverkusen	A	W2-1	van Bronckhorst,	2
(Germany)			Johansson	
	H	D1-1	Johansson	
Parma	H	D1-1	Wallace	3
(Italy)	A	L1-3	Albertz	
		1999-2000 EC		
FC Haka	A	W4-1	Amoruso, Mols 2	C
(Finland)			Johansson	
	H	W3-0	Wallace, Mols, Johansson	
Parma	H	W2-0	Vidmar, Reyna	C
(Italy)	A	L0-1		
		GROUP STAGES		
Valencia	A	L0-2		
(Spain)	H	L1-2	Moore	
Bayern Munich	H	D1-1	Albertz	
(Germany)	A	L0-1		
PSV Eindhoven	A	W1-0	Albertz	
(Holland)	H	W4-1	Amoruso Mols 2, McCann	

Opponents	Venue	Res	Scorers	Rnd
			UEFA	
Bor Dortmund	H	W2-0	Kohler og, Wallace	
(Germany)	A	L0-2		
		(Dortmund won 3-1 on penalties)		
			2000-2001 EC	
Zalgiris Kaunas	H	W4-1	Johnston, Albertz, Dodds 2	Q2
(Lithuania)	A	D0-0		
Herfolge BK	A	W3-0	Albertz, Dodds, Amoruso	Q3
(Denmark)	H	W3-0	Wallace, Johnston, Kanchelskis	
			GROUP STAGES	
Sturm Graz	H	W5-0	Mols, de Boer, Albertz, van Bronckhorst, Dodds	
(Austria)	A	L0-2		
Monaco	A	W1-0	van Bronckhorst	
(France)	H	D2-2	Miller, Mols	
Galatasaray	A	L2-3	Kanchelskis, van Bronckhorst	
(Turkey)	H	D0-0		
			UEFA	
Kaiserslautern	H	W1-0	Albertz	3
(Germany)	A	L3-0		
			2001-2002 EC	
NK Maribor	A	W3-0	Flo 2, Nerlinger	Q2
(Slovenia)	H	W3-1	Caniggia 2, Flo	
Fenerbahce	H	D0-0		Q3
(Turkey)	A	L1-2	Ricksen	
			UEFA	
Anzhi	N	W1-0	Konterman	1
(Russia)				
Moscow Dynamo	H	W3-1	Amoruso, Ball, de Boer	2
(Russia)	A	W4-1	de Boer, Ferguson, Flo Lovenkrands	
PSG	H	D0-0		3
(France)	A	D0-0		
		(aet, Rangers won 4-3 on penalties)		
Feyenoord	H	D1-1	Ferguson pen	4
(Holland)	A	L2-3	McCann, Ferguson pen	
			2002-2003 UEFA	
Viktoria Zizkov	A	L0-2		1
(Czech Republic)	H	W3-1	de Boer 2, McCann	
		(aet, 2-0 after 90 mins. Zizkov won on away goals)		
			2003-2004 EC	
FC Copenhagen	H	D1-1	Lovenkrands	Q3
(Denmark)	A	W2-0	Arteta, Arveladze	
			GROUP STAGE	
VfB Stuttgart	H	W2-1	Nerlinger, Lovenkrands	
(Germany)	A	L0-1		
Panathinaikos	A	D1-1	Emerson	
(Greece)	H	L1-3	Mols	
Manchester Utd	H	L0-1		
(England)	A	L0-3		

ST JOHNSTONE

Opponents	Venue	Res	Scorers	Rnd
		1971-72 UEFA		
SV Hamburg	A	L1-2	Pearson	1
(West Germany)	H	W3-0	Hall, Pearson, Whitelaw	
Vasas Budapest	H	W2-0	Connolly pen, Pearson	2
(Hungary)	A	L0-1		
Zeljeznicar	H	W1-0	Connolly	3
(Yugoslavia)	A	L1-5	Rooney	
		1999-2000 UEFA		
VPS Vaasa	A	D1-1	Lowndes	Q
(Finland)	H	W2-0	Simao 2	
Monaco	A	L0-3		1
(France)	H	D3-3	Leonard og, Dasovic, O'Neil	

ST MIRREN

		1980-81 UEFA		
Elfsborg	A	W2-1	Somner, Abercromby	1
(Sweden)	H	D0-0		
St Etienne	H	D0-0		2
(France)	A	L0-2		
		1983-84 UEFA		
Feyenoord	H	L0-1		1
(Holland)	A	L0-2		
		1985-86 UEFA		
Slavia Prague	A	L0-1		1
(Czechoslovakia)	H	W3-0	Gallagher, McGarvey 2	
Hammarby	A	D3-3	Gallagher 3	2
(Sweden)	H	L1-2	McGarvey	
		1987-88 ECWC		
Tromso	H	W1-0	McDowall	1
(Norway)	A	D0-0		
Mechelen	A	D0-0		2
(Belgium)	H	L0-2		

Ties finishing level on goals have been settled by: play-offs, toss of the coin, away goals rule (from 1966-67), penalty kicks or golden goal (from 2000-2001) or silver goal (from 2002-2003).

SCOTTISH JUNIOR CUP

1886-87	Fairfield (Govan) 3	Edin Woodburn 1
	(after protest)	
1887-88	Wishaw Thistle 3	Maryhill 1
1888-89	Burnbank Swifts 4	W Benhar Violet 1
1889-90	Burnbank Swifts 3	Benburb 1 ....
	(after protest)	
1890-91	Vale of Clyde 2	Chryston Ath.................0
	(after a draw)	
1891-92	Minerva 5	W Benhar Violet 2
1892-93	Vale of Clyde 3	Dumbarton Fern.............2
	(after a draw)	
1893-94	Ashfield 3	Renfrew V 0
1894-95	Ashfield 2	West Calder Wan. 1
	(after a draw)	
1895-96	Cambuslang Hibs 3	Parkhead 1
1896-97	Strathclyde 2	Dunfermline Jun. 0
	(after protest)	
1897-98	Dalziel Rovers 2	Parkhead 1
1898-99	Parkhead 4	Westmarch XI................1
1899-00	Maryhill 3	Rugby XI 2
1900-01	Burnbank Ath. 2	Maryhill 0
1901-02	Glencairn 1	Maryhill 0
	(after a draw)	
1902-03	Parkhead 3	Larkhall Th. 0
1903-04	Vale of Clyde 3	Parkhead 0
1904-05	Ashfield 2	Renfrew Vic...................1
1905-06	Dunipace Jun. 1	Rob Roy........................0
	(after a draw)	
1906-07	Strathclyde 1	Maryhill XI 0
	(after two draws)	
1907-08	Larkhall Th. 1	Q.P. Hampden XI 0
1908-09	Kilwinning R. 1	Strathclyde...................0
	(after a draw)	
1909-10	Ashfield 3	Kilwinning R. 0
	after protest)	
1910-11	Burnbank Ath. 1	Petershill 0
	(after a draw)	
1911-12	Petershill 5	Denny Hibs 0
1912-13	Inverkeithing Un. 1	Dunipace Jun................0
1913-14	Larkhall Th. 1	Ashfield 0
	(after two draws)	
1914-15	Parkhead 2	Port Glasgow Ath. 0
1915-16	Petershill 2	Parkhead 0

1916-17	St Mirren Jun. 1	Renfrew Jun. 0	
	(after a draw)		
1917-18	Petershill awarded cup, no final tie..............................		
1918-19	Glencairn 1	St Anthony's 0	
	(after a draw)		
1919-20	Parkhead 2	Cambuslang R. 0	
1920-21	Rob Roy....................1	Ashfield 0	
1921-22	St Roch's 2	Kilwinning R. 1	
	(after protest)		
1922-23	Musselb'gh Bruntonian ..2	Arniston R. 0	
1923-24	Parkhead 3	Baillieston Jun. 1	
	(after a draw)		
1924-25	Saltcoats Vics 2	St Anthony's 1	
	(after two draws)		
1925-26	Strathclyde 2	Bridgeton Wav. 0	
	(after a draw)		
1926-27	Glencairn 2	Cambuslang R. 1	
1927-28	Maryhill Hibs 6	Burnbank Ath. 2	
1928-29	Dundee Violet 4	Denny Hibs 0	
1929-30	Newtongrange Star ..3	Hall Russell's 0	
1930-31	Denny Hibs 1	Burnbank Ath. 0	
	(replay ordered, Denny failed to appear)		
1931-32	Perthshire 2	Rob Roy........................1	
1932-33	Yoker Ath 4	Tranent Jun. 2	
	(after a draw)		
1933-34	Benburb....................3	Bridgeton Wav. 1	
1934-35	Tranent....................6	Petershill 1	
1935-36	Benburb....................1	Yoker Ath. 0	
	(after a draw)		
1936-37	Arthurlie 5	Rob Roy........................1	
1937-38	Cambuslang R. 3	Benburb........................2	
1938-39	Glencairn 2	Shawfield 1	
1939-40	Maryhill 1	Morton Jun. 0	
1940-41	Perthshire 3	Armadale Th. 1	
	(after two draws)		
1941-42	Clydebank 4	Vale of Clyde 2	
1942-43	Rob Roy...................3	Benburb........................1	
	(after two draws)		
1943-44	Perthshire 1	Blantyre Vics. 0	
1944-45	Burnbank Ath. 3	Cambuslang R. 1	
	(after protest)		
1945-46	Fauldhouse Un. 2	Arthurlie 0	
1946-47	Shawfield..................2	Bo'ness Un. 1	
	(after a draw)		
1947-48	Bo'ness Un. 2	Irvine Meadow 1	

1948-49	Auchinleck Talbot 3	Petershill 2
1949-50	Blantyre Vics 3	Cumnock 0
1950-51	Petershill 1	Irvine Meadow 0
1951-52	Kilbirnie Ladeside 1	Camelon 0
1952-53	Vale of Leven 1	Annbank Un 0
1953-54	Sunnybank..................2	Lochee Harp 1
1954-55	Kilsyth R. 4	Duntocher Hibs 1

(after a draw)

1955-56	Petershill 4	Lugar Boswell Th. 1
1956-57	A'deen Bnks o' Dee ..1	Kilsyth R. 0
1957-58	Shotts Bon Accord 2	Pumpherston 0
1958-59	Irvine Meadow 2	Shettleston......................1
1959-60	St Andrew's 3	Greenock 1
1960-61	Dunbar United 2	Cambuslang R. 0

(after a draw)

1961-62	Rob Roy......................1	Renfrew 0

(after a draw)

1962-63	Irvine Meadow 2	Glenafton Ath. 1
1963-64	Johnstone Burgh 3	Cambuslang R. 0

(after a draw)

1964-65	Linlithgow Rose........4	Baillieston 1
1965-66	Bonnyrigg Rose........6	Whitburn 1

(after a draw)

1966-67	Kilsyth R. 3	Glencairn 1

(after a draw)

1967-68	Johnstone Burgh 4	Glenrothes 3

(after a draw)

1968-69	Cambuslang R. 1	Rob Roy..........................0
1969-70	Blantyre Vics 1	Penicuick Ath. 0

(ater a draw)

1970-71	Cambuslang R. 2	Newtongrange Star 1
1971-72	Cambuslang R. 3	Bonnyrigg Rose.............2

(after 1-1 draw)

1972-73	Irvine Meadow 1	Cambuslang R. 0

(after two draws)

1973-74	Cambuslang R. 3	Linlithgow Rose 1
1974-75	Glenrothes 1	Glencairn 0
1975-76	Bo'ness Un. 3	Darvel.............................0
1976-77	Kilbirnie Ladeside 3	Rob Roy..........................1
1977-78	Bonnyrigg Rose........1	Stonehouse Violet 0
1978-79	Cumnock 1	Bo'ness Utd 0
1979-80	Baillieston 2	Benburb 0

(after a draw)

1980-81	Pollok.........................1	Arthurlie 0

1981-82	Baillieston 0	Blantyre Vics 1
1982-83	East Kilbride Th. 2	Bo'ness United 0
1983-84	Baillieston 0	Bo'ness United 2
1984-85	Pollok......................3	Petershill 1

(after 1-1 draw)

1985-86	Auchinleck Talbot 3	Pollok............................2
1986-87	Auchinleck Talbot 1	Kilbirnie Ladeside 0

(after 1-1 draw)

1987-88	Auchinleck Talbot 1	Petershill 0
1988-89	Cumnock 1	Ormiston Primrose..........0
1989-90	Hill o' Beath 1	Lesmahagow 0
1990-91	Auchinleck Talbot 1	Newtongrange Star 0
1991-92	Auchinleck Talbot 4	Glenafton 0
1992-93	Glenafton 1	Tayport 0
1993-94	Largs Thistle 1	Glenafton 0
1994-95	Camelon 2	Whitburn 0
1995-96	Camelon 0	Tayport 2

(after extra time)

1996-97	Pollok......................3	Tayport 1
1997-98	Arthurlie 4	Pollok............................0
1998-99	Kilwinning Rangers ..1	Kelty Hearts 0
1999-2000	Johnstone Burgh 2	Whitburn 2

(aet, 2-2 full time. Whitburn won 4-3 on penalties)

2000-2001	Renfrew 0	Carnoustie Panmure 0

(aet, Renfrew won 6-5 on penalties)

2001-2002	Linlithgow Rose........1	Auchinleck Talbot............0
2002-2003	Tayport.....................1	Linlithgow Rose 0

(after extra time)

2003-2004	Carnoustie Panmure..0	Tayport 0

(aet, Carnoustie won 4-1 on penalties)

**CARNOUSTIE celebrate winning the OVD Scottish Junior
Cup on penalties against holders Tayport**

JUNIOR CONTACTS

ANNBANK UTD..S McCroskie, 01292 520394
ARDEER THISTLE ....P McBlain, 01294 471972
ARDROSSAN WINTON ROVERS ....T Ferrie, 01294 604264
ARTHURLIE ....J Docherty, 0141 881 3262
ASHFIELD ....T Robertson, 0141 944 0571
AUCHINLECK TALBOT.....................................H Dumigan, 01290 421785
BEITH ....R McCarter, 01505 503800
BELLSHILL ....P Henry, 07984 178772
BENBURB ....I Pope, 0141 633 1853
BLANTYRE VICS ....A McDade, 01698 323790
CAMBUSLANG RANGERS.................... W Miller, 0141 641 0255
CARLUKE ROVERS ....Ms C Kay, 01555 772154
CLYDEBANK ....S Latimer, 01389 382166
COLTNESS UTD ....J Devine, 01698 374606
CRAIGMARK BURNTONIANS.........................T Farrell, 01292 550093
CUMBERNAULD UTD.....................................A Robertson, 01236 451850
CUMNOCK ....G Morton, 01290 423992
DALRY...H Aitken, 01505 683558
DARVEL ....J MacLachlan, 01560 321487
DUNIPACE ....I Duncan, 01324 813463
EAST KILBRIDE THISTLE...............G Kirkpatrick, 01698 812247
FORTH WANDERERS ....J Kelly, 01555 840861
GLASGOW PERTHSHIRE ......Ms C Cunningham, 0141 419 9308
GLENAFTON ATHLETIC ....T King, 01292 478568
GREENOCK...L Falconer, 01475 797796
HURLFORD...W McMahon, 01563 821047
IRVINE MEADOW ....I McQueen, 01292 471884
IRVINE VICTORIA ....Ms S Thomson, 01294 468480
JOHNSTONE BURGH ....R Cantwell, 0141 561 6010
KELLO ROVERS ....D Cowan, 01659 67168
KILBIRNIE LADESIDE ....J Mathie, 01505 348083
KILSYTH RANGERS ....R Mackay, 01236 824462
KILWINNING ....A Tudhope, 01294 559465
KIRKINTILLOCH ROB ROY ....J Robertson, 0141 776 3618
LANARK UNITED...T Anderson, 01555 663796
LARGS ....K Smailes, 01294 465611
LARKHALL THISTLE ....S Thomson, 01698 884279
LESMAHAGOW ....D Logan, 01698 269532
LUGAR BOSWELL THISTLE ....K Young, 07967 907537

MARYHILL	G Anderson, 0141 563 096?	
MAYBOLE	A Meek, 01655 88341?	
MUIRKIRK	Ms U Stitt, 01290 66017?	
NEILSTON	H Blair, 0141 881 828?	
PETERSHILL	G Speirs, 0141 589 812?	
POLLOK	F McNeil, 0141 881 002?	
PORT GLASGOW	J McIlhinney, 01475 80205?	
RENFREW	J Barclay, 0141 884 614?	
ROYAL ALBERT ATHLETIC	P Higgins, 01698 88849?	
RUTHERGLEN GLENCAIRN	A Forbes, 0141 643 140?	
SALTCOATS VICTORIA	G Hunter, 01236 60282?	
ST ANTHONY'S	F McKenna, 0141 641 965?	
ST ROCH'S	T McIlroy, 0141 553 122?	
SHETTLESTON	M Scollan, 0141 554 880?	
SHOTTS BON ACCORD	W Quilter, 01501 77116?	
STONEHOUSE VIOLET	A Brown, 01698 79262?	
THORNIEWOOD UTD	J Miller, 01236 42146?	
TROON	G Dempster, 01292 31439?	
VALE OF CLYDE	J McKenna, 07961 013 962	
VALE OF LEVEN	A Wallace, 0141 840 155?	
WHITLETTS VICTORIA	I Dick, 01292 26540?	
WISHAW	R Watson, 01236 72504?	
YOKER ATH.	J George, 0141 951 107?	

Annbank Utd (New Pebble Pk), **Ardeer** Th (Ardeer Stdm), **Ardrossar Winton Rovers** (Winton Pk), **Arthurlie** (Dunterlie Pk), **Ashfield** (Saracen Pk), **Auchinleck Talbot** (Beechwood Pk), **Baillieston** (no curren ground), **Beith** (Bellsdale Pk), **Bellshill** (New Brandon Pk), **Benburt** (Tinto Pk), **Blantyre V** (Castle Pk), **Cambuslang Rangers** (Somervell Pk), **Carluke Rov** (Loch Park Stdm), **Clydebank** (Glenhead PK), **Coltness Utd** (Victoria Pk), **Craigmark Burtonians** (Station Pk), **Cumbernauld Utd** (Guy's Meadow), **Cumnock** (Townhead Pk), **Dalry** Th (Merskworth Pk), **Darvel** (Recreation Pk), **Dunipace** (Westfield Pk), **East Kilbride Th** (Show Pk), **Forth Wand.** (Kingshill Pk), **Glasgow Perthshire** (Keppoch Pk), **Glenafton Athletic** (Loch Pk), **Greenock** (Ravenscraig Stdm) **Hurlford Utd** (Blair Pk), **Irvine Meadow** (Meadow Pk), **Irvine Vics** (Victoria Pk), **Johnstone Burgh** (Keanie Pk), **Kello Rovers** (Nithside Pk) **Kilbirnie Ladeside** (Valefield), **Kilsyth Rangers** (Duncansfield) **Kilwinning Rangers** (Abbey Pk), **Kirkintilloch Rob Roy** (Adamslie Pk) **Lanark Utd** (Moor Pk), **Largs Th** (Barrfields Stdm), **Larkhall Th** (Gasworks Pk), **Lesmahagow** (Craighead Pk), **Lugar Boswell Th** (Rosebank Pk), **Maryhill** (Lochburn Pk), **Maybole** (Ladywell Stdm) **Muirkirk** (Burnside Pk), **Neilston** (Brig o'Lea Stdm), **Petershill** (Petershil Pk), **Pollok** (Newlandsfield Pk), **Port Glasgow** (sharing Ravenscraig Stdm), **Renfrew** (Western Pk), **Royal Albert** (Robert Smillie Memoria Pk), **Rutherglen Glen.** (Southcroft), **Saltcoats Vics** (Campbell Pk), **St Anthony's** (McKenna Pk), **St Roch's** (Provanmill Pk), **Shettleston** (Greenfield Pk), **Shotts Bon Accord** (Hannah Pk), **Stonehouse Violet** (Tilework Pk), **Thorniewood Utd** (Robertson Pk), **Troon** (Portland Pk), **Vale of Clyde** (Fullarton Pk), **Vale of Leven** (Millburn Pk), **Whitletts Vics** (Voluntary Pk), **Wishaw** (sharing Victoria Pk), **Yoker Athletic** (Holm Pk).

FA CUP WINNERS

1872 Wanderers 1 Royal
Engineers 0
1873 Wanderers 2 Oxford Uni 0
1874 Oxford Uni 2 Royal
Enginers 0
1875 Royal Enginers 2 Old
Etonians 0 (after 1-1 draw)
1876 Wanderers 3 Old
Etonians 0 (after 1-1 draw)
1877 Wanderers 2 Oxford Uni 1
(aet)
1878 Wanderers 3 Royal
Enginers 1
1879 Old Etonians 1 Clapham
Rovers 0
1880 Clapham Rovers 1 Oxford
Uni 0
1881 Old Carthusians 3 Old
Etonians 0
1882 Old Etonians 1
Blackburn R 0
1883 Blackburn Oly 2 Old
Etonians 0 (aet)
1884 Blackburn R 2 Queen's
Park 1
1885 Blackburn R 2 Queen's
Park 0
1886 Blackburn R 2 WBA 0
(after a 0-0 draw)
1887 Aston V 2 WBA 0
1888 WBA 2 Preston 1
1889 Preston 3 Wolves 0
1890 Blackburn R 6 Sheff Wed 1
1891 Blackburn R 3 Notts Co 1
1892 WBA 3 Aston V 0
1893 Wolves 1 Everton 0
1894 Notts Co 4 Bolton 1
1895 Aston V 1 WBA 0
1896 Sheff Wed 2 Wolves 1
1897 Aston V 3 Everton 2
1898 Notts Forest 3 Derby 1
1899 Sheff Utd 4 Derby 1

1900 Bury 4 Southampton 0
1901 Tottenham H 3 Sheff U 1
(after 2-2 draw)
1902 Sheff U 2 Southampton 1
(after 1-1 draw)
1903 Bury 6 Derby 0
1904 Man City 1 Bolton 0
1905 Aston V 2 Newcastle 0
1906 Everton 1 Newcastle 0
1907 Sheff W 2 Everton 1
1908 Wolves 3 Newcastle 1
1909 Man U 1 Bristol C 0
1910 Newcastle 2 Barnsley 0
(after 1-1 draw)
1911 Bradford C 1 Newcastle 0
(after 0-0 draw)
1912 Barnsley 1 West Brom 0
(aet, after 0-0 draw)
1913 Aston Villa 1 Sunderland 0
1914 Burnley 1 Liverpool 0
1915 Sheff U 3 Chelsea 0
1920 Aston V 1 Huddersfield 0
(aet)
1921 Tottenham 1 Wolves 0
1922 Huddersfield 1 Preston 0
1923 Bolton 2 West Ham 0
1924 Newcastle 2 Aston Villa 0
1925 Sheff U 1 Cardiff 0
1926 Bolton 1 Man City 0
1927 Cardiff 1 Arsenal 0
1928 Blackburn 3 Huddersfield 1
1929 Bolton 2 Portsmouth 0
1930 Arsenal 2 Huddersfield 0
1931 West Brom 2 Birmingham 1
1932 Newcastle 2 Arsenal 1
1933 Everton 3 Man City 0
1934 Man City 2 Portsmouth 1
1935 Sheffield W 4 West Brom 2
1936 Arsenal 1 Sheffield U 0
1937 Sunderland 3 Preston 1
1938 Preston 1 Huddersfield 0
(after extra time)

1939 Portsmouth 4 Wolves 1	1984 Everton 2 Watford 0
1946 Derby 4 Charlton 1 (aet)	1985 Man Utd 1 Everton 0 (aet
1947 Charlton 1 Burnley 0 (aet)	1986 Liverpool 3 Everton 1
1948 Man Utd 4 Blackpool 2	1987 Coventry 3 Tottenham 2
1949 Wolves 3 Leicester 1	(aet)
1950 Arsenal 2 Liverpool 0	1988 Wimbledon 1 Liverpool 0
1951 Newcastle 2 Blackpool 0	1989 Liverpool 3 Everton 2 (ae
1952 Newcastle 1 Arsenal 0	1990 Man Utd 1 Crystal P 0
1953 Blackpool 4 Bolton 3	(after 3-3 draw)
1954 WBA 3 Preston 2	1991 Tottenham 2 Notts Forest
1955 Newcastle 3 Man City 1	(aet)
1956 Man City 3 Birmingham 1	1992 Liverpool 2 Sunderland 0
1957 Aston Villa 2 Man Utd 1	1993 Arsenal 2 Sheff Wed 1
1958 Bolton 2 Man Utd 0	(aet, first game 1-1)
1959 Notts Forest 2 Luton 1	1994 Man Utd 4 Chelsea 0
1960 Wolves 3 Blackburn 0	1995 Everton 1 Man Utd 0
1961 Tottenham 2 Leicester 0	1996 Man Utd 1 Liverpool 0
1962 Tottenham 3 Burnley 1	1997 Chelsea 2 Middlesboro 0
1963 Man Utd 3 Leicester 1	1998 Arsenal 2 Newcastle 0
1964 West Ham 3 Preston 2	1999 Man Utd 2 Newcastle 0
1965 Liverpool 2 Leeds 1 (aet)	2000 Chelsea 1 Aston V 0
1966 Everton 3 Sheff Wed 2	2001 Liverpool 2 Arsenal 1
1967 Tottenham 2 Chelsea 1	2002 Arsenal 2 Chelsea 0
1968 West Brom 1 Everton 0	2003 Arsenal 1 Southampton 0
(aet)	2004 Man Utd 3 Millwall 0
1969 Man City 1 Leicester 0	
1970 Chelsea 2 Leeds 1 (aet, first game a 2-2 draw)	
1971 Arsenal 2 Liverpool 1 (aet)	
1972 Leeds 1 Arsenal 0	
1973 Sunderland 1 Leeds 0	
1974 Liverpool 3 Newcastle 0	
1975 West Ham 2 Fulham 0	
1976 Southampton 1 Man U 0	
1977 Man Utd 2 Liverpool 1	
1978 Ipswich 1 Arsenal 0	
1979 Arsenal 3 Man Utd 2	
1980 West Ham 1 Arsenal 0	
1981 Tottenham 3 Man City 2 (after 1-1 draw)	
1982 Tottenham 1 QPR 0 (after 1-1 draw)	
1983 Man Utd 4 Brighton 0 (after 2-2 draw)	

RUUD VAN NISTELROOY hi
a double in the FA Cup Fina

ENGLISH LEAGUE CHAMPIONS

1888-89	Preston NE	1936-37	Manchester City
1889-90	Preston NE	1937-38	Arsenal
1890-91	Everton	1938-39	Everton
1891-92	Sunderland	1946-47	Liverpool
1892-93	Sunderland	1947-48	Arsenal
1893-94	Aston Villa	1948-49	Portsmouth
1894-95	Sunderland	1949-50	Portsmouth
1895-96	Aston Villa	1950-51	Tottenham Hotspur
1896-97	Aston Villa	1951-52	Manchester United
1897-98	Sheffield United	1952-53	Arsenal
1898-99	Aston Villa	1953-54	Wolves
1899-1900	Aston Villa	1954-55	Chelsea
1900-01	Liverpool	1955-56	Manchester United
1901-02	Sunderland	1956-57	Manchester United
1902-03	The Wednesday	1957-58	Wolves
1903-04	The Wednesday	1958-59	Wolves
1904-05	Newcastle United	1959-60	Burnley
1905-06	Liverpool	1960-61	Tottenham Hotspur
1906-07	Newcastle United	1961-62	Ipswich Town
1907-08	Manchester United	1962-63	Everton
1908-09	Newcastle United	1963-64	Liverpool
1909-10	Aston Villa	1964-65	Manchester United
1910-11	Manchester United	1965-66	Liverpool
1911-12	Blackburn Rovers	1966-67	Manchester United
1912-13	Sunderland	1967-68	Manchester City
1913-14	Blackburn Rovers	1968-69	Leeds United
1914-15	Everton	1969-70	Everton
1919-20	West Bromwich Albion	1970-71	Arsenal
1920-21	Burnley	1971-72	Derby County
1921-22	Liverpool	1972-73	Liverpool
1922-23	Liverpool	1973-74	Leeds United
1923-24	Huddersfield Town	1974-75	Derby County
1924-25	Huddersfield Town	1975-76	Liverpool
1925-26	Huddersfield Town	1976-77	Liverpool
1926-27	Newcastle United	1977-78	Nottingham Forest
1927-28	Everton	1978-79	Liverpool
1928-29	Sheffield Wednesday	1979-80	Liverpool
1929-30	Sheffield Wednesday	1980-81	Aston Villa
1930-31	Arsenal	1981-82	Liverpool
1931-32	Everton	1982-83	Liverpool
1932-33	Arsenal	1983-84	Liverpool
1933-34	Arsenal	1984-85	Everton
1934-35	Arsenal	1985-86	Liverpool
1935-36	Sunderland	1986-87	Everton

1987-88	Liverpool	1995-96	Manchester United
1988-89	Arsenal	1996-97	Manchester United
1989-90	Liverpool	1997-98	Arsenal
1990-91	Arsenal	1998-99	Manchester United
1991-92	Leeds United	1999-00	Manchester United
PREMIER LEAGUE		2000-01	Manchester United
1992-93	Manchester United	2001-02	Arsenal
1993-94	Manchester United	2002-03	Manchester United
1994-95	Blackburn Rovers	2003-04	Arsenal

ENGLISH LEAGUE CUP WINNERS

1961	Aston Villa	1996	Aston Villa
1962	Norwich City	1997	Leicester City
1963	Birmingham City	1998	Chelsea
1964	Leicester City	1999	Tottenham Hotspur
1965	Chelsea	2000	Leicester City
1966	West Bromwich Albion	2001	Liverpool
1967	Queen's Park Rangers	2002	Blackburn Rovers
1968	Leeds United	2003	Liverpool
1969	Swindon Town	2004	Middlesbrough
1970	Manchester City		
1971	Tottenham Hotspur		
1972	Stoke City		
1973	Tottenham Hotspur		
1974	Wolves		
1975	Aston Villa		
1976	Manchester City		
1977	Aston Villa		
1978	Nottingham Forest		
1979	Nottingham Forest		
1980	Wolves		
1981	Liverpool		
1982	Liverpool		
1983	Liverpool		
1984	Liverpool		
1985	Norwich City		
1986	Oxford United		
1987	Arsenal		
1988	Luton Town		
1989	Nottingham Forest		
1990	Nottingham Forest		
1991	Sheffield Wednesday		
1992	Manchester United		
1993	Arsenal		
1994	Aston Villa		
1995	Liverpool		

BODO ZENDEN netted in Middlesbrough's League Cup victory